Praise for *The* **DEATH** *of* **MY**

"A sense of tenuousness—or, more specifically, of the fluid interplay between death and life—is a key factor in *The Death of My Father the Pope*, which opens with the death of the author's father, Juan, an artist and alcoholic who drank himself to death in Chihuahua, Mexico, in 2009, at forty-eight. Silva structures the book, his first, around his trip across the border for the wake and burial, but this is no linear reckoning. Instead, the memoir weaves back and forth in time, using memory and language to shade or expose the complexities of the father-son relationship."   —David L. Ulin, *Los Angeles Times*

"*The Death of My Father the Pope* is a masterful examination of the weight of patrimony; throughout the memoir, Silva meditates on the question of what he has inherited from his father."
              —James Penner, *Los Angeles Review of Books*

"An eloquent rendering of our times, told in a way that delivers in clear, precise thoughtfulness of la frontera and of what it means to be mestizo, what it means to be Chicano, Mexican, troubled, peaceful, courageous, and resentful, underscoring it all with what it means to be truly human. Everyone should read this memoir!"
              —Jimmy Santiago Baca, author of *A Place to Stand*

"Obed Silva's memoir is a magnificent and poignant achievement. Weaving the great literary giants throughout this narrative, Silva brings us to a rich and luminous excavation of the father wound, of the contours of death and the sure triumph of love. *The Death of My Father the Pope* is deeply affecting and a singular accomplishment. '¡Impresionante—*punto*!'"
              —Father Greg Boyle, author of *Tattoos on the Heart*

"Silva is a former gang member who survived a gunshot wound and though he is now paralyzed from the waist down, the strength of his character and charisma knows no bounds. This book shows how he turned his life around, ended up excelling in college, and became a man who embodies the spirit of redemption. Silva can make you laugh and cry at the same time."   —Mike Sonksen, *L.A. Taco*

MCD  PICADOR

FARRAR, STRAUS AND GIROUX   NEW YORK

The DEATH of MY FATHER the POPE

~

A Memoir

OBED SILVA

This book is dedicated to

THE SONS AND DAUGHTERS OF THE ALCOHOLIC
WHO STILL SUFFERS

MCD
Picador
120 Broadway, New York 10271

The Library of Congress has cataloged the MCD hardcover
edition as follows:
Names: Silva, Obed, 1979– author.
Title: The death of my father the pope : a memoir / Obed Silva.
Description: First edition. | New York : MCD / Farrar, Straus and Giroux,
    2021.
Identifiers: LCCN 2021031443 | ISBN 9780374539160 (hardcover)
Subjects: LCSH: Silva, Obed, 1979– | Children of alcoholics—Biography. |
    Alcoholics—Family relationships.
Classification: LCC HV5132 .S55 2021 | DDC 362.292/3092 [B]—dc23
LC record available at https://lccn.loc.gov/2021031443

Paperback ISBN: 978-1-250-85890-0

This is a memoir and a work of nonfiction. The names and identifying
characteristics of some individuals have been changed to protect their privacy.

CONTENTS

FOREWORD

When immigrant families produce published writers, those writers are revered, because they are a symbol of the resolve and intelligence of the people who raised them. The working people in those families sense a truth long stated by philosophers and scientists: that mastery of language is the defining element of being human. With words we tell stories, we pray, we curse. Our words express our empathy, our cruelty, our wisdom; they capture the beauty and the ugliness in our lives. We whisper those words, or shout them, or scribble them in notebooks or in poems to our lovers. When you grow up, as Obed Silva did, with stigmas of caste, race, and class attached to your person, the mastery of language elevates you. You read the stories that appear in the bound pages of a book, and you write your own stories, and you feel that these acts are essential expressions of your humanity.

Obed Silva is a Mexican immigrant who was raised by a single mother; she appears very briefly in the beginning of this book, where she offers the words of wisdom that set Obed off on his journey. And then she returns again in its final passages, where she appears in scenes that change the way we understand the entire story. Up to that point, Silva's memoir has focused primarily on his relationship with his father. It's a story about two men, father and son, struggling to hold on to their sense of themselves as decent human beings, even as circumstance and self-loathing cause them to slowly ruin themselves with drink. But the foundation of this book, its hidden scaffolding, is a mother's love.

When Marcela Mendoza arrived in California, in the suburbs of Los Angeles, one of her first jobs was picking celery, tomatoes, and strawberries in the fields of Orange County; sometimes her young son worked alongside her. She treasured literature, and when Obed grew older she gave him great classic books to read: *Les Misérables* and *Huckleberry Finn*, among others. She thought books might center him, teach him lessons about the world, even as he grew angry and embittered, as the children of violent and alcoholic men often do. She urged him to read even as he entered a path of self-destruction that would lead him into courtrooms, jails, and hospital beds. Sometimes, those books arrived in his hands when he was in his darkest state, in metaphorical and literal dungeons. The words his mother gave him rescued him. His desire to transform and master language gave his life new meaning.

Obed's journey to becoming an author is an improbable one. There is a hint of his past life in the inked skin showing under the collars of his shirts. His countenance, with its deep brown hue and shaved head, is one that causes a certain kind of American to recoil in fear, even though his full lips more often than not are formed into a broad smile. Cholo, they think. Gang member. He was in a gang, in fact, in another life, in the final decades of the twentieth century. But today he's a college professor, and on the days he teaches he wears a tie and pressed dress shirts, fresh from the dry cleaners. Underneath these shirts, his tattoos honor the novelists Victor Hugo and Fyodor Dostoevsky. Those old masters are important to Obed because their books tell stories with powerful echoes in his own life;

epic tales about inequality, degradation, and redemption. Stories about the forces of order trying to hunt down and crush
humble men and women. Stories about the demons that men
carry within them, and how those demons degrade them, and
how they wrestle with those demons.

The story told in this memoir begins well after Obed Silva's
rebirth from gang member to scholar was underway. I first met
him at about that time. He had just completed a master's degree in medieval literature at California State University, Los
Angeles. I was introduced to him by a professor there, Beth
Baker. Obed relayed to me the core elements of his recent life:
Orange County gang member at age twelve; shot and paralyzed
while taking beer from a liquor store at age seventeen; incar-
cerated at age nineteen and charged with attempted murder
after shooting, from his wheelchair, a rival gang member in the
leg; and eventually, the recipient of a GED diploma and two
college degrees. He was a longtime permanent U.S. resident, but
the government was trying to have him deported to Mexico for
shooting that gang rival eleven years earlier.

Not long after we first met, I was in immigration court to
witness the hearing that would determine Obed's fate. Twenty-
one witnesses had signed up to testify on his behalf. Michael
Calabrese, his professor at Cal State L.A., said, "He has the wisdom and the maturity of a natural scholar." The judge ques-
tioned Obed in detail about his life as a teenage gangster. How
and why, the judge asked, do young men join gangs? "You're
kind of courted into it," Obed explained. "You're praised.
You're given things. You come to see them as people who care
about you." The judge seemed moved by the thoughtfulness
of Obed's answers. But he did not rule after that hearing, and
Obed continued to live in the bureaucratic limbo the United

States imposes on thousands upon thousands of Latino immigrants. A few months later, in July 2009, Obed learned of his father's death. He made the journey to Mexico that he describes in this book.

In December 2010, the government finally dropped the deportation proceedings against him. By that time, Obed was deep into his new manuscript about his father's death. He sent me some pages to read, and later I visited him at his mother's home in Orange County. "You are a writer," I told him, because the power and the importance of the book were plain to see even in these early stages. His mother joined us for the conversation, and the three of us sat in her garage, where Obed had set up a studio to paint. (He was working on a large oil painting of Victor Hugo that he would later gift to me.) The talk turned, eventually, to Obed's father. "I came to this country to run away from him," Marcela told me. She described him as violent, stubborn, and obsessed with her and Obed—the woman who had abandoned him and the child he had fathered with her. When I asked her how she met him, she told a story that transported us to the Chihuahua of her youth. It was a story she had never told Obed, the secret of the circumstances that led to his birth. Obed was visibly shaken afterward. And yet, years later, he had the courage to place that story in the final section of *The Death of My Father the Pope*.

Obed's memoir is a book that brings together great erudition—a love and knowledge of literature obtained through much sacrifice and hard work—with a willingness to face the malice and the dysfunction inside and around him. There is a natural tendency among Latino writers to treat their works as if they were a public statement of the worthiness of an entire culture. We feel the xenophobes hovering over us, and we see our books and our stories and even our poems as if they were arguments in the national debate over immigration. Put another way, we feel the need to protect our people from the judgments of outsiders. Obed Silva realizes that to do so in his own work would be to deprive his art of its greatest truths. His book is a story about the pain and the sense of grievance and smallness that define masculinity among a conquered and exploited people. Obed's father can be warm and loving to his son and the women in his life at one moment; and then demean and strike them the next. Near the end of this book, Obed himself confesses to "the worst thing I've ever done in my life," an act of cruelty he committed when he was a mere thirteen years old. The candor and courage of this work of art, and its spirit of intellectual and moral questioning, are its great achievement. Time and again, Obed joyfully and incisively deconstructs the "toxic masculinity" (a phrase he thankfully never uses) around him, invoking Chaucer and others to reveal the secret smallness inside the male bully.

I saw Obed's joy and fearlessness on display at his very first post-publication reading, a book launch at an Orange County restaurant. He and his friends and family rented out the space for a night and filled it with more than a hundred people. Obed held court from a small platform, his friends having lifted his wheelchair up there. There was much cheering, shouting, and laughter—it may have been the most boisterous book launch in American history. Some of Obed's old friends from his gang life (guys in their forties, like him) were there, along with their families. When Obed mentioned that some of these "homeboys" had been in jail, as he had, one of the homies' wives covered her young son's ears. Obed introduced the audience to many of his uncles and cousins, and even the first girl he'd kissed when they were eight years old. The college professor who testified on his behalf in immigration court was there too, as was his Cuban American lawyer, who had once helped rescue Obed from what might have been a decades-long prison sentence. And, of course, Obed's mother, Marcela, was there, beaming from start to finish. Obed read several passages, and ended with one where he describes how his own drinking sabotaged his life and happiness again and again, even in the years after his father's death from an alcohol-induced illness. Without any fear in his reading voice, Obed bared himself in front of his loved ones, his homies, his blood relatives, and his mother. "I am two people," he began. It was the bravest thing I've ever seen an author do.

—Héctor Tobar
Los Angeles, 2022

Act 1
THE WAKE

"'THAT'S ALL! OH, YEMELYAN, YEMELYAN,' THOUGHT I,
'DRINK HAS BEEN YOUR UNDOING, AND NO MISTAKE!'"
—FYODOR DOSTOEVSKY, *An Honest Thief*

1

I'm asleep when the phone rings. I can hear it, but I can't make out whether I'm dreaming or if it's really ringing. I open my blurry eyes and reach for my phone. I can make out that the number on the screen is from Mexico. I rub my eyes with one hand and press the answer button with the other. Holding the phone to my ear, I hear my brother Aarón breathing heavily on the other end, desperately attempting to speak. "Se ... se ... se fue," he cries out between gasps—"Our father died." I say nothing, like the rays of the ascending sun breaking through the cracks in the curtains. What can I say? What am I supposed to say? My heart doesn't provide me with any words to speak. Slowly I bring the phone down to my chest and stare up at the white and empty ceiling, listening to my brother's cries as they break through the speaker. He's dead. My father is finally dead.

The urgent voice of a woman comes through the speaker. "¿Bueno? ¿Bueno?"

"Sí, ¿bueno?" I say calmly, when I again put the phone to my ear.

"Who are you, sir?" the woman asks with concern.

"I'm his brother. And you ... are you a friend of ..."

"No, no, I'm a nurse here at the hospital. I was here when your father passed. He *is* also your father, right?"

"Yes. He . . . he *was.*"

"Yes—of course, I'm sorry, I didn't mean to . . ."

"It's okay. Please, don't apologize."

"Where are you?" she asks. "Are you coming? This boy needs someone to be with him. He's in a lot of pain, and he doesn't know what to do."

In the background I can hear my brother still crying for our father, every new cry louder than the last.

"I'm in California," I tell her. "I'll be on my way as soon as possible." I'm still in bed and haven't made any effort to get up. With the phone pressed to my ear, I look toward the window and wonder how hot the day will be later. It's been terribly hot all summer.

"California!" she remarks with surprise. "Oh, no. You're too far! This boy needs somebody now. Can somebody come now?"

"I'm sorry . . . yes, of course. I'll call his mother."

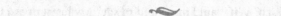

Aarón called me at exactly 5:34 a.m. I was the first person he called, the one who was also the farthest away. He'd called me the morning before to inform me that our father had been admitted to the hospital. "What's wrong with him this time?" I'd asked coldly, annoyed at having been awakened so early in the morning.

"The same thing as last time. He needs blood," my brother said with urgency, as if he'd been speaking to a representative at a blood bank and was about to place an order for a few pints.

"So give him blood. What's the problem?" I told him, with a direct voice, doctor-like. Little did I know that my father had run out of options, and filling him with someone else's blood was no longer going to help. In the months leading up to this moment, he'd been battling cirrhosis and hepatitis C. Going to the hospital every couple weeks because he was losing blood had become routine. But even more routine was his drinking, something he'd been doing daily since before he was a teenager. My father had been an alcoholic. He'd drunk for most of his life. Now, at forty-eight, his cirrhotic liver had finally stopped working, and he was dead.

It was sometime in January that my father's wife Cokis first called to tell me he'd been admitted to the hospital for losing blood. "He keeps vomiting and shitting it out," she said. "He can't hold it in." When I asked why, she very matter-of-factly told me it was because of his drinking. I'd thought it was no big deal. My father would get the blood he needed and be on his way, which, as it would turn out, is exactly what happened. The hospital kept him overnight and nurses restocked his body with blood. The following morning my father stepped out of the cold, white halls of the hospital into the warm light of a new day—body reenergized and hope renewed.

"All right then," I said to Cokis. "I'll send money tomorrow for whatever he may need, and tell him to call me as soon as he gets out." Money was all I could do for him. Every time my father had called to tell me about a problem he had, whether it had to do with work or the family or his health, I sent money. It would make me feel better, and my father always seemed to feel better, too. When I'd tell him that I'd be sending him a couple hundred dollars within a few days, he'd suddenly stop talking about his problem, because he no longer had any. "¡Gracias, hijo!" he'd say with excitement. I could see him smiling from ear to ear on the other end. I'd smile, too, knowing that my father was full of shit.

I'd debated whether to go to my father's funeral, and at some point had decided not to. Surprisingly, it was my mother who convinced me. "Ve," she said, "you need to go."

"Why?" I asked her. "What would be the point? He's already dead, and everything I needed to tell him I already told him while he was alive, like that I didn't love him, or that I wished he was dead."

"This is exactly why you need to go," my mother insisted. "You need to heal, and you can't do that unless you forgive your father. It's the only way you're ever going to close those wounds."

I thought about this idea. People always talk about healing through forgiveness, about not being able to move on unless you forgive. And although I didn't ask her, I wondered if *she* had forgiven my father. The grief I'd suffered at his whim was nothing compared to what he'd put her through. I couldn't imagine the pain that she'd had to endure living with my father for the few years that she did.

That morning, sitting across from her at the kitchen table, I had newfound admiration for my mother. This woman who'd raised me all on her own without asking for anything from my father—not a cent—was showing me what real strength looked like. It wasn't in muscles or in violence or in superiority; it was in meekness and humility, in simply saying I forgive you and moving on. Nothing gained, nothing lost, just moving forward with life and making the best of it for the ones you love. My mother loved me. Always. Unconditionally. Always. I'd been her struggle, her purpose, and later so were my sister Samantha and brother Roberto. She'd had to let go of any resentment and bitterness she'd felt toward my father if she had wanted to move on and create a better life for herself and her family, and she did. Fully self-made. Fully self-empowered. She knew her worth.

"If you don't go, you will regret it later," she said, "and you don't want to live with regret, son. It will hold you back. So go. Go and make peace with your father. Go and put him behind you."

2

The next day I'm on a flight to Chihuahua. I should be there by five p.m. By then my father will already have been buried. His funeral's set to be at three, exactly one hour from now. This is a good thing, because I don't want to be there among his mourners as he's being lowered into the ground, among those who loved him, and those who hated him—too many lies and too many tears. Some will cry and ask God why, but most will simply stare out at a cold casket and think of how the man inside had drunk himself to death. Someone will also uncap a beer and drink it on his behalf. "For you, Juanito! For you, my good friend! And for the many!" The mourning soul will raise a bottle to the sky as if toasting with my father's ghost; and then, as if holding the last beer on earth, will consume it in one long, savory gulp. "Ahhh!" will be the resounding proclamation of that quenched mouth.

Father, why can't I cry for you? Is it that you haven't left me yet? Is it that I still carry you with me everywhere I go? You're buried inside me. You've been there for some time now, and all the while you've managed to keep a smile—that devious smile of yours. Tell me: How was it when you left? What did you feel? Did you know it was time? Did you think of me? Did you see my face? I keep thinking that you simply closed your eyes; that you were tired and just gave up—peacefully. No more beers. No more battles. No more pain. "Ya 'stuvo," you said, "can't do it anymore, it's over—se acabó!" And so you left this world, and all of us, behind, to find our way without you.

Life was difficult for my father in the days leading up to his death, he was constantly vomiting and shitting out blood. The most difficult for him, however, had to be knowing he'd soon be dead, greeting every day as his last, killing every thought with a drink, trying to embrace his cruel fate. The condemned man's worst suffering, Dostoevsky declares in *The Idiot,* occurs on the day of his execution: It is in those moments before the end that the soul shudders with terror and clings most tightly to the flesh. The blade falls apace, as it was designed to do, but time, against every law created for it by man, slows down, and the anguish that fills him is amplified. The condemned man cries for the guillotine to do its job—to kill him at once, to end his suffering. Thus, my father went; ready, determined to never return. He'd been readying himself for some time. The idea haunted him; and those last days were too much, too long. It was all just moving too slowly. His death just wouldn't come fast enough.

I see you, Father, surrounded by golden lights and God's children, clear of mind and heart, free and light—and drunk no more! But tell me, mi querido viejo, whom I miss more than my own legs before they became useless, when I see you again, will you receive me with open arms after I have written all of these terrible words about you, after I have told the truth? Because like you, I am not far from death: feeding a thirst that won't recede, I drink and drink and drink.

The last time we spoke—a month before his death—my father sounded well. He did mention he was losing blood again, but he assured me that it was nothing. "I'm fine, hijo," he said. If anything, he made the fact that he was vomiting and shitting blood seem like nothing more serious than a passing cough. "La pinche sangre nomás, hijo. I keep losing it, but otherwise, I'm fine—de veras. I'll be back to my old self in no time." My father was like that when he spoke of any misfortune: aloof and apathetic. The man didn't care. "That's how it is, that's how God wants it to be," he'd say. "¿Para qué chingarle más?" I could never argue with that.

My father hadn't yet been buried when I arrived in the city of Chihuahua. As it turned out, his wife, my brothers, my sister Axcel, moved by good intentions, thought I might like to see him before he was stuffed in the ground forever. So they asked the owner of the funeral parlor for an extension, which he allowed without objection. So there was my father in a box inside the parlor waiting for me to come say my final goodbye. He couldn't have left without this moment. That's how I felt, like the whole extension thing had been his idea entirely, as if he'd been the one who arranged it, all for the purpose of fucking with me, his eldest son. "Just wait till he sees me," I could hear him saying with a smirk on his face as he snuggled in his box, rubbing his shoulders against the side panels, "Mijo's going to get a kick out of this!" See, my father was like that, too: he loved to fuck with your mind as much as he could, loved to torment you and make a mockery of every sensibility. Nothing was sacred to the man. And if you let him, he'd do it until you started wishing he were dead.

Outside the La Paz funeral parlor are dozens of people sitting and standing before the backdrop of a fiery-red descending sun. People who, with the exception of my brothers, sisters, and my father's wife, I'm not excited to see. They're mostly my father's family (many of whom I've never met); the rest are friends and acquaintances.

"¡Qué onda, raza?" I yell out of the truck's window as we pull up. Immediately, everyone stops what they're doing and turns their attention to me. The show has arrived.

"¡Es Obed!" my brother Danny announces when he sees my bald head hanging out of the truck's window. His brilliant smile, revealing his crooked teeth, complements the spark of light in his eyes. He's happy to see me, and so is the crowd cramming behind him as he walks toward the truck. They push and bump one another out of the way to get a look at me, fighting for my attention, calling my name. You would think I'm a ranchera music star or a telenovela actor the way they're receiving me. I prefer to think of myself as Monseigneur the Cardinal of Bourbon, arriving at the Palais de Justice in Paris on the Day of the Kings and the Feast of Fools in Victor Hugo's *Notre-Dame*. In the same way that Monseigneur the Cardinal, upon making his grand entrance into the gallery of the palace, took the attention of the crowd away from the morality play in progress, I, upon arriving at the curb of Funerales La Paz, this humble structure built for death scenes, take the attention of the crowd away from my father, who is in the middle of his last act.

While my uncle Chuy (my mother's brother) retrieves my wheelchair from the bed of the truck, I open my door and hang out one of my legs, careful not to let the white rubber bottom of my Vans connect with the dirt and trash that has piled up against the curb. The crowd watches as my leg dangles in the air, lifeless and beautiful, like an ornament hanging from a limp twig on a Christmas tree. Danny is the first to lean in to hug me, and when he does, others squeeze in behind him, throwing their arms around us both. I can feel the touch of many hands on my back and shoulders and the heat of different breaths assaulting my head and face. I feel as if I'm caught in the tentacles of a huge, sweaty octopus. All the while I'm praying to my sweet Lord that none of them starts crying on me or fucks up my neatly pressed blue polo shirt. And when Danny finally releases his grip on me and all the others step back, I thank Him for having answered my prayer.

My uncle pushes my chair up to me and I hop on it. I throw my black Anaheim Angels cap on backward on my head, making sure my legs are neatly tucked between the side bars leading to the footrest. The white rubber bottoms of my shoes are still clean, their white laces showing evenly from underneath each pant leg. I take a deep breath, and turn toward the sea of faces before me. Ugly faces. Each a different shade of melancholy and all part of the same unbearable collective face of the destitute. ¡Que bella vida! Life doesn't get more beautiful than this. I remember that I'm a Silva, too.

"¿Estás bien?" my tío Chuy asks me while tapping me on the shoulder and handing me my backpack. I tell him that I'm de aquellas!—all good, that he can leave now. And as he walks back to get into his truck, I pop a wheelie onto the curb, and without having to ask anyone, almost instinctively, there are more hands on me and my chair than necessary, lifting us both as one unit onto the cracked sidewalk—Obed has arrived, the one member of the tribe that all had been waiting for! Once on the sidewalk, I turn toward my tío's truck and say goodbye to his wife and son, who are peeping at me and the crowd through its back window. I can see their lips saying *Adiós* to me as they raise their hands and slowly wave, and I feel as if they're also silently praying for me. Que Dios me cuide.

I'm on my own, left to deal with what my father has left behind.

"I'm your tío Polo! Do you remember me?"

"And I'm your cousin Chuy! You probably don't remember me."

"And I'm your tía María!"

"And I'm your cousin Vero!"

"And I'm your tío Victorio!"

"And I'm this and I'm that."

"And I'm so-and-so!"

"And I'm blah! blah! blah! blah! blah! blah!"

¡Chingada madre! Where's the dead man? Come now, just lead me to the corpse.

I'm bombarded by a mob of excited Silvas who are all saying they're happy to see me. "¡Eres lo máximo! ¡Eres lo máximo! And we love you. We're all for one and one for all! There's always room for another Silva." I don't feel one bit of happiness to see any of them, not at this moment. I feel dry— real seco-like, like a fucking fish out of water, like a dying rose petal. All I want is to get it all over with: to roll through the parlor's doors, see my dead father, roll out, and shoot for the heavens with a bottle in hand. I want to get drunk already, re- ally fucked up. But that will have to wait.

I sling my backpack over my shoulder, turn toward the parlor's doors, grip my wheels, and the large group of grievers before me parts down the middle, as if commanded by Moses, making an opening for me to roll through into the parlor. I can feel every person fall in behind me as I pass them. They're so close to me that if I stop abruptly, they'll all crash into me from behind. At the door, Cokis is waiting for me with a smile and a tear, and somewhere close I know she's hiding a bottle. "I'm glad you're here," she says as she leans in to hug and kiss me. Any other time she might have held me and not let go, but not this time; her arms release me and point the way. "Go in, there's your father waiting for you, go and see him," she says meekly, with her arms and hands stretched out in front of her like ar- rows. And see him do what? I think, almost blurting out the words. But there's no need for such a senseless remark when my father's dead and in a casket only a few feet away from me on the other side of the parlor's doors.

3

It'd been almost four years since I'd last been in Chihuahua and saw my father. He'd been drinking terribly even then. He was consuming at least five thirty-two-ounce caguamas of Carta Blanca per day, and when he had the money for it, the occasional fix of cocaine. But beer, more than anything, had become something my father was incapable of living without.

In the mornings when I'd get out of bed I'd find him standing at the kitchen table before a cooling breakfast already sipping beer from a frosty glass mug he'd stored in the freezer the night before. I remember being sprawled out on the living room couch one morning and watching him act out this ritual. He'd be wearing only a pair of faded black briefs. Wrapped in the rays of the sun that flooded in through the kitchen window, he would, in a matter of minutes, sip one, then two, then three, then four mugs of beer before finally sitting down to have his now cold morning meal: a couple of scrambled eggs mixed in with yesterday's dry frijoles and just as dry corn tortillas. That morning, the wet sound of the food being smashed and squished inside his mouth made me squirm with disgust; and every time he swallowed, the thought of the masticated food making its way down into his beer-filled stomach made my own bowels churn and my body quiver. Yet I never once turned my eyes away. I watched my father until he cleared his plate and then moved on to finish the rest of his caguama. Like a voyeur who keeps still for fear of being discovered, I spied my father as he stood back up, wrapped his stubby hand around the caguama's thick form, lifted it, then turned it on its head until most of the sparkling yellow fluid smoothly streamed into the mug, rising quickly to the brim, pushing up a cloud of white foam. Eventually the stream became a drip and my father, twisting his wrist downward, shook the bottle violently up and down to make sure that every last drop of the golden elixir found its way into the mug. My father wasn't wasteful. Then came the gulp. One was all it took. In seconds the mug was empty; only scattered islands of foam remained lingering on the mug's inner surface. My father could've been a fucking magician the way he'd make all the beer disappear so quickly, so effortlessly. Good morning, world, I'm ready for you, bring on all you've got, you can't hurt me anymore. I could hear his heart sing as he brought down the mug from his lips back onto the table while letting out a long hiss through the hole in his mouth where teeth eight and nine once were. Then—for a moment—there was silence. For a few seconds my father stood at the table staring down at the empty bottle around which his hand was still tightly wrapped. Other than his exposed stomach, which seemed to be a living creature all its own because of the way it would puff out and then get sucked back in, no other part of his body moved. As I watched this scene stop time, I too continued to keep completely still for fear that if I did or said anything I might interrupt something big, something fucking enormous, something that would change the course of history. So, eager to know what that fucking enormous something was, I focused solely on my father's face and everything else around it seemed to melt away: the stained white refrigerator; the dirty brown cabinets with unhinged doors filled with cups and plates and old

cereal boxes and cans of food; the greasy stove with missing
knobs and just as greasy pots and pans piled on top of it; the
counter and sink next to it cluttered with more grimy pots and
pans and plates and cups and silverware; the crooked steel fau-
cet from which silent drops of water fell; the aluminum dining
table littered with even more dirty plates and cups, empty plastic two-liter bottles of soda, empty caguamas, including the
one my father still could not let go of; the table's three matching aluminum chairs, one of which had a bent backrest; and
even the dirty brown tile floor and the yellowy stained white
walls and ceiling, all turned into one big blur in which only
my father's face made sense, in which only his face had form.
His face held something secret and I wanted to know what that
something was. I wanted to know the truth. I wanted to know
why my father was the way he was and why I hated him so
fucking much but couldn't have him any other way. But more
than anything I wanted to know why at that moment he was
unable to remove his hand from that fucking bottle or turn his
eyes away from it. Had he fallen in love? Or was he wishing the
bottle farewell once and for all? I focused harder to try to break
through his dead expression and see what he saw; but before I
could, my father turned to me and said: "¿Qué onda, hijo? Do
you want to eat? The breakfast is good, real good."

And that was it. I blinked and everything was clear again.
I could see his hand releasing the bottle and moving up to his
mouth to wipe his lips; and I could also see the entire kitchen
again with him now at the center of it looking right at me with
a casual sense of being. He was perfect, and everything became
normal, everything the same. Only now the sun was brighter
and my father cooler than ever; nothing out of the ordinary
had transpired. And I quickly forgot what it was I'd been staring

at, what it was I'd been searching for, and all I could say to the absurd man was:

"No, güey, I'm not hungry yet. Thank you, anyway. You're too good to me."

❧

I ask everyone to step out of the funeral parlor before I enter. I want to be alone with my father. I don't know how I'm going to react when I see him, and I don't want anyone watching me. I also don't want anyone putting their arms around me or touching me anymore; or telling me that he'd been a good man and that he was also now in a better place. I don't want to hear any of it because none of it is true. It's all fantasy: procedural, fake; and I want to face the dead man with nothing but the truth I'm carrying in my gut and heart.

There I am, at the back of the room, fighting off the oppressive smell of jasmine and staring at the small casket a few feet away that contains my father. He hadn't been a tall man, about five feet five inches on his best days; but from where I'm standing, the casket seems even smaller than that. That shit don't look real, I'm thinking. Looks like a fucking toy. But I know that I have to roll up to it and view the body inside before all the eyes clinging to me from the doorway eventually make their way in and begin putting hands on me and spitting sympathetic nothings into my ears.

❧

"I didn't come to see you, I came to see my brothers!"

I said this to my father the last time I was in Chihuahua,

during an argument we were having over his drinking. The days when I'd come to Chihuahua because I yearned to see him were long dead. I no longer ran to his side or jumped for his arms, and not because my crippled body wouldn't allow me to, or because at twenty-six you just don't do shit like that anymore, but because my heart no longer had a pulse for it. That eternal flame that every son and daughter has burning inside their hearts for their father had been put out some time back, extinguished by some sickening image of the drunk it couldn't bear to see. "If it wasn't for my brothers," I told him, "I wouldn't be here. Fuck no, not to see you at least." I had to let my father know exactly how I felt and where I stood. Something inside me had exploded and given birth to hate. I cursed him and denied him, and not once during the entire argument did I ever refer to him as pa', papá, jefe, and especially not padre. I no longer felt like his son, nor did I want to be his son. He could've died then for all I cared.

The reality of my father being an alcoholic had become unbearable. I had become tired of always fighting with him and telling him to straighten out and do something for his family. I'd become tired of wanting to destroy him. "If you want to drink and kill yourself, then do it. I don't give a shit anymore— not about you or about anything you do. Just don't bother us with your shit." I spoke these words to his face.

I'd taken to calling my father güey, a term that evolved from the word buey, Spanish for ox. Originally, the term buey was used to refer to the husband of an unfaithful wife. The horns of the bull were emblematic of the wife's adultery and were said to loom over the head of the woeful husband, who, unlike those around him, was unable to see the horns, just like he was unable to see that his wife was tumbling in the hills with another man. Thus the townspeople of an older Mexico grew fond of making the cruel remarks: "Le pusieron los cuernos" and "Lo hicieron buey," whenever they came across a man afflicted by the calamity of having an adulterous beloved. The closest we have to this in English is the term cuckold, which finds its origins in the Old French word for cuckoo: *cocu*. The female of this bird—the cuckoo—was known for laying its eggs in the nests of other birds and gained the reputation of being unfaithful to her mate. Consequently, the French of the Old World would say that the husband of a straying wife was *cucuault*. Later the term would make its way into Middle English as cokewold. In "The Miller's Tale" in *The Canterbury Tales*, for example, Chaucer writes: "Who hath no wyf, he is no cokewold." And though cuckoos do not have horns, horns have always been associated with cuckoldry. Thus the cuckolded man is no different than el buey who walks around with horns he cannot see looming over his head.

But I digress. Because my father was no buey and he was no cuckold. He was in fact, just a güey: a fool, a ridiculous man. This, in its simplest form, is what güey has come to mean. Among the more lowly folk of Mexico, güey is often used as a less-than-formal term of address. In English you might hear someone, most likely a male teen, refer to his friend as fool. "Hey, fool!" he might call out to his comrade insouciantly, without malice; and in turn the comrade might respond: "What's up, fool. What troubles thee?" There is no harm in such a greeting. The same goes with the word güey. But like the word fool, which can also be used to insult someone, so too can the word güey. And because of this, güey is a term that a son should never use to address his beloved papá.

I was ten when I first referred to my father as güey. It happened during one of those summers when my mother would send me to Chihuahua for my vacation. I'd been spending the day with my tíos José, Chuy, and Juanito (three of my mother's four brothers) at their home watching them build a brick wall around the backyard. Around midday, when they took a break for lunch, I joined them for bean burritos and Cokes on the front stoop of the house. My tíos were cool, real suave dudes. As they munched they tossed around jokes and stories about adventure and female conquest, more specifically about the neighbors' two daughters, a couple of pale and homely looking Mennonites with whom the three claimed to have had their way at one time or another, each claiming to have taken the virginity of one of the girls at some point. Even I, at my young age, was intelligent enough to realize that one of them had to be lying since there were only two girls and three of them. But each swore that it was he who'd done the deed, who'd slimed the panties of one of these otherwise virtuous creatures who lived by the word of God. None, however, on account of the girls being twins, could say with certainty which girl he had in fact devirginized, which in a way worked to defuse the argument. Whatever the case, and regardless of who'd been telling the truth and who'd been lying, talking about these girls made them laugh and giggle and slap hands. With less enthusiasm and fewer body gestures, they also talked about how they were progressing in their work building the wall. There were times when they'd point to what was great about the wall and times when they'd point to what was not so great about it and shake their heads in disappointment. Other times they'd bring me into the discussion and ask what I thought about the wall and about the neighbors' daughters. They'd mostly laugh and go wild over the magnificent shit I said. This made me feel like I fit right in with them—real cool, like I was a real suave dude, too. And every time they referred to a male in one of their jokes or stories, they used the term güey. They threw it around like bolo at a Mexican wedding. Sometimes they'd even address one another as güey. This being the case, and me being the naive and wickedly amenable little gamin that I was, I began to softly utter the word beneath my breath and quickly took to liking it. It tasted something fresh on my tongue, new. And the more I uttered it, the more I grew in spirit and manhood. I could feel my little balls growing and I couldn't wait to use the word freely, out in the open, in front of my tíos. I'd be great in their eyes. They'd get a real kick out of hearing the word shooting forth from my sloppy mouth: "What a great kid this kid; he catches on quick; he's just like us." I imagined them giving me manly nudges on my chest and chin and high-fiving me. The scene played out in my head as concretely as the brick wall that was taking form before us.

It didn't take long for the perfect opportunity to present itself. My tío José, who has always been of a devilish mind, and who'd been sitting the farthest from me on a pile of red bricks and cement sacks, asked me: "Obed, ¿no extrañas a tu papá?" to which I gaudily replied: "And why would I miss that güey?" I'd done it! I'd shot the word right out of my bean burrito–filled mouth and into the dry Chihuahua air for my three suave tíos to hear. Without a snag my "güey" made its way right into their powdered-cement-dust-filled ears like red jalapeño peppers up their culos, causing them to let out a collective explosion of cacophonous laughter. Confused, chaotic shrieks came from their mouths as they clutched their pansas and kicked out their feet like fighting cocks. I didn't feel like that suave little vato I'd been earlier when they'd laughed at my silly wisdom. Instead, a sharp shiver shot up my spine, paralyzing me with ache and fear. The sound was ugly. It pounded in my brain like the bells of Notre-Dame in the brain of Quasimodo. Suddenly, I wanted my tíos to stop, to shut their mouths and swallow their laughter, which felt like a big hand gripping my neck and cutting off my air. I wanted everything to go back to the way things were only moments earlier. Suddenly, from some feet behind me, I heard a voice say: "¿Qué onda, hijo? Why do you call me güey? Soy tu papá." His words met my heart with the crashing force of a bowling ball hitting the floor. I immediately realized my mistake, my childish blunder. My innocence had been taken for a ride and I'd walked right into the trap these three Lady Macbeths had set for me. Even if my tío José had not been expecting me to call my father güey, he had been expecting me to say that I didn't miss him, my father, who everyone but I had noticed was making his way to our circle, and this would have hurt nonetheless—even if not as much as hearing me call him güey. And now, feeling small and alone, I didn't know what to do. All I knew was that I had to turn to face my father. And when I did, he was already wrapping his arms around my paralyzed body; his lips were already finding a place at the base of my forehead, providing me with the sense of security for which, at that moment, my whole being had been desperately yearning.

Meanwhile, my tíos kept laughing crazily. And it hurt. I felt it choking me. And I wanted to get away from the awful sin

I'd committed against the man who loved me unconditionally. I didn't know what to say to him, and by the way he pressed me against his body to protect me from my culeros tíos' awful laughter, I could sense that my father didn't expect me to say anything. In the security of his arms, with my ear listening to the heavy beat of his heart, I felt like a little culero myself, and small, very, very small. I'd called my father güey practically to his face, offending his paternal spirit. And still, my father offered me a smile and his arms. I didn't mean it, Papá, really, I didn't, I wanted to say to him. I don't even know what the stupid word means.

4

It's easy to escape into the bottle, to say fuck the world and all its problems—nothing to it. I got drunk last night for the first time after having returned from Chihuahua only a week ago. And this morning when I woke up with a hangover, the first thing I thought of doing was drinking again.

It was Sunday and I had nothing to do. I mean, there's always something to do—as my mother likes to say—you just have to get off your ass and do it. But I didn't. I didn't do whatever there was to be done because from the moment I awoke yester-morning all I could think of was how good it'd feel to have an ice-cold beer. So at about three in the afternoon, after arriving home from basketball practice (yes, wheelchair-people play basketball, too), I showered, dressed, and rolled my ass down the block to the friendly neighborhood liquor store. I wanted a thirty-two-ounce in memoriam of my father, a mean caguama to take down just for him. And not just any caguama, but a Carta Blanca, the same kind my father drank, Chihuahua's premium beer for the poorest motherfucker around. I thought I was a lucky guy when I saw it through the cooler's glass door. "Now would you look at that," I said as I reached up for it. "A real Carta Blanca caguama. Thanks, jefe, you must be watching out for your dear ol' son." I really thought that it'd been my father's doing; that somehow he'd put that Carta Blanca caguama there for me, like he now had some kind of magical power dead people get. "I'm going to drink it just for you, ya veras! We're gonna get real fucked-up today!"

At home I opened the garage door, sat on the La-Z-Boy facing the street, threw on some real cool borracho-time Mexican corridos, popped open the caguama with the bottom end of a Bic lighter, put its cool mouth to my lips, and began to drink. I could've been a commercial for misery the way I sat there with my happy-go-lucky face and Kool-Aid smile after that initial drink, for it instantly took away all the stress and pain that I'd been feeling and made me feel merrily alive again, real firme-like—even Jesus could've made me feel no better.

I drank and sang along to corridos like "Cruz de Madera" and "Dos Monedas" by Ramón Ayala, both of which had been sung by a triste pair of guitar-strumming compadres at my father's funeral, and both of which, in a sad and twisted way, aptly portray the way in which my father had lived and died: like a pitiful alcoholic nobody.

"Cruz de Madera," for example, is sung through the perspective of a poor man whose only wish when he dies is to have a lowly wooden cross mark his grave. He doesn't want any luxuries, or a mausoleum, or a coffin "que valga millones." Instead, he wants his mourners to sing him songs; he wants "la muerte de un pobre" to be turned into a celebration. And in keeping with the true spirit of the poor Mexican wino, midway through the song, el cool cantante asks that instead of holy water, tequila be poured over all four corners of his sepulcher:

> Cuando ya mi cuerpo esté cerca a la tumba
> Lo único que pido como despedida,
> En las cuatro esquinas de mi sepultura
> Como agua bendita que riegen tequila.

¡Vaya! What a way to go for this proud Mexican wino with an imaginary crown on his head, a beer in his hand, and not a peso in his pockets. Even in death he's king—rey! Even in death his delusions make him see glory in a bottle. Still, he's unable to let go of the show, of the character, of the bullshit macho identity he dragged through town for so long, scaring the mierda out of every woman and child who crossed his path to nowhere; pobre diablo with nothing more to hold on to than this dreadful image. But he needs to be justified, absolved of meaninglessness. He cannot have lived for nothing—and so he sings and lives in the words of a timeless ballad.

"Dos Monedas" is slightly different, though it, too, is driven by Mexico's other holy trinity of Drink, Poverty, and Death. Also sung from the perspective of a poor borracho, the song is a dark, melancholy tale of alcoholism and tragedy. Beginning with el borracho—the singer—modestly describing himself as el hombre "más desdichado en el mundo," or "the most unfortunate of fathers," as Herod said after murdering his own sons. The song quickly moves into the unforeseen and unforgiving, into the deepest and blackest crevice in every drunk's heart. El borracho begins to delineate in detail the story of when and how he lost his son. On a rainy night, he sings, while drunk inside his home, his son arrives, cold and empty-handed, from begging in the street, and pleads with his father not to torment him about it. But being completely swallowed by the booze and fiending for more, the father ignores the pleas of the son and instead beats him "hasta casi matarlo." He sends the child back into the street to do more begging while informing him that he will have neither a home nor a father if he returns with no money. And after the son leaves, the father continues to drink until eventually passing out. In the morning when he wakes up and notices that his son is not home, he opens the front door to find him curled up on the ground "muerto de hambre y de frío." In one of the dead boy's hands are "dos monedas," which he had brought home to give to his father so that his father could continue drinking: blessed be the heart of the child who loves his father and also fears him. And with the same modesty he expresses at the beginning of the song, el borracho—now the forsaken piece-of-shit father who's to blame for the death of his own son—feeling the nails of his sin, urges other soon-to-be-piece-of-shit fathers to not harm their own sons, to not do what he has done. He sings:

> Yo le quiero pedir a los padres
> Que no le hagan un mal a sus hijos,
> Tal vez Dios me mandó este castigo
> Por tirarme a la senda de vicio.

The song is terrifyingly sad, yet beautiful, and is the anthem of many a poor wino in Mexico. And when you sing along to it, you feel the imprisonment of the son and the sick desperation of the father; a battle between good and evil. And what do you do when it all becomes too much and your inebriated heart cannot bear *being* any longer? Well, you drink more, of course! Evil always wins, and you always *will be*. Bottle in hand, you surrender to the spirits. "Till the end, drunk man! Till the end!" You have seen it all play out in front of you one and a thousand times over, and you have come to realize how much more beautiful the story is when you sing like a karaoke singer with fleeting pathos. And so I kept drinking and I kept singing, pouring myself a cupful between songs, just like my father would do. This is how the child of the dead alcoholic grieves: like the father lived.

The crippled mess of me sitting on a La-Z-Boy at the threshold of my garage with my lifeless legs propped up on a wheelchair singing along to borracho ballads about alcohol and death while chugging beer from a glass, a curious spectacle to the handful of neighborhood children who'd gathered on my driveway in their dirty rags and with their crusty noses to watch me sing. This is it, kids, this is the future for many of you; if you have a father or if you don't, this is where you'll be some years from now. In my haze I looked out at their astounded little faces, amused and silent. I wanted to cheer with them, to toast with them, to cry with them. I wanted to tell them to always love their fathers no matter what. Be a son and love him. I wanted to pour the words into their little hearts: be a son and never forsake him.

I'd end up taking a trip for a second caguama, and eventually, at a bar with a few of my cousins getting more shit-faced than shit-faced, rolling up to complete strangers and telling them about my tragic loss. In my best shit-faced speech I'd say to them, "My father's dead, he died a few days ago, won't you cheer with me?" And they, being kind and shit-faced drunks themselves, would say, "My friend, I do not know you, but I'm sorry to hear that your father is dead." And most times, whether man or woman, they'd either put their arm around me or offer me a hug and say, "Here, please, let me buy you a beer." And without being too modest, I'd tell them that it wasn't necessary; that although I appreciated the gesture very much, they didn't have to. "No, no," I'd say, wagging a finger, "it's cool, really, my father was an asshole. He drank himself to death.

Please, you don't have to." But asshole or not, they'd insist and the beer would eventually reach my hands, and I'd eventually take it down with a boundless appreciation. "You're too kind, really . . . what? . . . cheer for my dead father again? . . . well, if you insist." Bottoms up. Bottoms down.

The next morning I woke up shirtless and with the sun in my face on a dirty-ass couch with ants and spiders crawling all over it and me on the back porch of one of my cousins' apartments. "¡Que mierda!" I cursed the sun, and with shame shook my head and uttered: "My father's dead, and I have a fucking headache!"

The closer I get to the casket, the more difficult it becomes for me to keep pushing. My arms become heavy and my heart begins to race. What the fuck—go, he's right there. But I can't. I can't make it all the way to the coffin. I stop about three feet short from the damn thing and turn my back to it. "What the fuck are you all staring at?" I say beneath my breath to all the sour eyes hovering at the door. I hate that they're still there doing nothing more than gawking my way as if I were about to do something miraculous, like bring the dead man back to life. Run along now, you scoundrels, there's nothing to see here, and miracles are for suckers. I turn back toward the casket, and this time I catch a glimpse of my father's shiny nose and forehead. I can't hold back any longer. I have to see all of it: the complete silence of the storm. Bracing myself for the inevitable, I push forward with the frail fortitude of a condemned man. I become steel in one breath and the dried-up petals of a daisy in another. The lifeless presence of the man I'd loved unconditionally as a child and had come to hate as a man is stirring in me a whirl of emotions I can't control. So much is dead there, forty-eight years of memories. The man in front of me had been my father, and the reality that he was now dead, which I'd been suppressing since the moment I first learned of his passing, is finally coming into being. The death was real. The masses had been telling the truth all along—my father was a corpse. He was dead. My father was dead. A flush of warmth rushes through me, and I feel a wave of tears wanting to break through the windows of my eyes. It's as though they'd been checked at the depths of my entrails and are now trying to make a break for it and there is nothing I can do to stop them. Fuck, Pops! Why'd you have to go and die for? What about the fish and all the sodas? Didn't you care anymore? I pinch my nose at the tip and wipe the tears away. I have to stop them. I can't give in. I can't let anybody see. The madness. The hell. What love can become. And just like that, I do. I seal the dam and stop the torrent. It's a new day. It's a new day. Remember the monster. Remember the fury. I bring my head up, shake off the fear, move closer to the coffin, stretch my neck out and glance at the corpse inside. There, stretched out in front of me, is a lovely and solemn image of silence. I take a deep breath and let out a long sigh. A smile comes over my face.

"So this is what you look like dead, eh, Pops?" I say to the body in the box as I place my hands over the plexiglass. "You look good, better than I thought you would."

But my father doesn't look good. I'm lying. Unlike the dead Ivan Ilyich's more pleasing countenance, of which Tolstoy writes, "as with all dead men, his face was more handsome, and most importantly, more significant than it had been on the living man," my father's face is a gross sight, terribly the same as the one he'd been lugging around long before his death. Aside from it now being bloodless and petrified, benumbed of life, the living man and the dead man share the same sickly face: a face that had aged too fast, a face that had already begun to rot while its cheeks still blushed. It was a century-old face, deeply brutalized through the years, trashed and corrupted. A scar for every battle and a wrinkle for every tormenting minute that had marked his life carries the tune, the shrills and grunts to its muted swan song. The crooked smile beneath the smashed and crooked nose that even in death reveals the one-inch gap where teeth eight and nine once were, is now testament to the unfavorable reality my father had put his face through. What is left of the hair on the head, like the mustache on the face, is mostly gray and sparse. He'd stopped dyeing them both. He'd stopped reviving those features that had once helped produce a handsome man and he'd settled with the degenerative jokes they'd become. The little bit of gray hair, the smashed nose and crooked smile, the missing teeth, the scars and wrinkles— Fuck 'em all, my father must've thought with delirium, what do I care for vanity when the high is much more wonderful! Fuck 'em all, indeed.

"What happened to your teeth?" I asked my father when I first noticed his top two front teeth were missing. And he told me he'd lost them as a result of eating too many sunflower seeds while working. "You have to break the shell to get to the seed, and after doing it so many times it eventually takes a toll on your teeth." But I knew better. He'd lost them as a result of the drinking and cocaine. And one after the other, the teeth came out.

"Shit," I told him, "those seeds must've been hard as rocks, and not the kind you smoke." He laughed and gave me his you-think-you-know-everything-mister-I-come-from-Washinton [translation: Washington] look. Commenting on my own teeth, he made the remark that the reason they were so white and straight was because I lived in the United States and had the money to buy toothpaste and see a dentist regularly. This explanation was laughable, though he had a point about me being able to see a dentist regularly while he could not. In Chihuahua, going to the dentist is a luxury that only a few have; as a result, it's not uncommon in that big city and state to see a young man or woman not even twenty years old with ugly brown teeth looking like they've been eating shit. Regardless of this unfortunate fact about the desert state, and perhaps about all of Mexico, I knew that my father was using it only because he was incapable of telling the truth. "It's this fucked-up country and this fucked-up poverty," he'd say, rather than admit he was mostly at fault. But having been around junkies enough on this side of the border, I'd seen first-hand what cocaine can do to a person's teeth, which are usually the first things to go. It'd been the combination of cocaine, alcohol, and constant disregard for proper hygiene that had caused my father's teeth to fall out, because even if my father had had the luxury and inclination to see a dentist regularly, he wouldn't have taken the dentist's advice to quit the cocaine and alcohol and to brush daily. He would've laughed at this little gem of wisdom, and as soon as he was out of that dentist's office would've been stomping his feet on the pavement, heading straight to the store for a caguama, and after that to the connect for a blast. This is the nature of the junkie: to disregard wise advice. And whether in Mexico or the United States of America, the junkie is the same. Always the same principles apply. His livelihood is only relative to his addiction. Everything else is inconsequential. Borders and boundaries are elusive concepts and life itself is one fleeting moment after another; the body's only a compressed clump of molecules and atoms driven by the fiend inside—the ailing soul. To the junkie, the outer appearance of the body means little to nothing, its maintenance nothing more than a trivial formality he'd rather not bother with, or be bothered by. Like the child who throws away his marbles when he feels he's outgrown them, when the junkie loses his teeth he tosses them to the wind and continues forward with his irrepressible march into the abyss of despair—straight into the hands of Hades. This is what my father had become. At full tilt had he marched into his own casket.

My father hadn't always been indifferent to his appearance. Even in his early forties, he had still made the effort to look presentable. He often dyed his hair and mustache jet-black and brushed his teeth daily. In a black-and-white photo I took of him in September of '04, this is strikingly apparent. Sitting on a concrete bench in front of his home and leaning casually against a wall, he looks stocky and strong, full of life. His chest and stomach are thick and taut under his dark blue workman's T-shirt and his veins protrude up and down his forearms like lines on a map. His wide neck looks solid. But nothing is more telling than his face. It is round and glowing, pleasant to look at. His hair, thick, full, and combed carelessly back, along with his dense mustache, are the blackest things in the picture—them and the black of his eyes, which stare out at you coquettishly like those of a man in love. Careful not to reveal too much, his smile is closed and slightly curved. And somewhere behind it, I daresay, though perhaps not in the best condition, is still a full set of teeth. At forty-two, my father looks like a healthy man who still has decades of life ahead of him. Nothing about it reveals the alcoholic that he was, or the dope fiend he'd soon become. Nothing about it speaks of death.

There is something else, however, that this picture does reveal, at least to me. A memory I'm compelled to relay in consequence of my own guilt. Two days before I took this picture, I arrived in Chihuahua only months after the last time I'd been there and found my father with an almost-full head of gray hair. Astonished by the sight, and true to my impetuous nature, I said, "¿Qué onda, jefe? You got old on me!" I didn't know it then, but these words would be enough to send my father into a midlife frenzy. So, later in the evening, when I returned to the house after having spent the day in el centro with my brothers, I found him sitting on a chair in the center of the living room with Cokis standing behind him coloring his hair black. My father let up a big grin when he saw me come through the door, as if he already knew I was going to say something hurtful, which again, I was quick to do.

"¡No mames, jefe!" I said to him with a saucy smirk on my face. "You're actually dyeing your hair? Only old women do that."

Here was my father, feeling the afflictions of old age as a result of my impulsively cruel nature, pitifully attempting to fight off time by buying himself a couple of years with cheap hair dye, and I was making a mockery of the whole situation with more distasteful and stinging comments. Certainly my father had only wanted to look his best for me, a fact I now recognize.

My father laughed and didn't say a word. Just looked at me with dejected eyes and laughed. *I still love you, son*, those eyes said, *and I always will*.

❧

I remove the plexiglass and, in doing so, cut my thumb. "Why the fuck would anybody put this here!" I quietly curse. I also note that the person who'd placed it there hadn't done a good job of gluing it to the coffin. It comes right off and I can see the clumps of yellow glue on the inner edges of the coffin's lining. "What a shitty job," I continue to say to myself while holding the glass above my father. "Only in fucking Mexico!" And after recalling a line from Octavio Paz's *The Labyrinth of Solitude*, where he separates the "carelessness" and the "negligence" of Mexico from the "precision and efficiency" of the other "North American world," I place it upright on the floor, lean it against the coffin, and begin to suck the blood from my thumb.

"Damn it, Pops," I say quietly. "Even in death you're fucking me up. No, I'll give you that, viejo. You never hit me. You never once raised a hand to me—I'll give you that. But look, now you're cutting my shit up, and all I want to do is touch you and run my hand over your beautiful face." I lean in, hang my arms over the edge of the coffin, and place my right hand on the left side of his left cheek. It feels cold and solid, and somewhat oily. Slowly, I begin to run my hand down to the bottom of his chin and then back up to the top of his cheek, softly, and then harder. "Wake up, viejo! Levántate," I say to him as I playfully tap both sides of his face. "Mira que ya amaneció," I sing to him. But he isn't waking up. He's a stiff and as stiff as a figure at Madame Tussauds wax museum. Yet, I feel that he's enjoying my game and silently laughing at my antics. I hear him say, "Stop fucking around, hijo! Can't you see I'm dead?" And I tap him again just to hear him again. "All right, hijo! I'm going to get up now, if that's what you want. Here I go."

I think of the mornings when Aarón would rest his head on our father's chest. I'd watch them from the couch as they lay on a blanket over the living room's concrete floor. Aarón would tap our father on the side of his face until he'd open his eyes, and when he did, he'd say, "Hijo, do you love me?" And Aarón, still with his hand on our father's face, and with puppy eyes, would reply: "Sí."

Someone has dressed my father. I wonder who. He has on a tacky, colorful long-sleeve button-down shirt with little light green, yellow, purple, and red squares. The jeans are old and faded, and I can't make out if they were once purple or blue. Whatever the color, one thing is certain, they're pants fit for a poor man, because like the shirt, they're something you'd find at the Goodwill or Salvation Army on this side of the border. "Shit, Pops," I say as I pull at his clothes, "in the States you'd've had on a suit and tie, and maybe even a crispy white handkerchief to go with it. We'd've made you up into a nice little lie over there, into a nice little gentleman. Not here, though. Here they're keeping it real with you."

Fuck the bullshit. My father had never been a gentleman, and the closest he ever came to having a white-collar job was when he drove around Chihuahua as a bill collector in an old pieced-together motorcycle and pounded on debtors' doors. He'd always been a man from el barrio who preferred to work with his hands. They'd been his livelihood, what had always kept food on the table for his wife and kids and a plump caguama for him at his side. My father had been a yesero till the day he died: El Cerro de la Cruz's premier plasterer. His hands said it all and his clothes told no lies. A suit would've been a laughing matter.

My father had been a plasterer for most of his life. He'd been good at it, too. I know this because I've not only seen his work, but I also had the privilege of seeing him work. As a testament to the quality of his work, his clients had often sought him over others when they needed additions or repairs done to their homes or businesses—that is, until he began to skip out on them with their down payments, at which point they blacklisted him for good.

When I was a young boy, I'd tag along with him and my tío Trini (my father's youngest brother) on some of their jobs. Sometimes I'd help out by carrying materials or mixing yeso in a wheelbarrow, wooden crate, or bucket. For the most part, though, I'd just watch. I'd take a seat on a cinder block or plastic crate in some corner, a Coke bottle in hand, and stare out at my father and tío intently as they splattered the white goo onto a raw surface and spread it out with large blades and long two-by-fours until it was completely smooth. Soon, walls and ceilings that had once borne the dull appearance of block, brick, or concrete would take on a white semblance of perfection, and my father and tío would look like they'd been assaulted by Jackson Pollock. They'd be covered in drips and globs of yeso from head to toe, and when I'd point and laugh at the million-dollar canvases they'd become, my father, turning to my tío and then to me, would shrug his shoulders humbly, raise his hands, and say: "We're poor, hijo. What do you expect? This is how we earn a living."

My father had also been an artist, and not in the generic sense that he was artful as a yesero. My father could draw and paint anything on any surface. As a young man, he'd been apprentice to Chihuahua's own Aarón Piña Mora, one of Mexico's great painters and muralists of the latter part of the twentieth century. "Piña Mora really loved your father," my mother always says when she tells the story about how we all once lived in one of Piña Mora's homes on what was then the rich part of Chihuahua while he taught my father to paint. "You were not even one year old when we lived there," she says. "You were barely learning to crawl. It was a big house, two-story. And all I had to do was take care of you. And your father, all he did was paint with Piña Mora. Piña Mora would teach him from morning all the way until sundown."

I'm an artist, too. Ever since I can remember, I've enjoyed picking up a pen or pencil and letting my imagination guide my hands. In elementary school, my teachers would praise me for my drawings and other artwork (which incidentally, is all my teachers ever praised me for); and throughout my elementary and middle-school years (I dropped out of high school in the ninth grade), art was the only subject in which I ever did well. "Wow, who taught you how to draw?" my chirpy teachers would ask, and my only response would be: "Nobody." But I was lying. Because although I never mentioned it to them, I knew that somehow, through some genetic principle, my father had taught me. Whether it was by copying a rose he'd drawn at the bottom of a letter he'd sent me on one of my birthdays, or by copying the Disney characters he'd drawn in black ink on a white handkerchief for me while he was in a Texas jail once for trafficking drugs, or by replaying some distant and vague memory in which he is sketching my portrait on a large square of whitewashed plywood, I knew that my ability to draw had come from my father, from my blood-connection to him.

Piña Mora, who died on April 19, 2009, approximately three months before my father, had been godfather to my father's brother Trini. During his younger years, my mother has told me, the famous painter had been a good friend of my grandpa Polo, my father's father. "Polo used to work in Piña Mora's furniture store in Cuauhtémoc. That's how the two met. And then, after some time, Piña Mora made Polo his personal assistant and driver. Your father was just a kid, about seven or eight years old at the time. And Piña Mora loved him. Bah! El pintor loved your father more than he loved his own godson Trini. He loved your father so much that he would give him everything. Later, when your father was a teenager and he and your abuelo Polo were living with Piña Mora in his home, Piña Mora had your father going to the best schools in Chihuahua. He paid for them and everything else having to do with your father's education. He saw your father's talent for painting as a gift that needed to be nurtured and guided. And that's what he always did for your father. But did your father appreciate it or take advantage of it? No! He goofed around more than anything else, and soon he stopped going to school altogether. And even though that hurt Piña Mora, he still didn't give up on your father. He continued to teach him how to paint and to give him everything he wanted. He always believed that your father would come around and see what a great talent he had. After I married your father and you were born and the three of us were living en la casa de las bolas [the house of the balls, the name my mother and father gave to the house in which Piña Mora let us live because of the two large glass half spheres that made up much of its roof to let in sunlight that was essential for painting], Piña Mora would always tell me to be patient, that your father would eventually change. And sometimes your father showed signs that would make us believe that he actually would. He would do what Piña Mora asked and produce beautiful paintings that showed promise. Some of the rich ladies from the neighborhood would even buy them from your father. They liked that they were done in Piña Mora's style and that they could buy them for much less. But as you can see, son, your father never changed one bit. He was too stubborn—too stubborn and too lazy. Plus, he couldn't stop drinking. He always preferred to drink than to paint."

And that was that. My father gave up. He'd never learn to be a great painter, and his talent, for the most part, would remain dormant for the rest of his life. Only a few reminders of his bastardized talent remain. In my mother's home in California, for example, a 20-by-15-inch oil painting of an arrangement of gray and blue samovars and some fruits hangs on a wall above the kitchen table. It's signed *Juan Jesús Silva, 1980.* My father was nineteen when he painted it, and I was one. And for as long as I can remember, the painting has hung above the kitchen table in every house and apartment I have ever lived in—whether with both my mother and father or just my mother—that one and the portrait of me done in graphite on a large square of whitewashed plywood. That portrait is signed *J. Jesús Silva Feb. 19, 1985,* only sixteen days after my sixth birthday. I like to think my father painted it with my birthday in mind, though I can't say with certainty. One thing I know for sure, though, is that he must've been happy and proud when he finally finished it. "My son," he must've uttered while rubbing his black-stained fingers and looking at it from a few feet away. "That's my son. My beautiful son." I wish I could remember the moment when he first showed it to me all complete. But I was too young. All I manage to see in my mind are his artist's hands moving across a white board, magically creating an image of a young boy whose deep black eyes are looking out at the face of his father: creator re-creating his creation.

It's disheartening to know that my father had the talent to be a great artist, painter—one of the greatest even—but that he let it go to waste. In Robert De Niro's film *A Bronx Tale*, Lorenzo teaches his son Calogero that "There's nothing sadder than wasted talent." He tells him that "a loser isn't someone who's stupid; he never had a chance, God made him stupid. A loser is a guy who could have made something of himself but didn't. A loser is a guy with wasted talent." In *Don Quixote*, Cervantes reminds us of this same maxim. In the marvel related by "the man conveying the arms," a regidor who is easily mistaken for an ass for his ability to bray like one, says to another ass-like braying regidor: "And I will further assert, that there are rare gifts going to waste in this world for the reason that those who possess them do not know how to make proper use of them." When I think of these words and those of Calogero's father, I cry; for like the borracho ballads I listen to every time I drink, they tell the tale of my father. They paint the truth. My father had been a man who did "not know how to make proper use" of his rare gift, and as a result became the "guy who could have made something of himself but didn't." My father had in fact been a loser. He'd been in the dark to what the bus driver and the ass-like braying regidor both profoundly understood and prudently expressed.

When I asked my father why he'd chosen not to continue to learn to paint under the instruction of Piña Mora, the only reason he could offer was that Piña Mora had been too strict. "He always wanted me to be painting," he said cavalierly as he stood before me outside his house holding a can of Carta Blanca. "I didn't like that, so I just left, with you and your mother." My eyes and face dropped, and all the blood in my brain rushed to the base of my cheeks, swelling and giving them a crimson coat from hell. He was too strict? Was my father serious? Was he really killing my day with this bullshit? I shook my head in disappointment and spit on the ground. I pushed the saliva out slowly and watched as it made its way down, as it crashed upon a parade of ants, ruining their enterprise. Where to go now that their course had been disrupted? What of their destiny? What of all the assholes in the world, the pricks who take it all for granted? Scatter, little ants! Run to safety! Find another way! I hated the sound of the crackling can in my father's hand, and I hated the shitty boots on his feet. I wanted to spit on them, too. They were dirty, filthy and fucking ugly, like the broken ground they stood on. It can't be, I kept telling myself. Just can't be. There has to be another reason. Something that makes sense.

"Are you really that stupid? Is that really why you left?" I asked him. "Come on, there has to be something else you're not telling me. Please tell me there's something else." But there wasn't anything else. He assured me that that'd been the only reason: Piña Mora had been too strict. He stressed it and even showed surprise at my inability to accept it as a good reason. He smirked and shook his head in disbelief at me. How was it that I couldn't recognize his plight?

"No, you just don't get it," he said to me. "You just don't know how he was with me. He never wanted me to do anything except paint. ¡Era cabrón!" That's all that my father could add: that Piña Mora had been an asshole. I didn't say anything more on the topic after that. I'd got it. My father was a man who could never handle discipline or order, a man who could never adhere to the principles that guide the relationship between master and apprentice, teacher and student. He preferred to laugh at greatness, to have nothing to do with it. To him a thing like greatness was too superficial, too detached from the chaos and misery he had such an affinity to. And there was nothing the artist could show him or teach him about life, because on top of everything else, my father was also a man who thought he knew it all.

5

Two weeks after I returned home from Chihuahua, Aarón called me to give me disturbing news about Danny. "He destroyed my dad's room," he said. "¡Lo madrió todo! He went in and started breaking everything. He broke the windows, the television, and all the shelves. He even ripped the bed apart."

"Why?" I asked Aarón. "Why'd he do it?"

"He was drunk. He's been drinking a lot lately, and every time he gets drunk and comes home he goes mad and starts to yell and break things, but this time he went too far. He broke everything in the room."

Before our father died, Danny had never displayed destructive behavior, and he'd never drunk much either. He'd always been quiet and withdrawn. "¿Qué onda, Danny?" I'd say to him in an attempt to pull him out of his silence and involve him in our discussions. "What's with you, man, why don't you ever talk?" My efforts, however, would go unrewarded, because all he was ever inclined to reply was: "Nothing. Nothing's wrong with me. I'm just here, listening." Unable to get more out of him, I'd turn to Aarón and give him a what's-wrong-with-this-kid look, to which Aarón would say: "That's how he is. He doesn't like to talk much." This being the case, I'd always thought of Danny as being like the shy kid at the school dance who tucks himself away in a corner and retreats into his own muted world, preferring to hear than be heard, to observe than be observed. So to learn that he'd put on this violent spectacle was shocking.

"What do you mean he's been drinking a lot lately? Danny doesn't drink like that," I said to Aarón.

"It's true," he continued. "He's been drinking almost every day for the past few days. Almost nonstop, and we don't know what to do."

Listening to Aarón's revealing words, I recalled how on the day that our father died, Danny, not realizing that I'd already received the news from Aarón only minutes earlier, called me crying to tell me that our father had passed. "He loved us a lot," he kept repeating, and all I wanted to tell him every time I heard him say those words was to shut the fuck up, because he must've not been talking about our father. I couldn't respect his pain. It seemed superficial, like an empty gesture for his dead father. As the eldest after me, I'd wanted him to be strong, to hold back his tears and take leadership of the family.

Aarón went on to tell me that the weekend before, Danny had shown up to our cousin Chuy's house, where Chuy and Aarón had been drinking with friends, and picked a fight with Aarón. "He got there drunk and began to hit me," Aarón said. "¡Me pegó!" These words sank to the bottom of my stomach like an anchor and began to stir there. There was something absurd about them, and it made me angry.

"Danny hit you?"

"Yes," Aarón went on. "He kept screaming at me and asking me why I'd hit my dad. He was mad because I'd hit him, and now he wanted to hit me. 'Why did you hit him, pendejo! Why did you hit my dad!' he kept screaming at me."

The news was becoming more alarming at every turn. Danny had attacked Aarón, and now I was learning for the first time that Aarón had hit our father. As it turns out, on many occasions when our father would show up drunk and belligerent to the house, wanting to start a fight with their mother, Aarón would step between the two and push him away. Of course, fists would start flying.

"You'd actually hit him, and he'd actually hit you, and with closed fists?" I asked Aarón.

"Pues sí," he said with peace in his voice, as if it were what he'd been put on this earth to do.

I didn't feel anger toward him when he told me this; on the contrary, I felt proud of the little guy. He reminded me of the little boy in Dostoevsky's *Crime and Punishment*. In Raskolnikov's dream, he attacks Mikolka and other drunk men after witnessing them horribly whip a helpless "puny mare" for thrills. Aarón, who's no taller than our father had been and weighs no more than a hundred and twenty pounds, like a fearless little vato and budding gentleman, stood up to protect his powerless mother. He took the hits from his father and gave them back tit for tat. The safety of his mother had been all he cared about. I pictured him raising his fists to his elbows and dancing around calmly with subdued adrenaline, like a young César Chávez, and telling our father to bring it, and our father, with his ominous eyes and slimy smile, spit on his chin, cowardly, taking up the challenge. "¿Quiere darse un tiro? ¡Pues vengase!" I could hear Aarón saying, and fiercely roaring like a cub in the wild, like a boy on fire.

All I felt toward Danny, however, was anger and disgust, like when he'd wept for our father over the phone. In my eyes he'd given up, and again he'd failed to lead. Instead, he'd let our father break into him like a demonic spirit. He'd drunk the fire and turned it into thunder, and in turn, just like Daddy, had cowered into hell.

Danny had gone as far as claiming that he was a better yesero than Aarón. When I asked Aarón why, he told me that this was a jealousy Danny had been holding inside for a long time; for Danny, unlike Aarón, had rarely done work with our father. Aarón had gone with him almost every time since the age of fourteen, when he'd stopped going to school. He'd been his young apprentice, and this had planted a seed of jealousy in Danny that he'd never been able to weed out, and that was now bearing the rotten fruits of hate. Now that our father was dead it gnawed at him to know that he hadn't been the one to accompany him. But who was he fooling? He was too late. Our father was dead, and frankly, he never would've given a fuck if Danny accompanied him on his jobs or not.

Axcel had also been a victim of Danny's drunken tantrum that night. When she arrived at the house, Danny, still fuming after having fought with Aarón, pulled her out from the passenger seat by the hair and began to pummel her with his fists.

"He beat her up, too," Aarón told me. "He dragged her out of the car by the hair and beat her in the middle of the street. Me and Chuy had to pull him off her."

I've tried to come up with a reason for why Danny acted out in this way, and every time I go back to those moments when I'd try to get him to talk and he wouldn't. There had to have been something behind those dreary eyes and that half-ass smile I'd mistaken for shyness that said he was suffering, that said he'd one day explode into a whirl of violence. There was, I suppose. Because knowing what I know now—about our father, and all the terror he created—I realize that it had more to do with the observation Victor Hugo makes in *Les Misérables* when describing Cosette's laconic personality. When Hugo wrote the line "nothing habituates children to silence like misfortune," he could easily have had Danny in mind. Like Cosette, who "had suffered so much that she was afraid of everything, even to speak, even to breathe," Danny had been afraid to open his mouth lest he open his soul for more suffering at the will of our father. Danny had seen too much. Countless times he'd seen the endless tears that spilled from his mother's eyes when they were met with the power of his father's fists; countless times he'd seen the lumps and bruises, and the blood that dripped onto the soiled floor from the head and face attached to the curled-up body against the wall; countless times he'd seen the way a scream materializes when the Devil appears holding hell in a bottle. This had been a recurring scene in my brother's home from the day he was born, and he'd been there to see it play out every time. Danny had continually been witness to the madness and the horror that accompanied our father when he'd come home. He knew the truth and could never bring himself to participate in a lie; he'd rather be silent than pretend that certain things hadn't happened and were sure to happen again. For him, moments of happiness had become ephemeral. He knew that they could never last forever, and because of that he could not allow himself to fully exist in them. Our father's will had been all he could ever count on as everlasting, and our father's will had always been violence. Violence: the only constant—the only sure bet. And with our father gone, that sure bet was gone, too, and Danny was having trouble living without it. For once a constant is gone, we tend to replace it with another. This is what Danny was trying to do. He was trying to bring that violence back.

A drop of blood from my finger falls onto my father's face and lands on his cheek just below his right eye. "Oh, shit! Sorry, viejo," I say, laughing, to the dead man. I put my thumb to my mouth and suck on the cut. With my other hand, I rub the drop of blood from his face and, after looking over my shoulder, wipe it on the sleeve of his shirt. "Fuck it," I whisper to him, "where you're going, this shit ain't gonna matter no more." I then tap his chest with the same hand and remember the tattoo on his left breast. I undo two buttons and spread the shirt open and there they are, tattooed in crooked cursive over his quieted heart. The years have faded away much of the cheap ink, but one can still make out the names: my mother's name, Marcela, on top, the Spanish conjunction *y* in the middle, and my name, Obed, on the bottom: *Marcela y Obed*. My father would say the tattoo had been his way of keeping us close to his heart "¡para siempre!" And every time he'd say this I'd think of the abhorrence that must've come over my mother's face when he first showed it to her. He: the pathetic lover. She: the disparaged woman who could only see in him the brutal beatings he was commonly inclined to give her. A tattoo of her and her son's names over his heart meant nothing.

I take my thumb away from my mouth, hang it over the

tattoo, and let it bleed until a couple of drops fall onto it. Then, with the index finger of my other hand, I softly dab at the two drops on his chest, blend them together like oil paints, and begin to spell out my name under the tattoo. As I do this, I quietly utter: "You were my father, and I am of your blood. I am your son. I am your son. Take it, Daddy, take your blood with you," and I finish with these words from Dostoevsky: "Tomorrow I will bury you. I have spoken."

I feel relieved when I finally leave my father and roll out of the parlor, like something big and dreadful has been done with, something like arriving at the final period in Joyce's *Ulysses*, like I could finally put this fucking book away forever. Life is a beautiful thing, and this is how it eventually plays out: every horror has its end. "Bye, bye, Daddy-O!" I say to my father before finally moving away from the coffin, without placing the plexiglass back over him. "I hope life's kinder to you on the other side, and *you* . . . are kinder to *it*." A rush of joy moves through me as I make my way out the doors and through the crowd. I could be rolling out of hell it feels so good.

The next time I'd come back into the parlor to see my father—which would be a few hours later—I'd be completely drunk, shit-faced, but happy, fully happy.

6

There's still light outside, enough for me to make out people's faces, though I hardly recognize any of them. Cokis, Danny, and Axcel are the first to meet me when I come out. They greet me with huge smiles, though Danny's quickly turns to a clump of shyness. Cokis and Axcel hug me and ask how I feel. "Fine" is all I say. I can sense they want me to say more by the way their smiles half disappear and their eyes open up when I don't. But I don't care. That's all I have. Besides, my tíos and tías and other people whom I don't know quickly move in and surround us. Like a thief, I want to sneak away to a tight corner where I can't be seen. I want to take a break and gently breathe in the sunset before it slips away behind the horizon. But no, such an escape is not happening. Because before I know it, I find myself again in the center of a circle of palpitating bodies lurching over my suffocating skin. The Silva scent is everywhere and there's nothing I can do to shake it. It's everything that I breathe. "Just be one with it," a voice in my head says to me. "Be one with it and bask in its stench—Silvas are beautiful, too! Remember that, and love the misery as it loves you!"

My father had been the sixth of nine brothers and sisters, nine Silva-Sánchezes, children to the great Apolonio Silva-Díaz and

Guadalupe Sánchez-Chávez, both of whom have long passed. The eldest of my father's brothers and sisters is my tío Victorio (b. 1949); next in line is my tía María (b. 1951); after her comes my tío José-Manuel, who was born many months later the same year my tía María was born; after him comes my tío Remundo (b. 1956); then my tío Apolonio (b. 1957); then my father (b. 1961); then my tía Guadalupe (b. 1962); then my tío Rumaldo (b. 1964); and, finally, my tío Trinidad (b. 1965). Of these nine original Silva-Sanchez children, only six survive; like my father today, two have been dead for some years now. My tío Rumaldo died in 1979 (the year I was born) at the young age of fifteen; and at the age of thirty-nine, in 1990, my tío José-Manuel died, too. But while my tío Rumaldo died after having been tragically struck and run over by a car, my tío José-Manuel died of the same disease as my father: cirrhosis, or better yet, alcoholism. My tío José-Manuel was the first to go from the disease and my father the second.

Of the six of my father's brothers and sisters who are still around, there are only two I know well: my tía Lupe (Guadalupe) and my tío Trini (Trinidad). Unlike the rest, they are the only ones who, like my father had, call Chihuahua their home. They've never lived anywhere else. Both have their families there. My tía Lupe is mother to a son close to my age and has been married to the same man for many years. They have a home and small candy store in El Cerro de la Cruz only a block away from where my father's house is. I love my tía Lupe, and I care much for her son and husband. My tía has always been good to me, a real sweetheart. She's plump and has white skin that is soft and always looks fresh. She smiles and laughs a lot, too. She also loves to hug me and pinch my cheeks every time she sees me in the same way fat aunts often do to the cheeks of their nieces and nephews in Hollywood movies. "¡Que chulo, mijo!" she says to me with a big smile on her moon face. "You are so handsome." I rejoice in her sentiments. But what makes my tía Lupe stand out from the rest of the Silvas is that she doesn't drink, at least not to the point of getting drunk. She'll have the occasional beer at the occasional party, but nothing more.

My tío Trini, however, is more like the rest of the Silva siblings.

"Let's go visit your tío Trini at his new home," my father would say to me when I was a kid on account that my tío Trini never lived in the same place for long. We'd always have to go for a ride in one of the many beat-up cars my father had owned throughout his life, or on one of Chihuahua's ever-polluting and sardine-packed piñata buses with the long snouts, rides that, though bumpy and long, I enjoyed because I was always right next to my father. Whether standing or sitting on the plastic seats, I was always holding on tightly to one of my father's legs, and he always had an arm wrapped around my shoulder, and every time the bus jerked when taking off he'd tighten his arm around me and I'd pinch hard on his pants. Once the bus caught rhythm and the jerking stopped, it was all good. I'd look up at my father, and he'd look down and smile, and I'd smile back, and then I'd look around at the people on the bus with all their belongings and worries. I was part of them, and they were part of me. We were all of the same class that needed this type of public transportation: undoubtedly bad for the lungs, but good for the spirit—because no matter how bad anybody had it, or where one might have been going, we were all in this loud and lurching beast together, moving through this small but dense city with our eyes wide open, taking all of it in. There were always many stops from El Cerro de la Cruz to El Centro. Buses in Chihuahua don't travel like the ones in the States. Where, in the States, buses tend to follow a linear trajectory, like a boulevard or main highway, in Chihuahua the buses travel in and out of almost every barrio, squeezing themselves through tight streets and stretching themselves around sharp corners like serpents. All the while, the passengers grip the ends of their seats lest they slide off, or hold on tightly to the rails along the ceiling if they're standing. And on Chihuahua buses there is no maximum capacity—the drivers keep letting people on even when they're being squeezed out the windows and doors. Often there are two or three men or boys hanging out of the open back door, fully exposed to the elements and balancing themselves on one foot on the door's step. I admired these desperate riders, and would watch them closely through the small gaps between the standing bodies, waiting for one of them to meet a tragic end. And as the bus moved down the road or made long turns they would jeer and shout and howl like wolves, with the thick air and smoke from the other cars and buses crashing hard against their dirty faces. I wanted to be like them, but I didn't really because I was too young to be so brave, too young to be so independent and wild and away from my father. But I enjoyed these bus rides nonetheless, even if I wasn't one of the ones hanging madly out of the bus, because Chihuahua meant so much to me, and it always had something for my eyes, which became a cinema screen of fleeting moments. Chihuahua is not famous for its architecture, by any means. There is nothing impressive about its downtown buildings. Most are similar in design: square and straight up. But it's not the buildings that matter, it's the people, the life that is always happening, just like in every other city of the world at every instant of time. Chihuahua moves, even if slowly. And it shines, even if roughly. And it always shone in my eyes. From La Vialidad to La 20 de Noviembre to La Libertad in El Centro. I'd be hypnotized by everything and everyone there was to see: from the people of all shapes and sizes, all more Mexican than I could ever imagine, walking down sidewalks along the rows of low-ceiling adobe houses and the big building structures closer to downtown. And the cerros were never too far away; you could see them from every direction lining the desert-valley town, from El Cerro Coronel to El Cerro Grande and every cerro in between. They, with the dense clouds, were always in the background of every barrio and every colonia we passed. It wasn't until we'd make it into El Centro, swallowed up by the high-rise buildings, that they'd all of a sudden disappear from my eyes. In just one turn they'd be gone, and we'd be in the belly of the city, where everything seemed to move fast, too fast for the young boy who held on for dear life to his all-knowing and protector father, who, once the bus had come to a stop, would say, "We're here, hijo," and take him by the hand and walk him off the bus and pull him through the masses of people doing what people do in big cities: speed up dying. And soon we'd be at my tío Trini's front doorstep.

My tío Trini also worked with my father as a yesero. Before Danny and Aarón grew physically capable of doing it as well, it had been only my father and my tío Trini slinging the white goo. For work they were always together, and for drinking they were always together, too. They did both at the same time.

I have to say something important here about my tío Trini. He's been clean since the last time I was in Chihuahua in 2007.

It was then that he got out of a detox center and started singing his praises to Jesus Christ his Lord and Savior. I know this
because at the time my father was singing his praises to Jesus
Christ, too, and joining my tío Trini at a local Christian home,
where on certain nights of the week drug addicts and alcoholics
gathered to support each other in their sobriety. Only problem,
though: Every night after those meetings, when I'd pick up my
father to bring him home, the first thing he'd want to do was get
a beer. And though I wasn't surprised anymore, I still had to ask:
"¿Para qué güey? Why go to the meetings if you're just going to
keep drinking? Why waste your time?" And my father would
say: "Well, to support your tío Trini, of course, why else?" Why
else? Of course why else, my mistake, what was I thinking
asking such a ridiculous question when it was obvious to see
that my father, with his kind heart, was only sacrificing a bit
of himself to save his brother—how naive of me. And now the
Good Samaritan is dead while my tío Trini's still singing his
tunes to Jesus Christ his Lord and Savior.

So here are my tío Trini and my tía Lupe alongside each
other, welcoming me with sweet words and big hugs, the first
two to step forward from the circle and embrace their little
dark-skinned nephew from el otro lado.

My tío Polo, on the other hand, who is also in the circle and
steps forward to embrace me after my tía Lupe and my tío Trini
step aside, looks like a man who still drinks heavily on a daily
basis and also indulges in other mind-altering substances. He
has the tired and weary face of the alcoholic and the fiendish
look of the junkie. And sadly, in this, he reminds me of my

father. Looks just like him the way he's standing before me in his white tank top and dusty blue jeans staring at me with his sunken yellow eyes and breathing his dragon breath onto me. He's no slice of heaven, no pretty cloud.

"Yo soy tu tío Polo," he says, extending his arms out to hug me. "Did you know about me?"

I welcome the hug, but because I hadn't been expecting him to ask me this question, I stammer in my response: "Ah . . . sí, sí . . . oh . . . of course." Truth is though, I knew short of nothing about the guy. Only thing I knew about my tío Polo at the time was that he and his son had both been shot at one night a few years back while standing outside of their home in Albuquerque, New Mexico. His son had been hit in the stomach and was in serious condition for a while. My sister Cecilia had called me about it when it happened. I remember growing curious about my tío Polo and wanting to learn more about who he was after that. Must be a crazy motherfucker doing crazy shit if people are looking to kill him, I thought at the time. Shit, must be a little like me. I'd wanted to meet him ever since. And now, here he is in front of me, standing as a man who, aside from being slightly taller, resembles my father in almost every unfortunate way, including in the fact that he too is missing his two upper front teeth. "¡Que loco!" I say to myself when he smiles and I notice the hole in his mouth. "I hope that shit ain't genetic." And putting my index and middle fingers up to my own two upper front teeth, I pray to God for them, for Him to keep them safe and forever where they belong—in my mouth.

My tía María and my tío Victorio are the next of my father's siblings that I have never met to greet me now. Both, like my tío Polo, resemble my father in many ways. My tío Victorio, I note the moment I see him, is like an aged version of my father, what he might have looked like had he lived another ten or more years, from the stocky frame of his body to every protruding bone on his face. Surprisingly, though, unlike my father and my tío Polo, my tío Victorio has all of his teeth. There's hope after all, I think when I peer into his mouth. I search for signs of alcoholism and drug use on him, too, but I can't find any. The man speaks clearly and appears to be in considerably good health. He gives me a hug and tells me, as the others had, that he's glad to see me after so many years, and that he's happy I've come to say goodbye to my father. As he speaks I notice his hands and fingers; they're thick and heavily scarred. I engrave the image of them in my mind and recall it years later, in early 2017, while speaking to his son Víctor-Manuel over the phone. He's telling me that his father had been a badass when he was younger, that the scars on his hands and fingers are the result of cracking human skulls with them. "Era chingón para pelear mi jefe," Víctor-Manuel says proudly. "Le gustaban los putasos." According to him, my tío Victorio had never lost a fight in his life, and he'd been in many, too many to count. Though I'm surprised by the undefeated element of it all, I'm not surprised about the violence. Violence is in our blood. And just as this thought crosses my mind, Víctor-Manuel says, "I guess that's where I got it from. I used to fight a lot too when I was younger." "Really?" I say. "Yes," he continues. "Where do you think I got this scar on my face, the big one across my forehead? Some dude hit me with a two-by-four because he couldn't beat me with his fists. I was on the verge of killing him." And then he laughs loudly, and I follow suit. Víctor-Manuel has a gift for telling stories and for making every one of them, no matter how sad or tragic, funny. We're having this conversation because my tío Victorio is in a convalescent home and wants Víctor-Manuel to take him out of it and back to Chihuahua. At this time, my tío Victorio is in Belen, New Mexico, Víctor-Manuel is in Las Vegas, Nevada, and I'm in Buena Park, California. My tío had had a stroke and was now recovering as best he could, but because he didn't like the young nurses cleaning his shit, he wanted to be taken to Chihuahua where family could care for him and not young nurses, which Víctor-Manuel is telling me over the phone is what he'd want one day: to have a young white nurse wipe his ass and feed him in bed. He laughs every time he brings this up. I laugh, too, especially since I already know what it's like to have a young white nurse wipe your ass and feed you in bed; it's not all it's cracked up to be. Takes away all your dignity and pride, so I can see where my tío Victorio is coming from. When I ask what may have caused my tío Victorio to have a stroke, he tells me that it most likely was a result of his drinking. "Really?" I say. "I didn't think my tío drank."

"¡Qué?" Víctor-Manuel says. "¡Como que no! Toma un chingo. Siempre ha tomado. ¡Toda su pinche vida!"

And when I tell him that the reason I didn't think he drank was because, at my father's funeral, I'd thought he looked well and sober, he tells me that that was because, at the time, he had been sober. "For some time he had stopped drinking, but it didn't last. In fact, he stopped a few times, but it never lasted very long. Siempre volvía a lo mismo." Made sense to me.

My tío Victorio goes on to introduce me to his children and wife. At first I think my tía María is his wife because the two introduce themselves to me at the same time. But when I ask my tía if this is the case, she laughs and tells me that I'm crazy, that she's my father's sister and that my tío Victorio, too, is her brother. "They're my brothers, hijo, and I'm your tía," she says, smiling and kissing me nonstop on the cheeks the same way my tía Lupe had done. "¡Que chulo muchacho!" she also says. After giving her a closer look, I'm able to see the Silva in her bulging cheekbones, protruding forehead, and deep dark eyes. And although I'm struck by her penciled-in chola eyebrows, I'm happy to see that she, like my tío Victorio, also has all of her teeth. Yes! Yes! How delightful it is to meet you, too, tía! You are beautiful in a Madame Thénardier sort of way, and I love you already.

Lastly, there's my tío Mundo, whom I've already met once seven or eight years before, but whom I hardly recognize when he steps forward to greet me. He doesn't look like the same tío Mundo who'd blessed me with one of the strangest experiences of my life the day I met him, which was a good thing because on that day he looked like a man who was on the verge of destruction, similar to how my father looked the last time I'd seen him alive.

"Soy tu tío Mundo. Do you remember me?" he says excitedly, as he leans in to embrace me.

"Oh, sí," I remark, slowly and with a curious smile.

"You don't, do you?" he says, noticing my memory fail me, and he provides the following clue: "You came to visit me in San Diego."

I laugh as the memory surges back, and pull him in to give him a big abrazo. How can I forget San Diego and my crazy-ass tío Mundo! I can't. He's the same man playing a trick on me, for the change is unbelievable.

My tío Mundo called me out of the blue those years ago, introduced himself and told me that he was my father's brother, news that wasn't quick to strike me as exciting. I mean, here was this person I'd never met, and had only heard briefly about from my father, calling me after some twenty-odd years of me being alive telling me that he was my father's brother, my uncle, and I was supposed to be excited or even slightly interested in the news? Not me. But my tío Mundo, unlike me, indifferent about my indifference and uninterested in my uninterestedness, was exhilarated over the idea.

"I've always wanted to meet you!" he said to me. "But I've never been able to because you've always lived so far. But I'm here in San Diego now, so I asked your dad to give me your phone number so that maybe I can drive down to see you, or you can drive over here where I am. How far are you from San Diego?"

Shit, I immediately started to think, this motherfucker's gonna want to hang out and try to bond with me. So I paused for a moment and estimated the time, which was unnecessary because I knew that San Diego was only an hour and a half to two hours away from where I lived; but I thought that pausing before giving him the answer would somehow make the distance stretch longer to the point where I'd be able to tell him, without feeling any guilt, that I was so far away from San Diego that it would be too difficult for either of us to drive anywhere.

It's not that I didn't like my tío Mundo—hell, I didn't even know the guy. But I knew that meeting him was not going to be anything special or life-changing for either of us. If we met, all that would be exchanged between us was a lot of small talk to fill in time, and I wasn't looking forward to that. He was my uncle, so what? What were we going to do once we saw each other—hug, kiss, maybe tell each other how much we loved one another? Fuck that. I already had uncles, from my mother's side, whom I'd grown up with all my life and whom I already loved, and I wasn't looking for another one. Yet I couldn't bring myself to turn him away; it just wasn't in my Silva heart to do so. After all, he sounded so excited. "About two hours," I told him.

"¿Dos horas? That's not too far," he said. "You think you can come over here?"

"Where, to San Diego?" I said in my most unexcited voice, hoping he'd get the hint. But he didn't. He only became more energized and continued with his plan to have me come out there, which, of course, had been his goal all along. His intention had never been for him to come and see me, as he had initially stated. He'd turn out to be much like my father in this way.

"¡Sí!" he said. "I'd go out there to see you, but I don't have a car right now. Mi vieja takes it to work every day."

I paused again and thought about the benefits of meeting him. Will it be worth it? I had to go deep to find the answer, which, when found, still didn't seem like the right one.

"All right, then," I finally said to him, already regretting my decision. "I'll come out there."

Two days later, I was on my way to San Diego, not knowing what to expect. I wondered if he looked and was anything like my father, and if I'd get along with him. And what would we talk about? I also thought about what we'd do besides talk.

I pulled up to a seemingly new apartment complex in a lower-middle-class neighborhood away from downtown. It was quiet. Not what I'd been expecting. I'd been expecting him to be staying in a run-down apartment in a barrio with raza all over the place and crying babies in dirty diapers running around unattended. Instead, I found myself driving up to an apartment complex with manicured lawns, trimmed trees, clean walkways, and residents who preferred to socialize inside of their homes rather than outside. Not bad, I thought, shit just might go all right and this dude might actually turn out to be pretty cool. Maybe I'll accept him as my tío after all.

When I reached his apartment, I knocked on the door. My tío Mundo answered quickly. What the fuck! My tío's a fucking tweaker, I mentally noted when I saw him appear from behind the door in black dusty jeans and a dirty white tank top. What I saw was a short and skinny man with a buzzed head wearing clunky black prescription glasses, who looked like he'd been up for one too many days. My tío, scraggly, greeted me with the same crooked smile as my father's, revealing a black hole where teeth eight and nine should have been. Bells started to go off in my head. Surprise! Surprise! The world is a stage and life a clown show: everyone's a fool. But of course, how could he be any different; after all, he was my father's brother—a Silva! It just wouldn't have been right had he been healthy looking and dressed in Dockers and a cardigan sweater pulled over a checkered wool vest—¡chale! God doesn't joke like that, and I'm glad, because as he was he was perfect: my tío Mundo. Mundo: world—¡vaya!

"Soy tu tío Mundo," were the first words out of his mouth. He leaned in to hug me. I tried not to breathe lest I inhale his odor. After, he took a step back and scrutinized me from top to bottom. For a second he paused on my wheelchair and offered a sympathetic smile. Tears began to form in his eyes. "Ah que Obed," he let out like a last breath; then, after raising his glasses and wiping the tears away before they could slip down his rough cheeks, he hugged me again. I welcomed this second hug more than the first, and I pulled him in close to me, and I breathed. It felt right, and he didn't smell bad. The blood in our veins had made the connection even before our minds, at least mine. "So qué—what do you want to do?" he proceeded to ask excitedly. I hadn't said a word yet and he was already moving into the future.

"Whatever, tío."

I called him tío without hesitation. Felt natural rolling off my tongue, and I believe it felt natural to him as it slid into his ears, because he seemed not to make any note of it; he just went on talking, something I'd soon discover he loved to do.

"How was the drive, good? Come in, come in. I'm all alone. There's nobody here." He walked in and I followed. "Can you make it? Do you need help?" he asked, looking back at me cautiously. But before I could answer he saw that I was moving with him and said proudly: "You don't need any help. You got it. ¡Eres chingón!"

The inside of the apartment was nothing impressive. The furniture was from your average discount Garden Grove, Korean, going-out-of-business-sale furniture store and the walls were bare of any picture frames or artwork. "This is my girlfriend's apartment," he said, moving about the place with ease. "Es Americana, una gabacha." He picked up a spotty silver-framed picture from one of the two lamp tables that stood on opposite ends of the living room couch and handed it to me. "This is her. She's a little fat, but she's nice. She's been letting me stay here." She was more than a little fat, but I didn't say anything. I also noticed a few toys scattered on the floor and asked if he had kids with her. "No," he said. "It's her son. He's little. He likes me a lot, too, just like his mom. He's at her mom's house—con su abuela. She picks him up after work. They'll be back later tonight. Are you going to stay till tonight? You can meet them if you do."

Nope. I had no intentions of staying. "Wish I could," I told him, "but I gotta go in a couple hours. There're some things I have to do. Plus, my girl's gonna be home in a couple hours, too, and she'll be waiting for me."

"Oh, you have a girl?" he asked curiously, and nodded his head approvingly. "I bet she's pretty, eh?"

"Hermosa," I told him, and he repeated the word after me, slowly, pausing for a moment after it had left his tongue, as if in contemplation, as if creating his own mental image of her. And then, without notice, as if unfrozen by a snap of the fingers, he got back into character and snatched the frame from my hand.

"Bueno, está bien," he said, sounding a bit disappointed. "The important thing is that you came. I'm glad to finally see you again. You were still a baby the last time. You don't re-member that, eh? Claro que no. You were just a baby. You can't remember."

What my tío Mundo and I ended up doing for the next couple of hours was drive around the outskirts of a suburban part of the city in his little red pickup truck. I didn't say anything to him about him having told me over the phone that he didn't have a car to drive because his girlfriend took it to work every day. I just let it be. After all, he wouldn't have been my father's brother if he hadn't also been a liar.

I didn't know where we were headed. He just asked me if I wanted to go for a drive and I said, "Yeah, sure, what the heck."

What else were we going to do to kill time, bond over crackers and tea? Sheee-it! Silvas don't work that way. No Cleavers here. No black-and-white American-dream family. So after only a few minutes of being at his apartment and me having a cup of water, we were off on a mission to seemingly nowhere. Our first stop was a liquor store, where my tío Mundo got off to buy a six-pack of beer. From outside the truck, he asked me if I wanted any kind in particular, and I, respectfully, informed him that he could get any kind he liked because I wouldn't be drinking any. By this, the man was stunned. He immediately leaned in through the truck's window with his eyebrows crunched over his eyes and stared at me like I was some kind of strange being, an aberration, a freak of nature even, a Silva like no other he'd ever encountered before.

"Are you sure?" he asked, hanging his head through the window and tapping his hands on the door.

"Yeah, I'm sure," I said to him, feeling a little disappointed in myself. For it was not that I didn't want to drink a beer with my tío Mundo in celebration of our nephew-and-uncle re-union, but rather that I knew if I started drinking with him I'd most likely end up really drinking and eventually be re-ally drunk, at which point I'd be forced into having to decide between whether to stay at his apartment overnight or drive home completely cara-de-mierda, and I didn't want to do ei-ther. And though my tío Mundo had initially shown surprise at my declining of his offer, he didn't press me to reconsider.

"Va pues," he said, stepping away from the truck. "I'll just have to drink them all myself. But how about a soda, you want a soda?"

"Yeah," I said, accepting his compromise. "I'll take a soda."

"A Coke?"

"Yeah, a Coke's good."

I stared at him as he walked away from the truck toward the store and lost myself in the idea that he was my uncle. I let it seep in. I thought I liked it. Didn't mind that he might be a tweaker or that he was an alcoholic, nor that, like many other Mexican illegals, he was living off a homely fat white woman. If anything, the whole thing made me laugh, and I indulged in the moment. I was already thinking of how I had to tell my girl and family back home in the County of Oranges about my crazy-cool tío Mundo, and of how he'd turned out to be nothing short of the ideal human being—a prince in my book, a soul without apologies.

He was all too happy drinking his six-pack of Budweiser beers alone as he drove me around, showing me the different luxury homes where he said he worked as a gardener. He was also happy to be the one doing all the talking. Between sips, he'd point to different houses and tell me about how he worked on them and about the people who owned them. "They're all güeros," he said, "and they all have lots of money. And they all like me, too. And the wives are all a bunch of horny viejas! Some of them walk around the house wearing almost nothing—and I like that." He was in love with his words, and after a while, I began to fall in love with them, too, the way they flowed so rapidly from his lips like a fountain. I enjoyed watching him, the way he drove with one hand on the wheel and the other atop the beer can resting between his legs, constantly pulling and turning the pull-tab, and often turning to me to give me a great big toothless smile.

Also enamored with the people he worked for, he told me about all the gifts they'd given him throughout his career as their gardener, even showed me some as proof. There was the gold-rope chain around his neck and the silver college graduation ring with a black stone he proudly sported on the middle finger of his right hand (he didn't look like a college graduate, or even a high school one for that matter), and then there was the autographed hardcover book of a certain San Diego Padre he pulled out from beneath his seat. I couldn't believe it. "Mira," he said with a grin, "I work for this guy. He plays for the Padres. Open it. It's signed and everything!" It *was* signed, and dedicated, too. It just wasn't signed by the player and it wasn't dedicated to my tío Mundo either. The book, as I'd come to learn through close examination, had been a first print and had been given to the player by his manager. The short dedication written in black ink on its title page were a few endearing words from the manager to the player. And from what I was able to discern from the penmanship, they mainly expressed the manager's wish for the player to have the first copy of the book. So of course the signature was the manager's and not the player's. My tío Mundo was evidently unaware of this. Probably unable to read English, he'd had no clue of what the dedication said and only assumed it'd been written and also signed by the player. "¡Mira! ¡Mira!" he said as he pointed to the signature. "That's him, he signed it!" All I could do was smile and chuckle inside, though I wanted to burst with laughter; I mean, here was God being more than a jester, he was being downright malicious, cruel to this unenlightened crook who spun tales to exalt himself. As I stared at the oblivious man sitting next to me and listened to his boasts, I couldn't help but think about how much he reminded me of my father, of the way he, too, was full of

himself and his lies and thought it all great. And just like with
my father, I wanted to call my tío Mundo on every lie he was
telling me. Bullshit! Nobody gave you these things. You stole
them and you know it—everything, you stole; from the neck-
lace to this book, you stole it! But I didn't say a word. Instead,
I looked away from him and out the window and let his words
turn to mush in my ears. I let him ramble on without paying
him any mind. I wasn't delighted to hear him anymore. I didn't
love his words. The whole fucking thing was now beginning to
stink. I was realizing that he was as empty as the crushed beer
cans at my dead feet. There was nothing intriguing there, only
lies and crazy talk, shit I'd heard a million times before from a
million other fucked-up junkies who loved to give meaning to
their lives by spitting bullshit accounts of their fruitful exploits.
This shit's fucking amazing, I thought to myself as I began to
zone out. This motherfucker's crazy; he really believes this shit,
and what am I doing here again? I'm feeling thrown off now,
confused, totally fucked with, like my tío Mundo's turning out
to be exactly what I'd expected, a man too similar to my father.
Alas, the romance has disappeared and the mush is making me
twitch; it's tickling my eardrums like a spider creeping into my
brain. I want to be home now, with my girl, loving her, kissing
her, sucking on her white breasts and brown nipples, telling her
how she means the world to me, and not in this fucked-up gardener's truck driving on this San Diego back road scoping out
rich people's homes like a crook while listening to this madman hemorrhage from the mouth. No! Not here. And so my
mind runs away, to look toward a better day: for some fucking
dream made up of another fabric to wrap myself in. My father's
face comes to me and escapes me, laughing and screaming that
I'm a sucker with a soft heart. It rolls down richly green hill-

sides and bumps into bountiful tree trunks. It takes me home
and back on a fragrant wind that reminds me of childhood. It
turns into many faces, into many memories, and then to more
mush. I love you, Mamá, my heart is screaming now. You, my
queen. You, the birth point of my every thought. And I love
me this dirty white bitch. Lo! How pleasing is whiteness to the
shitty eye! She's driving the car next to us at a stop waiting for
the light to turn green. I envy her face, her car, and everything
she represents. She's beautiful. Like she's easy to talk to. With
skin the color of candles and hair the color of Ponyboy from
The Outsiders. She doesn't have much makeup on, and she
doesn't need it. Her fingers with fake French-tipped nails on
the steering wheel are long and lustful, like ones I'd love to have
in my mouth circling my tongue. She's doing that tapping thing
on top of her steering wheel that women do when they have
long nails and are anxiously awaiting something. I'm taking
in every wave in slow motion. First her pinkie nails drop and
then the rest follow, like a human wave at a professional baseball game. Shit's turning me on. I imagine them working their
way down my pants, and then her lovely Marilyn Monroe lips
making the same trip. I want her to see me. I want her to turn
my way and connect her eyes with mine. Because I don't get
it. I don't understand. How the fuck is it so? How is it that the
ugly and the beautiful can meet at a street signal and have the
union go unnoticed, unmarked by history, untold by any hand?
It must happen all the time and everywhere the higher class
have the poor clean their shit. So what gives? Should someone
not tell the world about it? And what the fuck am I doing in
this shitty truck that smells like a Mexican cantina listening to
this crazy tío of mine whom I just met not even an hour ago rant
on about opportune robberies and fleeting glory when I should

be sitting shotgun in this rich bitch's silver E-Class taking in her Chanel all the way to her home atop the hill where satin sheets are the norm, and all the while holding her hand in mine on my lap, softly feeling the tips of her fake-ass crazy-glued-by-a-non-English-speaking-Korean fingernails? "You're great, God, real swell," I quietly utter to the Man in the sky after the light turns green and she hits the gas, leaving me behind. I'm crushed because she never turned my way, because she will never know I exist.

We've been driving for over an hour, and if I'm going to keep listening to my tío and his amazingly ridiculous stories, then I'm going to need a beer. There's still three left. Fuck it, I grab one and pop it open.

"¡Ah, no que no quería el muchacho?" my tío is quick to remark.

"Just this one," I tell him, already regretting the fact that I hadn't been able to keep up my resistance.

"That's fine, nephew, enjoy," he says, encouragingly, while also giving me a look that says he'd known all along that I was a Silva just like him, and that it'd be only a matter of time before I showed it. And maybe this is why he now feels free to ask me the following question:

"Do you do drugs?"

A junkie has no limits, no grain of shame. I take a swig from my beer and shake my head no. But I'm lying of course; because at the time there was nothing I enjoyed more than a fat fucking joint. I was smoking a little more than an ounce of pure chronic a week those days, real stoner-like. In fact, I'd smoked two joints right down to my fingertips in the car on my way down to see him. Nevertheless, this isn't something I want him to know about me, at least not this soon. I don't trust that easy. He, on the other hand, has no scruples telling me about his own drug problem. "I like speed and rock—¡piedra!" he informs me real super-enthusiastically, as if he were about to bust out a glass pipe or piece of radio antenna with burnt Brillo wire pushed into it and start smoking from it right there in front of me. But he doesn't. Instead, he droops a little. Then, with a shake of his head, as if to free himself from a dragon: "I've been hooked on it for a little while now. Like for two years. I'm still trying to stop, but it's hard. That stuff's the Devil—¡hiiijole! When it gets you, it gets you. It doesn't want to let you go—¿sabes?"

"Yeah, I know." I take a long fucking swallow from my beer.

The sun's gone down. My tío's at the end of his fifth beer and I'm at the end of my one and only. We're pulling into the parking lot of his apartment and all I want to do is get back home. I've done what I'd come here to do. It's now time for me to be on my way and find my road less traveled. Our goodbyes are short and dulcet, nothing less than tender. He tells me how great it is for him to have finally seen me again and to have had this opportunity to get to know me a little. I tell him, "Yeah, I feel the same way." We hug, we lament, and we finally depart. And as I roll away toward my car he tosses in one last question:

"Hey! Do you have a gun?"

Perplexed by its randomness, I stop and turn to look at him with a what-the-fuck-did-you-just-ask-me expression on my face, and I remark, "A gun?"

"Sí, una pistola. You got one?"

"No, not on me," I tell him.

I don't have one at all, but I want to see where he's going with such a question. "Why, you need one?"

"No. I just wanted to know if you had one. Be good, nephew, maybe I'll see you again."

Crazy is as crazy talks. My tío Mundo was fucking crazy.

The next time I'd hear from him would be a couple of years later when he'd call me from a hotel in Los Angeles to ask me to come out and see him there. "I'll only be here for one night. I leave tomorrow back to New Mexico after I pick up what I came here for," he said in the same overly excited voice he'd had when he called me from San Diego. But oh no, I wasn't going anywhere this time. As soon as he said he was in Los Angeles just to pick something up, I instantly knew what that something was, and I wanted no part of it. So I played it cool and told him that I couldn't make it, but maybe on another occasion. "Can't do it, tío. I got shit to do over here. Maybe next time you come around."

But there was no next time. The months passed and eventually the years, and not another peep from my incredible tío Mundo. That is, until now.

Here he is in Chihuahua like me, to say farewell to my father. But he doesn't look at all like the crackhead I'd met in San Diego. Not in the least. The man has aged quite a bit and, more importantly, has cleaned up nicely. He looks healthy. He's put on a few pounds and has grown his hair out, which is completely gray like his thick mustache; and he's dressed decent, too. Has on a crisp, short-sleeve, button-down shirt with white and brown squares and clean light-blue jeans. And while his eyeglasses once added to his freakishly junkie look, they now make him look more like Geppetto than anything else. Teeth eight and nine are still missing though. I guess there's no helping that.

"¿Cómo estás, hijo? Don't you recognize me?" he asks.

I don't. There's no way for me to tell it's him. The man is a miracle in the flesh, a modern-day Lazarus. He's sober now—as I'd later learn—and glowing with life. Will you look at that, I think to myself, my dad's dead and my tío Mundo's more alive than ever.

I begin to fade away as more faces arrive and their eager smiles call for my attention. The red sky melts into a purple acid dream and everything and everyone around me turns into one black shadow. I'm off to another world, one made of a pretty face and dazzling moonlike eyes.

7

"Obed! Obed!"

"Yes. Yes. How are you?"

"I'm all right. And you? Didn't you hear me calling your name?"

"Yeah. I did. I just spaced out for a second."

"She's pretty, huh?"

"Who?"

"That girl you were staring at."

"What girl?"

"Don't play stupid with me. I was just watching you stare at her."

I laugh but say nothing.

It's my sister Cecilia. I'd seen her earlier sitting alone on the concrete bench on the side of the parlor when I first arrived. I'd meant to go talk to her but the others had prevented me from doing so. All I could do then was offer her a semi-sympathetic smile, which she kindly offered back. She understood. But I'm happy to have her standing in front of me now. She's a breath of fresh air, a cup of cold water to my parched soul. She brings something new to the scene, a little bit of Uncle Sam, some brightness to this gloomy portrait of disparaged Mexico. Fuck the Spanish, I could speak English with her, take myself back to my mean Orange County silver streets and talk up a lively mess of uncensored nonsensical bullshit in my un-native language. I see the United States in her face, my newly elected Black president and the red, white, and blue, wars and fast cars and just as fast-moving people, of all colors and tongues. She takes me away for a moment: no funeral, no Mexico, only the *"gleam of the morning's first beam."* I'm transfixed by the spark in her speak and sent spiraling into her dainty heart. I pull her in to hug her and tell her that I'm so very happy she's here.

"I'm glad you're here, too," she says, wrapping her warm arms around me. "I feel like I don't know anybody, and I've been feeling really lonely ever since I got here."

My poor little sister, not knowing how dark night can get, too, had followed the sun south to wish her dead father farewell.

Sister, you've come to watch your father's last act and can barely understand a word from the blizzard of words being spit at you from all these mouths. But let me ask you: What is there to understand? Do you wish to learn more about your father from those who knew him best? I'd sit at the back of the class and pretend I didn't exist if I were you. Truth is dangerous enough to kill your spirit if you don't know how to use a smile and how to dance around pain. See, Papá was a rolling stone and hated having to love; it was too heavy for his heart and so he fought against it to the end. And now he laughs from his little box, knowing that all his offspring have gathered today to weep for him. So wipe away those terrible tears, what purpose do they serve? Look! the sun is setting and there is a red blaze upon your face. I'm sorry to have to tell you this, my little sis, but your daddy's probably going to hell! No, not probably. He is most certainly going to hell.

I call Cecilia my half-white sister because her mother's a straight-up gabacha from Albuquerque, New Mexico—All-American pan blanco, with, I've heard, a little bit of some type of American Indian. I don't know how my father pulled it off, but he did. Must've been his ever-flourishing romantic sensibilities. Bullshit! Who am I kidding? My father simply found himself at the right bar in the right state in the right country at the right time, inebriated, overcome by lust, and without a condom. And the white girl—though it doesn't speak well of her taste in men—must've liked what she saw in the chapito. Daddy probably played it cool, told her a joke or two, maybe even told her she was beautiful in his paisa English and bought her a beer, just enough for him to get his foot in the door, and then his—well, a child was born.

Cecilia was born on October 13, 1985, but I didn't meet her until she was sixteen. Before then I didn't even know she existed. One day, however, in 2001, when I was twenty-two years old, while I was home doing God knows what, the phone rang, and when I picked it up I was greeted by a woman who said she had something important to tell me, that there was someone with her who wanted to speak with me, and when I asked her who, she, very casually, said, "Your sister."

"My sister?" I remarked with surprise, thinking she was talking about my sister Samantha, who at the time was twelve and in middle school. "What happened, is she all right?" I asked the woman, thinking she was either a teacher or the principal from her school calling to inform us that she was in some sort of trouble. "Samantha?" I eventually said, seeking confirmation that it was actually Samantha the voice on the other end was talking about.

"No. I'm talking about your sister Cecilia, who lives over here in Albuquerque, New Mexico." It now became clear to me that the woman was talking to the wrong person.

"Oh no, you got the wrong number, lady. I don't have a sister named Cecilia who lives in Albuquerque. My sister's name's Samantha, and she lives here, with me, in California." I felt confident the woman would recognize her mistake and hang up, but she didn't. And the reason she didn't was because she'd made no mistake. She was cool and continued on the line.

"You're Obed Silva, right?" she said with that added confidence in her voice that one gets when one feels absolutely certain about something. I, on the other hand, upon hearing my name come through the speaker, felt my own certainty that she'd mistaken me for someone else slowly diminish. As a result, I had to force my response, forbearingly pushing out each subtle syllable of the word: "Ye-ah."

"Then no, I don't have the wrong number, Cecilia's your sister. She's your dad's daughter. Juan, he's your dad, right?"

¡Puta madre! When I heard her say the viejo's name I felt like someone had slapped me across the face after telling me a cruel joke and was now encouraging me to laugh. What the fuck! You've got to be kidding me. But there was no kidding.

The woman was telling the truth. My dad, my sneaky little dad, was guilty.

"Juan, yeah—of course, that's my dad." And I'm his son, the pendejo you're talking to.

"Me and your dad, we were together sixteen years ago and I got pregnant with your sister." She came out with it just like that, like it was no big deal to her. And though the shit was surreal to me, it wasn't all that unbelievable. This was, after all, my father she was talking about. Of course he'd been with her and gotten her pregnant all those years ago and had never bothered to mention to me that I had another sister this side of the border. It all made perfect sense after a few deep breaths. It was in my father's character to hide his mistakes. In this case his mistake was not that my sister had been born, but that he, for whatever reason, had exempted himself of all responsibility as a father to her from the moment he'd found out she'd been conceived.

The last time I'd seen Cecilia was a couple months after I'd received the news about her existence, which was also the only time I'd ever seen her before now.

I drove to Albuquerque to meet her and I bought it right away. She had our father's face, from his passionate cheekbones to his large, round, dark eyes, and wide mouth. There was no disputing it. She was a Silva all right: the product of a man who'd never care or provide for her in any way. A phone call every few years was all she'd ever get from him. And now, here she was at that man's funeral, doing the most decent thing a child can do for their parents when they die—show up.

Don't count on me to give you the rundown on dad, little sis. He was how he was and died because he lived the way he did: loving his drink more than he loved his children. All I can tell you is welcome to the family. This is it. Look around you; befriend the misery and you'll be able to make a star out of every tear, music out of every cry. Grab someone by the hand and laugh with them until you understand their plight, until you know from whence their sorrow comes. It's a beautiful thing once you recognize it, like the sweet and insatiable fragrance of dark chocolate as it shoots endorphins straight up to your brain and arouses the senses. You then not only open up to it without fear, but embrace it like an empty couch on a lonely night. It all becomes a sickly joke that belongs to all of us and that keeps us all the same. For better or for worse, you are your father's daughter—you, too, are a Silva.

There is grief in Cecilia, but it has nothing to do with our father's death. Her grief is one born of an ignorance imposed on her; for here she is surrounded by people who carry the same last name as she, yet she barely knows any of them. She's the secret that was never meant to be revealed. But here she is now, all alone, looking shocked and confused, as if having finally found her way back home after being lost in the wilderness for many years, making note of every face and wanting every face to make note of her.

"Did you see Dad yet?" I ask her.

"Yeah," she says, bringing her eyes to her chest.

"And, what did you think, how'd he look to you?"

"I don't know. He looked fine, I guess."

"Handsome, eh?"

"Sure."

"Did you cry?

"No."

"Why not?"

"I couldn't."

Of course not. Why would you cry for him? It wouldn't make any sense.

～

Drunk off some cheap four-dollar wine, I'm back at home and writing this. And I'm stuck because I don't know shit about how my father met Cecilia's mother or what the circumstances were in which Cecilia was born. So I send her a late-night email asking her to tell me all she knows. But the next day when she writes back all I get is a short and unsatisfactory "I don't know anything." So I write her again and press her to find out, to ask her mother. She does. And the following day when I check my email I discover this short and heartbreaking tale of a little girl who never had a father:

> They met at a bar on New Year's Eve 1985. I was con-
> ceived January 12, 1985, after Dad went looking for my
> mom at my grandparents' house. Dad paid my grandma
> to babysit my brother and sister while he and my mom
> went out to have some drinks. Margaritas. They stayed
> the night at my mom's place and I was born nine months

and one day later. My mom said [our father] should
have a burn scar on his butt from where she kicked him
and spun him around and he bumped into the wall heater
and he burned his butt! They stayed together for a while
after that, living at my mom's house. But they were kicked
out a few weeks later. The landlord didn't like Mexicans.
So my mom went with Dad to his place. I don't know if he
had the place already. But they stayed in a studio apartment that only had a bathroom. The kitchen was in the living room/bedroom! So my mom told him he had a month
to get them all a bigger place, my mom already having
two kids from a previous relationship. He couldn't get a
bigger place, so on the thirteenth day my mom moved
out. She moved all the way to Roswell, New Mexico,
and stayed there until she was seven months pregnant.
Then she returned to Belen, New Mexico. My mom said
she would see Dad around town but they would not talk.
My mom didn't have a car, so she would walk to the
store and other places. And Dad would not pick her and
my brother and my sister up, Mom being all pregnant.
She had me there in Belen. My grandmother watched
my brother and my sister while she was in the hospital,
but left right when my grandpa brought her home. That
night Dad went to my mom's house doing doughnuts in
the yard and yelling out "My daughter! My daughter!"
but never stopping to see me. When Dad finally came
to see me I was one year old. I don't remember how
that went. Then again when I was five years old. This
time he took me to the store and got me a Barbie! My
brother went with me because my mom wouldn't let him
take me alone. Then the next time I saw him I was about

seventeen. I went and saw him in Belen. At the time I lived in Albuquerque, about fifty miles away. He came to Albuquerque to work the next day and spent a couple of days with us at our house. This was kind of awkward because I didn't know him. When he went back to Mexico he didn't even call to say bye. I did talk to him a few times on the phone but that was short and not so sweet. We never could communicate. The last time I saw him was at his funeral. Got any more questions?

Cecilia

No. There was nothing more I needed to know. From beginning to end, it had my father all over it. I could see him in every sentence: his shamelessness, his inability to feel anything for his daughter or for the woman who'd given birth to her. My father had been a selfish man, wickedly arrogant in his own ugly skin, for him to think that he could impregnate a woman and not do his part as a father, as a man. Sure, he hadn't had the means to support a family, and perhaps he'd never planned to have a child with a woman he'd only known for a short while. The unexpected always happens, and he probably tried. He had, after all, shown up at the woman's house on the night she'd come home from the hospital with her child yelling "My daughter! My daughter!" while doing doughnuts on her lawn. Yes, my father had shown up all right, but probably drunk and only because in his drunkenness he'd been unable to resist his narcissistic impulse to make a scene, to let it be known that Juan Silva was a man who'd made a child, that he was un hombre muy macho.

Thinking about Cecilia and my father, I can't help but think of my own life as a little boy. I have trouble connecting the two.

How could the father who'd always been warm to me have been so cold to her? A Barbie when she was five and a few "not so sweet" hellos when she was a teen. This man who on countless occasions had told me that he loved me while pressing his stubbly cheek against mine had been the same man who'd left this little girl to wonder what had become of her father. Did he even love her?

Sometimes my mother drops a jewel on me when I least expect it, like on the day she heard me singing "Hermoso Cariño" along to Vicente Fernández: "Hermoso cariño que Dios ha mandado nomás para mí . . ."—"My beautiful beloved that God has sent only for me . . ."

I'd been listening to this song in my room while grading my students' essays when she walked in, put her hand on my shoulder, and said, "You want to know something?"

I laid down my red pen, turned down the music on my phone, and asked her, "What?"

"When you were born," she said, "your father would sing that song to you almost every day. He would hold you in his arms, swing you from side to side, and sing this song to you from beginning to end. And you would never cry. You would just stare up at him with your big, wide eyes. Maybe that's why you like this song so much, because your father would sing it to you."

8

I've been asking for Aarón since I arrived at the funeral parlor. "Where's Aarón?" "Why isn't he here?" and "When will he be back?" I keep asking the crowd, but all anybody can tell me is that he left to pick up a friend only minutes before I arrived. I haven't stopped worrying about him ever since the moment I first heard him crying over the phone. I can't bear the thought of him being in pain. So the more that time passes and he still isn't here, the more desperate I get. I keep looking around for him, often ignoring the voices that fight for my attention. "Yeah, yeah, but where's Aarón?"

Finally, out of a mouth of people, he appears. He breaks through the crowd with a glorious smile aimed directly at me. Without saying a word, upon reaching me, he wraps his dark skinny arms around my thicker but just as dark arms and trunk as if he were a bounty hunter and I a fugitive he'd just captured. Squeezing me with all his might, he buries his face in between my neck and shoulder and begins to sob. This time, however, I don't pray to God for him not to start crying or for him not to fuck up my shirt. This time, I don't care. Let this boy cry. Let him make hell of my shirt. I don't say a word to him, and he doesn't say a word to me. We say nothing to each other. We don't have to. The pounding of our hearts speaks for the two of us; they say *I love you* to each other, and *I am happy to finally see you*. We remain embraced for a couple of minutes that, beneath the dark and melancholy Chihuahua sky, make up for the last two years we've been apart. My brother's tears are now running down my neck. I can feel them making a trail. There is no distance between us—no time and no border. His whimpers are at the base of my ear. They feel like quiet screams from a baby, echoes of a broken heart yearning for repair. *Your father is gone but your brother is here*, my heart screams back.

When we finally allow space to come between us and the world to reenter our lives, Aarón's first words to me are: "¿Cuándo te vas?" Already he wants to know when I'm leaving. Already he's preparing himself for what is sure to come. Reality has been cruel, and now he has to protect himself from it by mitigating the pain it sends his way. Every time I come I never stay, and every time he has to see me leave hurts him; it's something he can never grow accustomed to. And this time it will be worse. This time, it will hurt more. Even before our father died, every time I'd speak with Aarón over the phone the last thing he'd ask me before we said our goodbyes was "When are you coming back?" And every time I'd have to tell him that I didn't know, but that I'd make it there as soon as I could. Now he's asking me when I'll be leaving. If only I could say never.

I put my hands on his shoulders and place him at arms' length. I stare at him, his small frame and round brown face. I take my right hand and wipe his tears away, then run it over the angled scar on his forehead, a memento left from a car accident my father had caused as a result of him driving while drunk. Five-year-old Aarón had been sitting in the front seat, without a seat belt, between my father and Cokis, when my father, unwilling to listen to Cokis's cries to stop the car, ran a red light and sideswiped another vehicle. Aarón flew and crashed headfirst into the windshield. Unconscious, he was

taken by ambulance to the hospital and treated for a head injury. My father and Cokis would walk away from the accident
unscathed, though Cokis would suffer emotionally for many
years after, blaming herself for the accident, believing that it
had been her cries that had distracted my father from driving, causing him to run the red light.

"In a few days," I tell Aarón. "I can't stay that long, but I'll
be back." He lowers his head and continues to cry. I pull him in
and wrap my arms around him once again.

Before returning for my father's funeral, the last time I'd been
in Chihuahua was during the summer of '07. Since then I'd
been prevented from returning by my United States government. The only way I was going to return to Chihuahua after
that summer was if I were officially deported from the country or if I were granted a pardon by an immigration judge. For
though I'd lived in the United States all my life since the age of
one, and had been a legal permanent resident since the Reagan
administration, I was now, after this last trip to the land of the
Tarahumaras in '07, once again officially a wetback, a straight-up
mojado "subject for removal" at any time. I was like the annoy-
ing piece of masticated gum that sticks to the bottom of your
shoe and pushes itself completely into the grooves lest it be discovered, scraped off, and tossed into the gutter.

It happened when I flew into Dallas airport on my way back
home to California. At one of the gates I was met by a Department of Homeland Security agent who demanded I show her
my green card, which I did, and happily. I'd never had a problem before, so why would this time be any different? However,

after the inquiring agent ran my name through the system, everything changed—something was different. She quickly put up a rampart between me and the country I loved and led me to a room where I was to be interrogated by another agent. "What gives," I said quietly to myself as I followed the obese Black woman past various doors and down cold hallways away from the flow of travelers. Feeling nervous, I began to perspire heavily beneath my fake Panama hat and made-in-China gray guayabera I'd bought at Olvera Street in Los Angeles from a pushy Hondureña who said I looked like a real guapo in it the day before I had departed to Chihuahua. I couldn't have chosen a worse day to look like a wannabe Cuban communist or a Miami drug pusher.

In the room I was met by an older white male agent who was sitting at a wide metal desk in front of a computer. He was bringing a blue coffee cup with the Department of Homeland Security emblem stamped on it down from his lips when the sista walked me in.

"What do we got, Shirley?" the white agent asked, looking at me and my wheels and then back at Shirley, who was now at my side handing him my card.

"A possible subject for removal" was all Shirley said, before quickly exiting the room.

What the fuck did she just say? Removal from where, and who is going to be removed, and removed how, and removed when? I turned back to look at her as she walked away, hoping she'd say something more. But nada. She just turned and disappeared.

"What did she say?" I asked the white agent as he examined my card. But he didn't say a word. Fucker was as cold as the room. It was not until after he'd put his cup down and typed all of the information on my card into the computer and then intently looked over all that came up on its monitor that he finally turned to me and acknowledged that I was more than just a face on a card or a bunch of words on a screen.

"It seems you have quite a history, Juan. Is that your name, Juan Obed Silva Mendoza?"

"Yeah," I said, staring at the left side of his face. There was nothing interesting about it, just plain and white. I gripped tightly on to the nylon straps of my backpack and looked around the quiet room, but there wasn't shit to look at, because like the agent's face, it was plain and white as well, empty of anything unique or the slightest bit appealing.

"Then this is all you here?" he said, tapping at the monitor's screen with his long and lanky white finger.

"I don't know what that is." I played stupid because by now I had a hunch as to what was transpiring.

"Have you ever used a weapon to injure another person?" he said, looking suspiciously into my timorous eyes the way cops do when they want to catch you in a lie: like they lost some shit behind your eyeballs and are trying desperately to find it.

"Yeah," I said, carefully, giving him the best pitiful look I could muster. Maybe he'd see that the person on the monitor and the person sitting meekly before him were two different people. Maybe.

"A gun?"

"Ye-ah."

"How long ago?"

"A long time ago. I don't remember."

"And you are also a member of a street gang."

"No."

"Were you ever?"

"Ye-ah."

"But you're not anymore?"

"No."

"Hmm."

"Hmmm."

"Hmmmm."

"Hmmmmm."

"And where are you coming from?"

"Chihuahua."

"And what were you doing there?"

"Visiting my father."

It's true. I'd been a member of a street gang, and in 1999 I'd been convicted for shooting a gang rival. What was jumping out at this agent's prying blue eyes from the monitor was an extensive criminal record that went back to when I was thirteen. It was bad. So bad that even as I sat there staring the agent in the face with my own uninteresting cara de palo, answering his questions, I was serving out a three-year probation sentence for an assault-on-a-peace-officer charge I'd been convicted for only two years earlier after having been arrested at a protest in the city of Garden Grove against a group of beaner hunters who called themselves the Minutemen. These two criminal acts I'd committed as an adult, and apparently were now cause enough to return my defected brown ass back to Mexico. I had lots of explaining to do, from every detail pertaining to every crime I'd ever been convicted of to the reason why I was in a wheelchair. This would go on for hours. I'd miss a dozen flights to Los Angeles before the interrogation was over. At one point, much amused by what he was hearing, the agent called in a fellow agent who'd happened to be passing by in the hallway so that he, too, could indulge in my grief.

"Go on, tell him what you told me just a few minutes ago

about how you ended up in that chair," white agent number one, who had now kicked up his boots on the desk and was leaning back on his chair as if he were enjoying a movie, said to me as I now tiredly found myself staring at another agent with a similar, uninteresting pale face.

"I got shot, that's all," I said, shrugging the whole thing off, hoping we could move on, that I could be let go and sent on my way to move freely about the country. But white agent number one wasn't having it; he wanted me to recount this whole fucking part of my life all over again just so white agent number two could get a kick out of the extraordinary. Nothing about the part where I was a scholar working on an MA in English, or about how much I loved to spend hours reading French and Russian novels in trendy coffee shops while sipping on five-dollar lattes next to other Americans who shared my affinity for the bohemian lifestyle. Nothing about my poetic inclinations or about my talent for writing plays—nothing.

"But tell him who shot you, and why, what you were doing," white agent number one persisted, now with his hands behind his head. Meanwhile, white agent number two kept looking at me and my wheels with morbid fascination. From where he stood in the doorway, he'd often twist his head to one side and look down at me with a bewildered expression on his face. When he'd do this, he'd squint his eyes and tuck in his lips. I take it he didn't know what to make of me and my fashion. Maybe the Vans and black baggy jeans threw him off; or maybe it was the guayabera and the Panama hat; or maybe it was the whole fucking ensemble.

"I got shot by a gas-station attendant. Me and a friend were running away from his store with two cases of beer each that we hadn't paid for when he followed us out and shot me."

"In the back?" said white agent number two, taken aback by what he'd just heard.

"Yeah, right through my spine. The bullet almost came out through my front, but my skin stopped it."

"Ain't that something? Some good ol' American vigilante justice," interjected white agent number one with no less excitement in his voice than when I'd first relayed the story to him.

"Sure is," said white agent number two, now leaning back and crossing his arms. "And how old were you when this happened?"

"Seventeen."

"Just a kid," said white agent number one, smacking his lips and shaking his head.

"Pretty terrible," said white agent number two, doing the same, though with a more sympathetic expression on his face.

"Yep," agreed white agent number one, picking up his cup of coffee and holding it out in front of him, "and all for some beer."

The interrogation quickly became a sideshow. In their government-issued royal-blue uniforms, the two agents began to take great liberty with their questions and made no apologies for the delight they took in asking them. But contrary to how I felt when the interrogation first began or when white agent number two was called in, by this point, I'd begun to not mind it one bit; because if I remembered anything about cops and the like, it was that it's always best to keep them happy, to be the pony they want you to be. So no matter what questions these two paddies asked me from this point on, I was quick to answer them without restraints. I loosened up and began to breathe again. I'd come to the conclusion that if amusing was what they wanted, then amusing was what I'd give them, anything to relieve the tension and anxiety I'd been feeling since the moment I was pulled out of the line to freedom by Shirley and her enormous culo. Play it cool and play it charming, I said to myself in my big head, and you'll be out of here in no time, shit's nothing. And plus, I reminded myself, you're as American as they are, only darker.

"But that's not all," continued agent number one to agent number two after taking a sip of his coffee. "It gets better. Apparently this guy's quite the shooter, too. Get this, a year after having been shot himself, he went out one night and shot another gangster. Shot him right in the leg." He was retelling all of this with a smile. Motherfucker could've been reading the shit from a book he told it so well. You could see the glee in his yellow, coffee-stained teeth every time he opened his mouth. Agent number two, on the other hand, seemed stupefied by what he was hearing. Who was I and how could all this violence come out of this oddly dressed cripple were, I imagined, the questions formulating in his head.

"Wait a minute," agent number two said to me, "you mean to tell me that a year after you got shot by a store clerk for having robbed him, you then went out and shot somebody yourself?"

"Yes," I said matter-of-factly, while pushing up the brim of my hat with my left pointing finger like a cowboy in a western.

"But weren't you in a wheelchair then, too?" he continued, revealing his keenness for observation.

"Yes."

"So you had a gun on you and you shot someone from your wheelchair?"

"Yes. But not because I wanted to." I felt the need to explain to him the circumstances of the situation lest he and his partner began to view me as a danger to society and decided to throw me back into Mexico right then and there. "I didn't mean to shoot him. I just wanted to scare him."

"Scare him? Why? Did he have a gun, too?" said white agent number two.

"No—I mean, at the time I didn't know if he did or if he didn't, but I suppose he could've. Plus, he had about fifteen of his friends with him, and some of them had other weapons that were visible. They had chains and bottles and knives. And they were going to attack us."

"Who's us?" said white agent number one.

"Me and my cousin and two other friends. Oh, and my girl-friend. Shit, ain't no telling what they'd've done to us all if I hadn't pulled out the gun and shot. We were outnumbered."

"So you just pulled the gun out and shot the guy closest to you?" asked white agent number one, inquisitively.

"No. I pulled it out and shot blindly to the right of me as soon as they charged at us. I had no choice. I had to do some-thing to keep them from attacking us, especially my girlfriend. She's beautiful, you know, a real doll. Unfortunately, it just so happened that one of them got hit in the leg as he was chasing after my cousin, who, incidentally, still got his ass kicked by them after me, my girl, and my other friends took off. So they really could've done worse to us."

"You say you took off," said white agent number one, reveal-ing his own talent for keen observation. "You weren't appre-hended that night?"

"I was," I continued, "at a friend's apartment. Somebody told the police where we were hiding. They came in, arrested me, and took me in. I was charged with attempted murder that night and bailed out by my mom the next. I went to court for about two years and in '99 the judged sentenced me to five years' gang-terms probation with twelve years of prison time hanging over my head. Said that if I violated any of the terms of my probation for any reason he'd have me sent straight to prison, no questions asked, to serve out those twelve years. He wasn't fucking around."

"No kidding," said white agent number one. "But you got off pretty easy, wouldn't you say? Hell, I've never heard of someone getting only probation for shooting another person. Sounds unlikely. Plus you're a gang member."

"*Was.*"

"Of course—*was,*" said agent number one, cracking a smile.

This was what the interrogation would be like for the rest of my time with them: one of the two agents would ask me a question and I'd answer it the best I could. Eventually I'd also describe to them in detail the night of the protest in Garden Grove, during which I was observed by two white undercover officers in civilian clothes chucking marble-size rocks from my wheelchair at a line of deputy sheriffs on horseback. (I was really chucking them at the hicks behind the deputy sheriffs who were screaming out anti-immigration racist epithets at the protesters. But ¡que será, será! I had to stick to what I'd pleaded guilty to.) But it wouldn't be until I presented the two agents with a written permission letter to travel to Chihuahua signed by my probation officer and after I repeatedly expressed to them that I was a changed man on my way to academic and literary greatness that I'd finally be sent on my way to baggage claim and to catch the next flight to Los Angeles.

"I swear to you," I said pressingly to the two agents, "I'm not a criminal. I'm a scholar, can't you see? Look inside my backpack, all I have is books, books and catheters I use to take

a piss." I was hoping they wouldn't look though. I was reading *Che* at the time and thought that if they saw the book they
might take me for a communist, if they hadn't already by the
way I was dressed all Cuban-like. Then I'd really be fucked.
To government agents like these the only thing worse than
an ex–gang member is an active communist. But they didn't.
White agent number one, convinced of my aspirations, just
handed me a form to sign that said I promised to appear before an immigration judge in Los Angeles on a specific date.
I did, and was free to go. My time with these two paddies had
finally come to an end. And although I was elated that they'd
allowed me to remain in the country, I was now facing deportation. I'd been stripped of my green card and sent home with
a piece of paper that said I was in "proceedings for removal."
¡Que mierda! I felt unbearable sorrow. After all the years of
pledging allegiance to the flag! I was hurting inside. The only
consolation I got came from the customs agent who searched
my suitcase after I retrieved it from the luggage claim. After
he, with stern demeanor, rummaged through it with his gloved
hands and had his Lassie sniff around it and my person, and
was done questioning me about how I was able to afford a TAG
Heuer watch, he calmly removed one of his black leather gloves
and paternally placed his white hand on my shoulder and said:
"Welcome home, son." That was more like it! Oh, America, if
only you knew how much I love you!

9

I'd been itching for a beer since I first got off the plane and felt the scathing heat of the Chihuahua sun blanket my skin. My first thought was that I'd come to a funeral in hell, and that the only way I'd be able to survive it would be by drinking my way through it. Immediately, therefore, I resigned myself to the deceivingly refreshing pull of a cold beer. At the bar in the airport lobby, however, there wasn't any beer. All they served to my not-so-displeased surprise was liquor. And so, from a plethora of rich names and without any misgivings, within a half hour's time—the time it took for my uncle Chuy and his wife and kid to get there to pick me up—I had five unflinching shots of Buchanan's whiskey—straight to the gut. And just like that, feeling the chill on my cheeks from the airport's high-powered air-conditioning system and the revolting warmth of the Scotch whiskey in my throat and stomach, I was ready to roll out past the military guards into the Chihuahua sun once again and head to my father's closing act.

And now, almost three hours after those initial drinks, I'm ready for more. I send Danny for beer and a fifth of whatever tequila he can find. "What kind of beer do you want?" he asks me as I hand him a wad of dollar bills. I tell him to get a couple of Carta Blanca caguamas in memoriam of our dead father. He cracks a smile that says he likes the idea, and without further ado walks away to retrieve my order.

When he comes back, I drink one of the caguamas within minutes. I can't wait. I need to not give a fuck in a hurry. I need to turn this death scene into a party, even if only in my mind. The other caguama I give to Danny and Aarón to share with their friends and some of our cousins who are there looking miserable, like children forced to go to church. They all thank me for the gesture and toast with me every time I take a drink from the fifth of Hornitos tequila, which is quickly passed around and empty sooner than it can make its way back to me. So it goes. But I can't stop. Not now. I'm on a roll and feeling chingón, al cien, as they say. I have to stay like this. There's nothing good otherwise. So I send Danny to get another fifth and more caguamas. This time five. We're taking flight.

I drink in front of everyone. Shamelessly, without a care. I give not one flying fuck about who sees me give in to the drink. Am I not a Silva? At one point, gripping a caguama in my hand, I turn to Cokis and, pointing my finger in the direction of the parlor's doors, say to her: "That man in there, mi padre, he'd be doing the same shit—¡la misma mierda! In fact, he's probably wishing he could have a drink now, even being as dead as he is." Cokis agrees with me, laughs, leans in, grips me tightly, tells me how right I am, takes the caguama from my hand, and takes a long drink from it herself. "That's the spirit," I tell her. She joins in the celebration, and soon my sister Axcel and even Cecilia join, too.

For the rest of the night the tequila and beers keep coming and the music keeps playing. From a stereo in a small white '90s Chevy pickup that belongs to one of Aarón's friends and is parked beside the parlor, we listen to old Vicente Fernández songs my father had loved to listen to when he drank. Our toasts and cheers join the ensemble of chance sounds that fill the barrio's night sky. Our laughter and meaningless talk are accompanied by the laughter and talk of young women and men clinging to the night on the beds of old trucks that roar by. Our yelps and cries swirl with the yelps and cries of the men drinking in front of the houses across the street and of those drinking in the distance and somewhere around every corner. The voice of Vicente Fernández fights against the wild screams of warring children. Sound is everywhere, finding refuge in the darkness. Life is taking place: footsteps here; a bottle breaking there; sizzling grease and whistles everywhere. Chihuahua is alive, and *we* are celebrating death.

I get my buzz back in no time. The caguamas are going down smoothly and I'm becoming energized. "Para mi papá," I scream out every time after I take a drink. The tequila has murdered all my inhibitions and I have murdered *it*. "Turn up the music!" I yell boisterously while puffing my chest. "¡Que se oiga por todo Chihuahua! Let everybody know that Juan Silva has died! That the eagle has finally chewed up his liver for the last time! Let them know that Prometheus is no more! That the firewater has finally killed him!"

Surrounded by Cokis and my brothers and sisters, I feel like the patriarch of the family. I'm at the center of each of their worlds and they look upon me as their only hope—ME: this drunk cripple at their feet who's rambunctiously screaming at the night sky. For every one of them, with the exception of Cecilia, who looks more bewildered by the event unfolding before her than anything else, stares at me with the look of lost children: sad and pitiful. "What are you going to do now?" is what every one of the weary eyes is saying to me. "Please, tell us something comforting. Have you heard that our father is dead?" But I have nothing for them, no plan, no vision for the future. All I know is that things are certain to get better. And aside from putting on this drunken spectacle, all I can say to them is not to be so sad—to cheer up. "Everything's going to be just fine," I promise them with a smile. As soon as I say this, Cokis, who has not left my side, places her arm around my neck and in her soft and childlike voice, optimistically whispers into my ear: "Really? Is it true?"

My certainty comes from having seen Cokis suffer, even more than my brothers and sister Axcel, at the hands of my father. On more than one occasion I'd told her to leave him, to get as far as she could from his reach. And although she always assured me that one day she would, she never did. I take it the blows and tears had hardened and their weight had burrowed her at his side. But he was dead now and there was no way he could ever hurt her again.

"Yes, Cokis, I promise," I say to her, looking into her devastated eyes. "I promise, I promise, I promise." I take the caguama from her hands, take a drink from it, and pass it to her again: "Tome," I tell her. "Drink for the hell inside, and don't worry about tomorrow, because tomorrow we bury this man."

Sad woman. Sad widow. Sad mother. Sad sight. Drink for your dead beloved. Let him know that your sorrows are still connected to his life. Show him that your misery still lives. But kill him! Kill him with another drink! That a girl! He must not live again! He must not rise at dawn with the rest of the spirits!

Turn him into a memory and leave him in the past! And laugh! Laugh with me! Laugh with all of us! Let us hear you laugh hard with the bottle in hand! Raise it like the Olympic torch and wave it around for everyone to see! Be proud and show the world! Tell it that your beloved is dead and that you drink for the hell inside! Be free, sad bird. Be free!

10

In one episode of HBO's *The Sopranos*, Tony Soprano remarks that "remember when . . ." is the lowest form of conversation. To the wise monk and to the sagacious scholar, and even to the boss of an Italian crime family, perhaps, this is true, but not to the drunk; to him there is no form of conversation with greater value than "remember when." Hell, to him, "remember when" is the *only* form of conversation. The past is the only subject he is capable of discussing at length, and there is no future there— not one glimmer of hope. But he doesn't mind this. Because what cares he for the future? Any vision of the future is an obstacle: too much work, too much thought, too much time away from the drink. Now there's an unbearable reality and the drunk desires to have no part of it. So he looks firmly to his past, to his memories, to where he feels safe. There are no surprises in the past for him, and no need for him to plan for the unexpected; in the past he is free of responsibility. In his memories he can move freely, picking and choosing moments he wishes to relive: moments in which he's the superhero, the great lover, the best friend, the brave comrade in the face of danger, and of course—the exceptional drinker. A great many tales, "bēore druncen"—as Bēowulf says to Unferð after Unferð reminds him of the contest he had with Breca—the drunk is able to tell. He can spend hours at a time reveling in his memories, retelling them over and over without respite. And always he's the skilled orator, the master storyteller; and always he begins every tale that slips through his sloppy lips with: "remember when."

But the drunk is not alone in his fanatical appreciation for talk about the past. The mourner, too, takes great solace in reliving memories. But where the drunk retells the past to exalt himself, the mourner retells it to exalt the dead. It is his way of easing the pain that comes with losing someone, his way of keeping a part of the deceased alive. He cannot mourn without reliving certain moments of the dead person's life, moments that, like the drunk, he chooses carefully. Because when the mourner lets out the phrase "remember when," what follows is a story that paints the deceased in glorious light. The deceased, in these stories, is a great friend, son, daughter, mother, father—a great everything. Alive the dead person did no wrong, and it is now left to the mourner to let it be known, to tell the world about it. And so "remember when" springs forth from the mourner's tongue as often as it does from the tongue of the drunk. The two are equal in their pity.

And what of the mourner who is also a drunk? Well, let all intelligent and productive talk keep vigil at the door, as there is no place for it here; for when the mourner drinks and becomes the drunk who mourns, every "remember when" tale is accompanied with a sobbing spectacle of uncontrollable emotion—he becomes an explosion of pathos. In mourning the drunk is a passionate animal who builds monuments to his feelings; he's both sensitive and delicate, and the bearer of all of the world's pain, and he weeps to no end to show it. "Remember when?" he cries out, and before he can begin to articulate his memory the tears are already streaming from his eyes. He's a disturbing mess, a fountain of misery.

And let us be a fountain of misery. Why not? The patriarch is dead. Let us sing on his behalf; and sob. Let us make fools of ourselves for this fragment of time. Soon the pain will pass. And soon the stories will be forgotten. Soon this man will be dead again. But not tonight! Because tonight we tell a tale. And we cry. And we drink. And we cry and drink and drink and cry. And yet again we tell another tale! Hurrah! Hurrah!

I don't remember how it happened. I never do. No drunk or mourner ever does. Somebody just begins, and somebody else follows. But it always begins with the words:

Remember when . . .

Telling words. Full of wonder. Can do no harm. Because indeed my father had been a great man while he stumbled carelessly upon this earth. It's true. I tell no lies. He really had been something beautiful. And the stories we share about him on this night, on this broken sidewalk, in our drunken state, say it all—that the man was a flower, our flower. Of the circle, everyone, with the exception of Cecilia and some of Aarón's friends, recalls something good about my father, something that had been lost in the chaotic world of the drunken character he'd created. With every weeping word that flies forth from our mouths we paint a man, a good man, and we give life to a god!

"Obed, remember when your dad used to take you fishing when you were little?" Cokis, impassionedly, says to me with tears rushing down her face. She's clinging to my arm and resting her head heavily on my shoulder, and somewhere deep down I am crying, too.

I remember. They were some of the happiest moments I'd ever spent with my father. There'd never been a time when I visited Chihuahua as a child that my father didn't take me fishing. He'd mostly take me to La Presa Chihuahua (the Chihuahua Dam), which is only a short drive away from El Cerro de la Cruz. Other times he'd take me to El Granero (Chihuahua's other dam), which is much farther away but better for fishing. It was always certain that we were going to come away with dozens of fish when we went to El Granero. But because my father had never in his life owned a reliable car, one that could get us from point A to point B and then back to point A without taking a dump somewhere in between, most often we settled for La Presa, which was always fine by me. I loved it there.

I'm on my knees, and I have my arm elbow-deep in mud and shit. From a few feet away I can hear my father say to me, "¡A las lombrices les gustan la caca!" He, too, is on his knees and digging deep into this paradise of mud and shit for what we'll soon be using for fish bait. "Look!" my father says to me triumphantly. I turn to look at him without pulling my arm out of this shitty earth. He's still on his knees but now has his arms extended in front of him holding two fists full of mud and shit

with earthworms squiggling out from them like snakes sprouting out of Medusa's head. He has a brilliant smile. From where
I am, I can see his teeth sparkle from the hot sun. "Let's see!
What did you get?!" he yells to me. I pull out my arm and in
my little hand I'm holding my own fistful of warm mud and
shit with wiggly worms squiggling out from it. There must
be dozens of them in this small fistful, all of them alive and
squiggling with urgency, fighting for survival. Any other time I
would be disgusted by the way the slimy critters feel slithering
between my fingers, but not this time. This time I'm overjoyed,
thrilled even, to see so many wiggly and slimy worms squiggling out from the ball of mud and shit I'm holding in my little
hand: I'm a prince in paradise, and my father my king.

"¡Yo también!" I yell to my father. "I got a lot of worms,
too!" My father laughs and I laugh with him. We're both on
our knees in a muddy brook that receives the sewage from a
small rancho a couple of kilometers away from La Presa, and
we couldn't be having a happier time together: father and son
loving the stench of pig and human shit meshed with warm
and wet soil on a hot summer day.

At La Presa, my father takes out a few rusted tin cans that
at one point had contained fruit juice and pokes a hole on
the top side of each near the mouth. He loops fishing line
through the holes and mouths and then wraps a few yards
of it around the cans' cylindrical shapes. When he's done, he
hands me one and tells me to put the sinkers on.

"Where?" I ask him. And after snatching the can back from
my hands he unrolls some of the string and begins to pinch
the pellet-size lead balls onto it. They look like little silver Pac-
Mans that he pinches onto various points on the string, first
with his teeth and then with a pair of rusted pliers he pulls

out from the back pocket of his old cutoff stonewashed denim shorts with slits on the sides.

"Like this, hijo," he says to me. "This is how you do it. It's really easy."

Mi papá knows what he's doing. He's probably done this a thousand times before and now he's teaching his son how to do it, too.

"Esto es todo, hijo—that's it, there's nothing to it," he says, speaking like an expert. "You don't need anything else, none of those fancy fishing poles they use over there en Hontinton Beesh [translation: Huntington Beach]. No, aquí no. Here, all you need are these old cans, this string, and these tiny weights and hooks, and of course the worms. Here we fish like the poor, son—como los pobres."

What a picture: my father, the proud poor man standing at the feet of a fiery sun that shines behind him against a blue sky like a blazing halo that has somehow gotten separated from an angel—¡vaya!

"Remember, Obed, and you, Mamá, when we went to the bull-fights with my dad," Axcel chimes in. She sounds like an excited little girl about to relive a memory she experienced only moments ago. But she's not a little girl. She's twenty-four and the memory goes back some twenty years. I stare at her as she holds a half-empty caguama in her hand and I wonder how she's able to recall that day.

I was ten and Axcel four. On this day Cokis and my father took us to the bullfights at La Plaza de Toros La Esperanza near El Centro. We spent most of the day in the scorching sun,

watching burly men sporting sombreros and huge silver and
gold belt buckles and pointy leather boots get knocked off bulls,
and bullfighters in sparkly flamboyant outfits tease and taunt
the raging beasts. Ranchera music singers, clowns, dwarfs, and
professional charros in traditional charro attire with elaborate
gold and silver trimmings who did incredible tricks with their
horses were also part of the spectacle. Axcel and I sat on each
side of my father on a concrete bench, and along with the other
spectators, the three of us, including Cokis, shouted at the en-
tertainers. In unison we showed our approbation of this traditional Mexican pastime. And when we weren't shouting and
cheering, we were chomping down on baked pumpkin seeds my
father had bought from an elderly Tarahumara woman outside
the stadium. There was a lot to remember there, and Axcel re-
lived every moment for us with intensity. She talked about An-
tonio Aguilar and his majestic and tamed horses, about how
silly the clowns and dwarfs were and about how the bulls were
gruesomely brought down by rope handlers and matadors. But
even so, it wasn't the time we spent inside La Plaza de Toros La
Esperanza that was most memorable to her, but rather the time
we spent outside of it at the placita directly across the street.

"Do you remember the fountain?" Axcel asks me.

"Yes, I do."

Chihuahua is full of placitas, small oases where Chihua-
huenses go to escape the drab confinements of their homes
or the dreariness of their workplaces. Here, people gather to
enjoy the shade from trees, or to listen to músicos sing old
ballads for a few pesos, or to get their shoes shined by men
who are masters at the art of conversation, or by ten-year-old
boys who've been hungry their entire lives, or to eat an elote
on a stick or in a Styrofoam cup purchased from one of the

many vendors of different types of easy-to-eat finger foods (including cold treats like raspados and paletas) that fight for customers on any given day, or to simply interact and socialize with total strangers. And at the center of every placita is a concrete water fountain. And while some are bigger than others, depending on the size of the placita itself, and while some have a large bronze statue of one of Mexico's heroes at their center while others don't, they all make for great bathing pools, at least to Chihuahua's undesirable children.

"Do you remember how we bathed in it?" Axcel says.

"I do."

On this day, Axcel and I became two of Chihuahua's undesirable children, and our father one of Chihuahua's undesirable men. We couldn't help it. The heat had taken its toll on us and we were looking for instant relief. And the sight of the undesirable children—those boys and girls with skin the color of dirt and eyes that reflect a dying civilization, and who sell Chiclets and newspapers on the street, or who throw themselves on top of cars to clean windshields all day to make enough to eat, and those who beg for it—joyfully splashing and sinking beneath this particular placita's fountain's water, inspired Axcel and me to ask our father if we could jump in the fountain, too. And while Cokis was busy being firmly against it, arguing that it didn't look right, that the other people in the placita would talk, and that perhaps the undesirables had already filled the fountain with dirt, germs, and even urine, my father was already removing his clothes and walking toward it. "I think it's a great idea," he said, revealing his burly torso and chest and impressively robust but short and hairy legs. "¡Ándale!" he added, encouraging Axcel and me to do the same. Before anything more could be said, the three of us were in the fountain splashing and submerging our heads and bodies beneath its shallow water. And while some of the people who were near shot disapproving stares our way, especially at my father, who like Axcel and me was wearing only underwear, the undesirables welcomed us with splashes and explosive laughter. "¡Báñense! ¡Báñense!" the lot of them (I don't remember how many there were, but there were a lot) said to us, handing the three of us little pieces of Ariel laundry soap to wash ourselves with, which we gladly accepted.

"¡Ay, Juan!" Cokis complained to my father from a green cast-iron bench a few feet away from the fountain where she sat next to an elderly couple who couldn't take their eyes off of us. "Are you really going to wash yourself with that soap in public, in this fountain, and are you really going to let the kids do it, too? Can't you see that everyone is staring at you?"

But Cokis could've complained until the sun went down or until her mouth dried up, because my father wasn't about to change his mind and get out of the fountain for any reason. As far as he was concerned, he was a free man in a free country and could do whatever he wanted, and that included bathing with his two kids in a fountain at a public park. "¿Y qué? Who are these people to tell us anything?" my father said to Cokis as he leaned against the fountain's round centerpiece and rubbed the small piece of Ariel soap over his face and hair. "If these kids can find joy in this fountain, then why can't we, and besides, ¡hace un chingo de calor!"

"¡Ay, Juan!" was all Cokis had left to say.

With that, my father bent his body forward and dipped his soap-lathered face and hair into the water. And after one, two, three seconds, he brought it back up and shot his sight toward the sun with his hands pressingly moving from the front of his face all the way to the back of his head, wringing out as much water as he possibly could from his hair. The man could've been David Hasselhoff rising out of the waters of a Los Angeles beach on an episode of *Baywatch* the way he so casually looked around afterward, shooting every person at the park a glance and a smile, beads of water jumping off his face in every direction.

That day, Axcel, my father, and I arrived home cleaner than we'd left it, smelling like freshly clean laundry. Cokis, on the other hand, not so much. The sun had done a terrible job on her, and much of her makeup seemed to have melted into her skin.

It's Danny's turn.

"My father loved the water," he quietly utters, humbly looking around at the disheveled yet lively faces surrounding him, every one of them now captivated by his quiet voice. "Remember when we'd all go to Los Balnearios on the weekends?"

When Cokis, Axcel, Aarón, and I heard the name, we each let out a loud and cheerful yes in unison. The memories of us and our father at this place came rushing into our minds. Undoubtedly, the image of our father in his tiny cutoff stonewashed denim shorts (the same ones he'd wear when he'd go to La Presa) splashing happily in a swimming pool manifested itself in each of our minds at the same time.

Los Balnearios Robinson, which is the official name, is a swimming park with lots of pools of various sizes, shapes, and depths. And during Chihuahua's hot-ass summers, it's the place to be, and we certainly were. When I was a child, my father would often take all of us there as a family to spend the day picnicking and bathing. It was one of his favorite places for a family outing and relaxation, second to La Presa and El Granero. And while Danny went on to relay what he remembered most about our father at this ambitious water park, I couldn't help but let my mind drift into my own memory of el viejo and me at this magical place.

"Hold on tight, son."

"But I'm scared."

"Don't be. I'm your father and I'm not going to let anything happen to you. Do you trust your father?"

"Yes."

"Then?"

I say nothing more, just wrap my skinny dark arms around my father's stout neck and press my face hard against the back of his head, burying it as much as I can into his heavy wet hair.

"Relax, hijo. There's no need to press so hard. Just close your eyes and hold your breath. That's it. Are you ready—¿listo?"

"Sí."

"¡Vámonos!"

There's a hop and then a pull, like something's just sucked us into the water. My eyes are closed so I can't see. All I can do is feel. It's a feeling I've never felt before, like I'm flying, moving through clouds of gelatin. My arms are relaxed, my father's hair like fingers teasing my face. We're moving downward, going deep; my father's arms and hands are digging through water, and his legs and feet are rapidly kicking and flapping. I can feel all of it, the entire movement of his body, like I'm riding on the back of a wave. In the darkness of my mind I imagine a dolphin, fish, sharks, and even gigantic whales. I feel safe, like nothing can touch me. I twist my head forward and slowly open my eyes. We're at the base of the pool, streamlining an inch above its white concrete bottom, nothing but water all around us. I can see the movements now, and the hair reaching out to me like tentacles from an octopus. Suddenly my father turns his head to the side and I can see his profile; he's looking at me with one eye, the only one I can see. Then there are bubbles. They're coming from his mouth. Is he smiling at me? Yes. But he's also saying something. His lips are moving slowly. I make sense of two syllables: "mi-jo"—son.

"Remember how he used to flip us into the air?" I hear Aarón saying, taking the torch from Danny and bringing me out of myself. "Really high we'd go, and then into the water—*splash*!"

"Bien chingón," Danny says, fighting back the tears. "He would flip everybody, even kids he didn't know. They would line up and he'd flip all of them as many times as they wanted. He was always happy to do it."

Danny was right. Whenever a boy or girl—after seeing him flip one of his own children—came to him to ask him to flip them, my father would quickly extend his hands out in front of him and say, "Well, what are you waiting for? Put your feet on my hands and hold on to my shoulders." Then he'd bounce them once, twice, and on the third he'd push them, with all his strength, right up and over behind his head and into the air from where they'd either dive or flop into the water. And regardless of how they'd make it into the water, there was never a time when any of them came out with anything other than a laugh or a smile on his or her face. Happiness was what, at Los Balnearios, my father offered these children and us. Here he was the father every child wished for.

~

"¡Pinche Juan loco!" Víctor-Manuel loudly interjects. "He was like one big kid. He always liked playing with us in the street. Do you guys remember when he used to have water-balloon fights with all the kids in the neighborhood on el día de San Juan? ¡Se hacía un desmadre cuando salía Juanillo con sus globos!"

I had only experienced these water-balloon fights once, but apparently, judging by the way my brothers, Cokis, and my sister Axcel reacted to Víctor-Manuel's recollection, my father had participated in this infamous tradition every year when el día de San Juan came around.

According to legend, on June 24, 1549, the Spanish explorer Francisco Vásquez Coronado prayed for rain while standing on the dry banks of the Santa Cruz riverbed in Arizona. And when the rain came, he marked it as the day on which the summer rains would come every year after that. Consequently, because he is the patron saint of water, San Juan (Saint John) was quickly associated with this day. And while in many parts of Mexico and even in some Mexican American communities in the United States this day is celebrated by paying homage to this saint with music, dance, and prayers, in Chihuahua it is celebrated in a manner more befitting: every Juan must get wet.

My memory of the only día de San Juan I got to experience with my father begins with the two of us in the bathroom pouring water from the showerhead into one of my father's yeso-blotched buckets. I'm small and at his side, tugging hastily at his yeso-splattered pants, urging him to hurry. We're completely soaked in water and it's dripping from our shorts onto the floor. But we don't care. All we care about is filling up the bucket with water and getting back into the street to join in all of the action.

"Hold on, hijo! We have to let it fill to the top. This way we can really get them," my father says to me as he runs his hand through my hair.

Once the bucket is full, he lifts it up to his shoulder and tells me to shut off the water and then to follow him. We move quickly through the hallway and past the living room; our soaked shoes squish through the pools of water on the concrete floor. My heart races with excitement. I'm in on something big. I rub my hands with devilish design as I break through the home's front door behind my father. Suddenly there is a loud roar and my father starts charging out into the street. I try hard to keep up with him but the man is out of control. Like a bull that's just been freed from its corral, my father moves chaotically, looking for his target. But there are too many of them and they're all scattering, trying frantically to find refuge from our offense.

"Here he comes! Here he comes!" they're all yelling. "Run! Run!"

I'm a little bull myself, fierce and unafraid of the repercussions, shirtless and dark, loving the heat, the dirt, the yelling, and all the rambunctious laughter. I'm running behind the man who gives me orders, who encourages me to enjoy life the way a seven-year-old boy should. On fire! Shamelessly! Without ever having to say I'm sorry. Without ever having to cry. Only on fire! With my fists to my bare chest and my feet on terra firma!

Splash! My father has found his target: a bent-over body hiding silently behind an old junked car raised on cinder blocks. "Ahhh!" the body cries out as it extends itself back to life. "You got me, Juanillo!" the body screams as it runs away, looking down at its now-drenched clothes. He's one of a countless number of the neighborhood boys who've joined together to accomplish one thing on this day: to get my father—un Juan—wet.

From the moment they'd first laid eyes on my father, this band of brothers had issued their attack, launching water balloons our way from every direction. He and I had been walking back home from the store with a couple of Cokes and bologna sandwiches when the first water grenade landed at our feet. Caught by surprise, my father and I looked at each other and then at our surroundings. What our eyes captured was a group of boys—some fully clothed and others shirtless and barefooted—posted at different points of the barrio heavily armed with water balloons of different colors, ready to catapult them our way.

"Órale, hijo, ya estuvo," my father calmly said, leaning in to my ear. And before he could say anything else, one of the boys yelled for his entire squadron to attack and the balloons began to land on us like rain.

"¡Un Juan! ¡Un Juan!" was all we could hear from the mob as we gripped our sodas and sandwiches and hurriedly made our way toward the front door of my father's house. "¡Van a ver, cabrones! You're going to get it!" my father laughingly yelled back at them while protecting his face with his raised arm. But his defense, like mine, was useless; because by the time we reached the door of the house and made it inside, the two of us were completely soaked, and our sandwiches, which had turned into sponges, were falling apart.

Safely inside the house, my father and I laughed hysterically as we removed our shirts. "It's on, son. They got us and now we have to get them back," my father said as he walked to the backyard. And curious as to what he had planned, I followed him. Out back he pulled out a yeso-speckled bucket full of tools from inside a heavily dented and also yeso-speckled wheelbar-row. As he dumped all the tools onto the ground, he said, "It's war with these cabrones! They messed with the wrong Juanes!"

It caught me by surprise. He had used the plural form of his name. Up until that point, it hadn't hit me that I, too, was a Juan.

Everyone is teary-eyed, some are even weeping, including Cecilia. She's looking at me while wiping tears away. Probably wondering how the man in the box could be the same man we're telling such stories about.

"He loved us all," Danny says.

"Con todo su corazón, hijo," Cokis says. She's crying, too.

And it's fucking dark. Time has passed and we've made no note of it. And I want to say something because I'm afraid we might be out of beer again. I look around and notice that all the caguama bottles are carefully placed on the floor against the wall in a perfect queue, each completely empty. I also notice that most of the people who were not part of our little circle are gone. Only a scattered few remain standing and talking in front of the funeral parlor's doors or sitting on the curb, all mostly young people unwilling to bid farewell to the night.

"¿Qué horas son?" I ask anyone who will answer.

"Three o'clock," Víctor-Manuel says, looking at the invisible watch on his wrist.

"Not true," Cokis quickly interjects, looking at her own real watch and wagging her finger at him. "It's barely eleven thirty."

"Oh, really?" says Víctor-Manuel, tapping his wrist. "Then it's also time for me to get a new watch."

"Pinche loco," says Axcel, and we all laugh.

"I'm not crazy. What, you don't like my watch?" continues Víctor-Manuel with his act. "I bought it in El Centro from a little Tarahumara girl."

"Oh yeah, and how much did you pay for it?" Axcel asks him, playing along.

"¡Mil pesos!"

"¡Mil pesos!" Aarón cuts in. "No seas mamón. When have you ever had mil pesos?"

"Well, right before I bought this watch of course!" Víctor-Manuel says, raising his bent wrist into the air.

We're all laughing again. It's what we needed to escape the gloom we'd been creating moments before. But even as I find myself laughing along, my mind remains consumed with the dilemma that is now upon us. Familiar with the laws that govern the sale of alcohol in Chihuahua, I'm well aware of the fact that, being the time that it is, we are way past the last call for alcohol, and if the party is to continue, then something must be done, and soon.

11

Irony sometimes resembles absurdity. Nowhere is this more true than in Chihuahua's ley seca—dry law: prohibition. Because although Chihuahua's a state in which you can't go more than a block or two without passing an expendio (mini-mart that specializes in selling beer) or licorería (liquor store that specializes in selling wine and hard liquor), it has strict laws that regulate times and days when alcohol can and cannot be sold.

Every night at ten o'clock expendios, licorerías, and all other stores that deal in the drink must lock up their coolers. Additionally, every time government elections come around on July 4, the sale of alcohol is suspended twenty-four hours before voting begins until twelve hours after it ends, or until the following day. Anyone caught violating this law is subject to seventy-two hours' jail time. The government does this to prevent disorder while this most democratic of processes is taking place; and also to make sure that every citizen who votes does so sober. Can't have a ballot intended for el PRIista (member of the Institutional Revolutionary Party) going to el PANista (member of the National Action Party) because Juan Doe was too drunk to know what name on the ballot he was checking.

But how effective are these precautionary measures?

Let's see. Before every election day, every newspaper in the state prints a front-page reminder of the upcoming day of ley seca to keep drunks from showing up to their preferred beer and liquor depot only to find it either closed or restricted from selling alcoholic beverages. Yet what ends up happening is not that the drunks take heed of the law and go a day and some hours without drinking because they respect it, or because they realize that in a matter of hours they, too, with the rest of the citizenry, will be voting for their favored politician and therefore will have to stay sober. No. Instead, what ends up happening is—yes, you guessed it, a furious frenzy of stock-piling. As happens during the seventh-inning stretch at a U.S. professional baseball game when almost everyone gets up to use the bathroom and to get their last beers, suddenly every drunk in the state is on a rampage to fill his hands, pockets, coolers, refrigerators, and cabinets with as much beer and liquor as possible. The disorder the government is attempting to prevent from manifesting on Election Day takes place on the day before ley seca goes into action. This is Chihuahua's version of the United States' Black Friday on steroids. Because while on Black Friday the frenzy of mostly middle- and working-class persons out for a big sale on mostly clothes and appliances tends to die down by ten in the morning—at the latest, noon—the frenzy of mostly overeager alcoholic men out for anything that'll get them drunk on the day before ley seca lasts until every beer-and-liquor-selling store either closes or runs out of product.

Ley seca frightens the alcoholic. It's a disruption to his life, an infringement on his right to be drunk. "What do you mean you're going to stop selling beer for a couple of days because of elections?" he doth protest. "Fuck the elections! They're all a bunch of crooks anyways—¡puro pinche ratero!" To the alcoholic Chihuahuense there is no difference between el PRIista and el PANista when it comes to the state's halt on the sale of alcohol; because although both el PRIista and el PANista shit on different sides of the aisle, to the alcoholic, they're both still shitting on not only his right but also his need to get shit-faced.

Trucks and cars of all makes, models, and years are left unattended, idling in the middle of streets while their drivers run into expendios and liquorerías carrying cream-colored plastic cartons with the Carta Blanca insignia stamped on their sides, filled with either twenty-four twelve-ounce or twelve thirty-two-ounce envases (recyclable bottles). (In Chihuahua, as well as in every other state in Mexico, people still turn in their envases upon purchasing new bottled beverages; this exempts them from having to pay the few extra pesos for the bottle, too.) On some streets traffic is backed up for blocks. Honking and engine revving are accompanied by an endless "chinga-tu-madre" and middle finger. And you can always count on a few good fistfights because every alcoholic must fend for himself. There is no love for one's brother here, or mercy or pity, only chaos and insatiable thirst. Every capricious man is as responsible for his own welfare as he is for his own brown envase.

And hope is never lost, because even when all is said and done and every expendio and licorería has shut its doors or stopped selling alcohol for the day, there are always las clandestinas: clandestine beers and other alcoholic beverages sold on the black market.

I was fourteen when I first heard the word clandestinas. I'd been out drinking past midnight with my cousins the twins (my mother's older sister Guadalupe's sons, who also lived in Chihuahua at the time) and some of their friends

when one of them suggested we go for "unas clandestinas."
In Spanish every noun is either masculine or feminine, and
many feminine nouns end with *a*. So naturally, when I heard
the phrase "unas clandestinas," my young brain automatically associated it with prostitution. Thus my response to my
companions was: "That sounds like a great idea, but shouldn't
we get condoms first?"

How was I supposed to know my cousin had been referring
to illicitly sold beer? If at that age my English was terrible, my
Spanish was worse.

Today clandestinas are still big business. As soon as the
legit businesses like expendios and licorerías stop selling beer,
Chihuahua's modern-day speakeasies open for business. But
unlike the speakeasies that flourished in the United States
during Prohibition, where people would have to walk down a
dark alley and then down concrete steps to get to the back door
of a commercial business's basement that had been turned into
an underground nightclub or bar, these speakeasies are more
conveniently located in the humble homes of some of Chihuahua's lower-class citizens. Where there's hunger there's hustle,
and in Chihuahua there's a lot of hunger. When I was out with
my cousins and their friends, we didn't have to go a block to
get clandestinas, nor any other time I'd been in Chihuahua and
found myself out of beer and thirsting for more way past last
call. There was always at least one house on every block that en-
gaged in this after-hours profession. All one had to do was quietly creep up—with envase or envases in hand—to the home's
main window, give it a few light taps, wait for it to be cracked
open, and hear the low voice on the other side say, "¿Qué vas a
llevar?"—what would you like?

So when the laughter subsided and I turned to Danny and

asked him if he could get more caguamas, he knew exactly where to go.

"¿Cuántas?" he said.

"Another five," I told him, handing him another wad of green bills.

Run along, little brother, the night is still young and there is still lots more drinking to do.

12

There she is again. She's coming up the street alongside another girl and two children. I'm able to make out her slender
figure as the four bodies casually pass beneath the glow of a
streetlight; and again I wonder who she is and what she's doing
coming back here. Did she know my father, or was she simply
somebody's friend?

I pull Aarón close to me and whisper into his ear, "Who's
that . . . the girl in the red coming this way with the other girl
and the two kids?"

My brother laughs and shakes his head. "That's Rocío," he
says. "Lucy's friend. And that's Lucy with her. Don't you recognize them?"

I'm drunk, so no.

But now that he's mentioned it, I do recognize Lucy,
Danny's wife, and even the two little girls: one is Estrellita, Axcel's daughter, and the other Alady, Danny and Lucy's older
daughter, both my nieces. But I still don't recognize the girl
with them, the one Aarón called Rocío.

"Rocío," I quietly mutter, trying to remember. I even squint
and rub my eyes as I stare out at her. Still nothing. The image of
the beautiful girl who's quickly advancing and whose face I can
now see clearly doesn't register in my mind. Frustrated, I look
up at my brother and say her name one more time: "Rocío?"

"¡Sí—Ro-cí-o!" he says firmly, impatiently stressing each

syllable of her name as if teaching a child how to pronounce it for the first time. "That's her," he says after. "Don't you remember how you promised her a bike for her birthday?"

I'm drunk, so no.

"A bike for her birthday?" I repeat after him, confused, pondering the absurdity of the idea of me having promised this girl, whom I don't recognize and who's getting closer to us with every step she takes, a bike for her birthday.

"Sí," Aarón adds with a tinge of annoyance in his voice. And for the few seconds that follow, our exchange goes like this:

"¡No mames, güey!"

"¡No mamo, güey!"

"I promised her a bike, really?"

"Sí."

"Get the fuck out of here."

"De veras."

"A real fucking bike?"

"I think so. Why would you promise her a fake one?"

"You see . . . you are fucking with me."

"I'm not. I'm telling you the truth. You really did promise her a bike."

"Okay then, what kind of bike did I promise her?"

"No, ¿pues yo que sé? You never mentioned that part. Maybe a small bike. She was little before."

Finally, after we both break into laughter after this last jab from Aarón and he finally realizes that he isn't going to get any further with me unless he provides more details, he says: "Mira, one of the last times you were here, you told her that if she got As in all her classes at school that you would bring her a bike from the United States the next time you came." And suddenly, I know exactly who Rocío is. The memory of the moment when I'd made her this fantastic promise is quickly coming back to me, providing me with one of the soberest instances I'd have throughout the rest of the night. I could see it all so very clearly now.

I'd met the little girl at my father's house. She'd been there with her older sister visiting Lucy, and she'd come riding on an old beat-up bicycle; one so demoralized that the foam cushion and vinyl covering of its metal seat had been completely torn off and it had also been missing a pedal. At one time its mostly rust-covered metal frame could've been pink or red, but most of the paint that remained was faded. I remembered that when I saw it leaning against the wall, sustaining itself upright by the tip of the wasted rubber handle that barely gripped the wall's stucco, I'd laughed at its mournful condition. "Look at this piece of shit," I remember saying to Aarón, who'd been standing next to me at the time the same way he's standing next to me now. "I feel sorry for the poor kid who owns it." And when Aarón told me that it belonged to the little girl who'd been sitting on the couch between Lucy and her friend and whom I'd passed on my way out without noticing, driven by the sudden desire to repair such a misfortune, I went back into the house to meet her. I wanted to meet the Don Quixote who rode up and down the streets of El Cerro de la Cruz on this Rocinante.

"You have a beautiful bike," I said to the little girl after introducing myself to her and her sister. She blushed and curled herself into a ball of embarrassment with her hands tucked tensely under her bottom; then she lowered her head and with only her eyeballs looked around to her sister, to Lucy, and to Aarón, hoping to find the meaning of my words in their faces. But their faces betrayed her inquiring eyes; because all they offered up were silent stares that said they, too, didn't know what I meant by them. Thus, it quickly occurred to me that given the obvious condition of the bicycle, my words could've only been interpreted by everyone in the room, including the little girl, as cruel. Cruelty, however, hadn't been my intention. Because although the bicycle, when viewed as a mere object, was a pitiful sight, when viewed in this case in relation to the little girl who was blushing bashfully before me, it was something to admire. It was the pure and uncorrupted face of childhood poverty, of blissful ignorance; the reason why the meek shall inherit the earth; because the little girl knew no better, only that this bike she rode on belonged to her and that it was more than most kids she knew had or would ever have. Sweetness was in her heart and in her eyes, and in either there weren't any complaints. "Really," I went on, "it says a lot about you: que ves lo maravilloso en todo. You have what none of us have anymore, eyes that only see beautiful."

The little girl smiled shyly and said, "Gracias." Everybody else, though, looked at me like I was full of shit, which was fine with me, because maybe I was; for sometimes even the man who's full of shit is full of shit only because he wishes things were different. And if I promised her a bike that day, it was only because in the moment I'd been completely overcome by the desire to fill her heart with hope: a hope that only a stranger from el otro lado could provide a poor child like her. Because while to her and the others in the room the fifty to one hundred dollars I'd spend purchasing the damn thing from a Walmart or swap meet was considered a fortune, to me it was what I'd usually spend on a night of drinking—it was nothing. Knowing this brought the philanthropist out in me, and I told myself that the next time I'd come to Chihuahua I'd bring this little girl the raddest little bike she'd ever seen. It'd be pink all over and have the most comfortable seat her bottom had ever felt. And she'd ride through all of El Cerro de la Cruz with her head held high and her long black hair blowing in the wind, and she'd be the envy of all the other wretched children from the neighborhood. She'd be amazing in all of their eyes: the little girl who had it all.

But Rocío had grown up on me. She was no longer that little girl to whom all those years ago I'd made a promise I wouldn't keep. Because after that day when I met her, I'd only see the little girl one other time, and it'd be from the passenger seat of my uncle Chuy's truck. Driving through the streets of El Cerro on our way to his house one sunny afternoon, I caught her through the corner of my eye, walking on the sidewalk with a two-liter soda and a small bag of chips. As we zoomed past her, I turned back and watched her until she became small in the distance and eventually got lost in a whirl of dirt and black exhaust smoke. Seeing that something had caught my attention, I remember my tío Chuy asking me, "What is it?" And though I thought, It's the little girl who was at my dad's house with the ugly bike the other day, to my uncle, I said: "Nothing. Just thought I saw someone I knew."

"How old is she now?" I ask Aarón.

"Eighteen."

"Eighteen! Son of a bitch! I'm getting fucking old!" I run my hands over my face with urgency as if afraid it might melt away any second. Time is suddenly precious to me again. I'm caught in between youth and death.

That day at my father's house, Rocío had been only days away from her twelfth birthday: a sprouting flower with no signs of spring. Now, spring had come and gone and behind had left this beautiful rose.

"She's pretty, isn't she?" Aarón says.

"Está hermosa," I reply.

And I'm shamefully laughing inside, because I'm suddenly thinking I should've bought her that fucking bike.

Estrellita and Alady are quick to greet me. "¡Tío! ¡Tío! You're here!" the two bellow excitedly as they run up to me and drop their little heads on my lap. Being just as excited to see them, I wrap my arms around their tiny bodies and bend forward to give them each a kiss on the back of the head. They smell like peaches. But when I tell them so, they quickly perk up and correct me. "¡No, no olemos a durazno, olemos a fresa!"

"Okay, then strawberries it is," I tell them while playfully pinching their rosy cheeks and making a grin. As I'm doing this, Lucy comes from behind them to greet me as well.

"Hola, Obed. ¿Cómo estás?" she says in her soft voice.

"I'm well," I say to her in my drunk one. "I couldn't be better. Can't you tell?

"Pues sí," she says, clutching her hands in front of her.

"And you—how are you, Lucy?"

"Pues bien también."

"Que bueno. I'm glad to hear that. Well is always good." And looking at the girl standing quietly behind her, I say: "And this, who is this with you?"

"My friend Rocío. ¿No te recuerdas de ella?"

Right before I answer, I check myself and pretend to search my memory bank for her name. "Do I remember her?" I ask myself aloud while clutching my chin and staring into the stranger's eyes—they're waiting on me, pleading to me to remember. "But of course I do. How could I ever forget little Rocío? I believe I still owe her a bike—no?" Everyone laughs, including Aarón, who looks at me like I'm one great big asshole.

Up close Rocío is more beautiful than I first perceived her to be. Her skin is pink and creamy and her face unblemished. Her eyes are dark brown and her eyelashes thick and long, like her silky black hair, which she wears pulled back into a ponytail. Her eyebrows are as dark black as her hair and are precisely plucked—not too thick, not too thin. All in place. I admire it: the passion in the care, the delicacy in the presentation, the effort in the gracefulness. I'm staring at godly perfection on this ghostly night. I'm a madman in love with youth—with life all over again. There is hope after all, I say to myself, even in the shittiest of places. I'm drunk. I'm drunk.

"Hola, Rocío," I say to her while again staring stupidly into her eyes.

"Hola, Obed," she replies softly, cool, composed, as if unmoved by my broken promise.

Turning my attention back to my two nieces who are still on my lap and yanking at my shirtsleeves and backpack straps, I say to her, "You grew up on me, and fast. Eres toda una mujer."

I kiss my nieces again and continue to pinch their cheeks. They giggle and I do, too.

"Pues sí, pasan rápido los años," Rocío says.

I couldn't agree more. I want to tell her this, but I'm slowly fading out. I'm clearly in this moment and then I'm not. Something's happened from the time Danny left to get more beer to this moment when I'm talking with Rocío and missing my youth. Estrellita and Alady are laughing and jumping up and down in front of me. Aarón is still at my side and I'm listening to Lucy continue to say something I don't register. I gotta go and I gotta go quick because somehow I realize that I'm already gone. The madness has arrived and the drunk man has no clue; the drunk man has no sense.

13

For a few minutes that seemed like seconds it'd gotten dark, and when the lights came back on I was once again inside the funeral parlor, hanging over my dead father's casket.

I'm shit-faced now.

My father, on the other hand, hasn't changed a bit. He's still stiff and in the same angelic position he'd been in when I last saw him. "Still trying to fool the world, eh, Pops? Well, you can try and fool the world all you want, but you ain't fooling me. I'm your boy. Your drunken piece-of-shit boy who does as you did: drink, motherfucker, drink! So far apart, yet so alike, blood is a motherfucker! God makes no mistakes, you can be sure of that." Tap. Tap. "Who put this fucking glass back over you? Motherfuckers mustn't want anybody to touch that ugly fucking face of yours. I'm drunk, Pops, drunk—¡bien pedo! ¡Hasta la chingada! But you know how it goes, you understand, when nothing else, have a beer, or two, or three—fuck it, drink as much as the heart desires! Isn't that what you used to say? Drink—drink until we die! ¡Hasta la muerte! Hurrah! Hurrah! Time to shine, Daddy-O! Like a lonely star in the vast and black sky. We're all lonely. Every one of us. Lonely and drunk. Just the way you left us. The whole lot of us. Pieces of shit all. And shedding tears for the worthless, the meaningless piece of shit that you were. Because you left nothing. Nothing worth fucking repeating. Nothing worth fucking holding on to. Nothing worth the shit. ¡Mierda todo! ¡Todo mierda! ¡Como lo quiso, Juan, el pinche Pito Pérez, el pinche Papá Juan!"

I'm cursing my father directly to his face. But I don't cry. Can't cry. All I can do is smile. I am one big, drooling, sloppy smile—firme fucking smile.

Alady and Estrellita appear at my side. For a moment all they do is look up at me with curious eyes, as if wondering why I'm so happy. And then, unexpectedly (as children tend to do things), Estrellita, getting on her tiptoes and extending her neck trying desperately to see inside the casket, pulls at my shirtsleeve and says, "Quiero ver a mi papá." And although her words and actions are, in this moment, teaching me what unconditional love looks like, I'm not quick to oblige her. For a moment I let her struggle to get her eyes over the top edge of the casket, just enough to get a glimpse of the dead man. She puts all her weight on her tiptoes and pulls herself up with her fingertips, which she uses to cling to the casket's edge. She presses so hard on it that I can see the blood rushing away from her hands. Soon Alady is doing the same. The two go up and down like pistons on a well-greased engine, but no matter how much they try to get their little noses over the casket's edge, they just aren't tall enough. There's no way they're going to be able to see their papá without my help. So when they give up on their efforts and turn to me with exhausted expressions on their angelic brown faces and Estrellita tells me again that she wants to see her papá, I give her a conceding smile, point inside the casket, and say, "Which papá? This papá? You want to see *El* Papá?" And without saying another word, she promptly nods her head.

"Well, come on then, come see *El* Papá," I say to her while hooking my hand beneath her armpit and bringing her up onto my lap. And because one child always follows the other, I pick up Alady and sit her on my lap, too.

"Look, there's *El* Papá," I say to the two as they stare into the casket with eyes that have never seen death before tonight. They peer into it as if peering into an empty tunnel. There's wonderment and curiosity in their eyes, and, to my surprise, no fear. The two place their hands over the glass and gracefully move them around in circles. Then they begin to lightly tap it. "Shhh, you're going to wake him up," I tell them, "and it's not time for him to wake up. He must sleep for a long time, a very long time." After I say this, they both look at me and giggle, because they know that I'm being silly. They know that I'm lying. They know these things because they know that *El* Papá, *their* papá, is dead and is never going to wake up again.

"Lo quiero tocar," Estrellita says, and then Alady says the same thing.

"You want to touch him?" I repeat after them.

"¡Sí! ¡Sí! ¡Sí!"

"Okay, then, touch him you shall. Are you sure, though, you might wake him up and then he's going to be mad, and you know how he gets when he's mad. Roar!" I gnarl at them while tickling their bellies. The two giggle and bounce on my lap.

I bring each one down gently and they stand quietly away from the casket as I once again remove the plexiglass, all the while hoping I don't drop the fucking thing in front of them or break it over the old man. (People shouldn't handle big pieces of glass, even plexiglass, when drunk; it's not safe, especially around children.) But I manage. I get it down safely and again place it upright against the casket, and this time without cutting myself.

"All right, who's first?" I ask, and Estrellita is quickly climbing up my leg. But there's no way I'm going to be able to have them touch the old man one at a time, because as soon as I sit Estrellita on my lap, Alady is right there begging for me to lift her up, too. So up she comes as well to touch her papá.

This time, in addition to curiosity, upon seeing their papá's corpse without the plexiglass over it, their faces bear a splash of excitement: the plastic covering has been torn off the box and they're now able to touch the product inside, which they do, eagerly. The two reach in and grab at his face and body. Estrellita, who's sitting on my left leg and therefore closer to the corpse's face, is able to reach it without a problem; she touches its cheeks and squeezes its nose and pulls on its right ear. "He can't feel it," she comments while looking back at me.

"Nope, he sure can't," I tell her.

Meanwhile, Alady pounds on her abuelo's chest with her little fists and pulls at the end of his shirtsleeve. "He doesn't move," she says, also while looking back at me.

"Nope, he sure doesn't. But don't worry, he knows you're here playing with him."

"¿De veras?" the two reply with surprise.

"Yes, really. And do you know why?"

"¿Por qué?"

"Because from where he's at, he can see everything. He can see the three of us now looking at him and touching his face and body, and he likes it."

"¿Cómo Diosito?" Estrellita, who's as bright as her name,

says, making equals of her very dead abuelo and her very om-
nipresent God. To her, dead people equal heaven and heaven
equals God; and if God can see everything from heaven, then,
logically, every dead person in the history of the world can see
everything and everyone from heaven, too—just like God.

If only I could've made this deductive leap; if only I could've
been so pure; if only; if only; if only; then saying goodbye to
this man would not have been so easy.

"Obed! Obed!" Aarón is at the door calling me. "Danny's back
with the beer."

"Great! I'm coming."

I tell Estrellita and Alady that they need to say goodbye to
their papá because it's time to go.

"Ba-bye, papá," the two quietly say to the corpse and wave
their little hands at it as I bring them down from my lap. As
I grab the plexiglass to put it back where it belongs, the two
scurry out yelling, "We touched our papá, we touched our papá
in his box!"

I don't say anything more to my father after I'm left alone
with him again. I just carefully place the plexiglass over him
again and silently roll away. This is it. Never will I see my father
again.

I don't remember getting back to the circle.

With one hand I'm holding an almost-full caguama and with
the other I'm receiving a pint of mescal from someone who's

handing it to me. I don't know who it is. I can't see clearly. The world's a blur. My brothers and sisters are all around me and someone's snapping pictures. Everyone's laughing and talking loudly, but I can't make out what they're saying. I'm drunk. They're drunk. We're all drunk. The world is drunk.

Black Out.

INTERMISSION

YA 'STUVO. SE LO ACABÓ EL TRAGO.

—VÍCTOR-MANUEL

14

You get tired of the same ol' shit. Nothing ever changes. Then the body calls. Because it can't stop. Becomes restless. The mind follows. Says that it needs it: Come on, one more time, there's nothing else, not even life. Then you try to measure the bad with the good. But there is no good. Ever. It's all bad. Always. And nothing matters anymore. Let us drink, for tomorrow we die! Everybody drinks; everybody disappears. Was my father a good man? Am I a good man? When drunk, it doesn't matter anymore: all is equal; all is lost forever! It's a sickening thing, like the image of a god that doesn't care. Every Silva must make his grave and fill it.

It's 2:06 a.m., and I'm taking the last drag from the last cigarette I'll smoke before going to bed when the phone rings. And because I know who's calling and why, I hurriedly flick the cigarette butt and roll past the front door toward the phone. Too late. I missed her call; but before I can return it, she calls again. I answer.

"¿Bueno?"

"Ya se nos fue."

It's Veronica, and she's informing me of what could not be put off for any longer.

"He's dead?"

"Sí."

Pause.

"He died at 1:48 a.m."

My tío Mundo died on his bed in his home in Las Cruces, New Mexico, surrounded by his closest family—all Silvas. Hours before he died his liver and kidneys had stopped working, leaving him only with a few last breaths and heartbeats. On the night of November 10, a Thursday, while on most American news stations and radio shows, people speculated on what November 11, 2011, would bring to those who believe in silly superstitions, my tío Mundo was fighting for his life at a hospital he'd been admitted to after having spent much of the morning and day vomiting and shitting blood. And on November 11, a day on which nothing spectacular happened and on which every baby born was being celebrated for nothing other than having come into this world, the hospital sent my tío Mundo back to his home because there was nothing more they could do to save his life. Mundo was in God's hands now.

At home he quickly worsened and became unconscious. His spirit had escaped him and he was reduced to nothing more than a breathing body.

> Goodbye, fellow spirit
> And farewell;
> May you find your place
> In the vast abyss
> Of
> Memory,

And say hello to my father for me—
It's saddest when a death comes as no surprise.

Mundo had started drinking again. According to my cousin Víctor-Manuel, whom I spoke with over the phone a couple days after Mundo was cremated, he'd tried hard to abstain from drinking since my father's passing, but in the end the urge had finally consumed him. "He just couldn't stay away from it. He had to drink," said Víctor-Manuel. "He would drink and then stop and then drink again. But this time there wouldn't be an again. Ya 'stuvo. Se lo acabó el trago."

Mundo died on a Saturday and was viewed at his home the following Monday. I wasn't there. I thought about going, but in the end decided not to. I used work as an excuse. I didn't feel like reliving my father's funeral all over again, exchanging sorrows with the remaining Silvas, who, according to my sister Cecilia, with the exception of my tío Polo, who'd been deported back to Mexico months earlier, were all present. "They were all there," she said as she described the scene over the phone the day after, "and they were all drinking, even my tía Lupe, though not as much as the rest. And they all took it pretty hard, just like Dad's death. But his kids took it the hardest, especially Adriana. At random moments she would cry out for her dad in Spanish. Her mom, Marcella, tended the kitchen most of the night. Lots of friends and family brought food. And it was very crowded, because he (Mundo) had a tiny two-bedroom house. His sons Jr. and Anthony drank straight from the bottle all night and had everyone singing at times in honor of their dad. Unfortunately, the toilet got clogged early in the night so everyone had to piss outside. My uncle Manuel and someone else tried to fix it for hours. But I'm not sure if they ever succeeded. Between breaks they would take hits from a joint that Adriana's boyfriend, Jesús, provided, which was cool because it helped kill the smell of shit. And all his kids spoke. Tía Lupe did, too, along with a couple of his friends from the neighborhood who also played their guitars and sang songs for the family. No one got crazy while I was there though, or that I heard of after. And Adriana said she paid for all of the arrangements because his other five kids didn't want to pitch in because of hard feelings."

Cecilia stopped there, said, "This was about it. Nothing much else went on." When I asked her if she knew when he'd be buried, she told me that he wouldn't. "He's going to burn. They're going to cremate him tomorrow."

On Wednesday, four days after he died, my tío Mundo's body was pushed into a furnace and reduced to ashes from which no phoenix would ever rise.

Act 2
THE BURIAL

~

DEATH DEFINES LIFE; A DEATH DEPICTS A LIFE IN
IMMUTABLE FORMS; WE DO NOT CHANGE
EXCEPT TO DISAPPEAR.

—OCTAVIO PAZ, *The Labyrinth of Solitude*

15

I awake in my father's bedroom. I'm still in my clothes and my mouth tastes like shit; my shoes and cap are all that have been removed (had I removed them, or had someone removed them for me?). I'm also still wearing my watch. It's 7:12 a.m.

"Fuck," I say, pressing my hands against my forehead. "It's time to bury this motherfucker and it's so fucking early! Give me a few more hours, Pops," I say, trying to squeeze away the pain at my temples. But "¡Nel, ni madres! Bury me now! I'm tired of people crying over me. Por el favor de Dios, bury me already!" I hear my father saying in response. "Okay. Okay. If you want to be buried now, then we shall bury you now. Just let me get ready and take a shit first. Then we'll be on our way."

But before I do these things, I sit up on the edge of the bed and take in the room. Sunlight's already pouring in through the window and glass sliding door; it's bright all over and time's moving slowly. And though my eyes are having trouble adjusting to the brightness, I curiously look around the room. It hasn't changed much since the last time I was in it four years earlier. The bed is still the same ripped-up shitty mattress with metal springs popping out from it. The curtains are the same ugly orange veil-like drapes that do little to keep out the sun, and a thick film of dust and dirt still covers everything from the brown tile floor to the old box-television set with missing knobs resting on the corner shelf above the white wooden desk that comes out from the wall. And the small two-drawer dressers on each side of the bed are also still covered in dirt and dust. On one of them is an old digital alarm clock that keeps blinking 12:00 AM and a pack of Faros cigarettes with a few Faritos still in them. I think about my father sitting where I am and smoking them while drinking away and staring at the clock—time passing him by. He's thinking about nothing, worrying about nothing, or maybe—he is. Of me. Yes, of me. Of the years gone by. Of the time we never spent together, and of the time we did. He's taking a puff, pinching the Farito with his thumb and index finger, sucking its life out. His fingernails are yellow and the skin of his hands is caked with yeso. He's drunk. Rocking back and forth, falling sideways, struggling to sit up straight. He's been drunk for days. Once in a while he lets out a laugh. Hypnotized by the bright red 12:00 AM that keeps blinking in front of him, he falls back onto the bed. He remembers that he once had dreams, that he hadn't always been this way. Or had he? But there's nothing he can do about it now. It's too late. Too fucking late. No turning back. No way of fixing what's already broken. "Vámonos," he cries, "a la chingada con todo. Ya hice y deshice, ya no hay más. ¡Los quiero, hijos, a todos!"

I notice that someone has ripped out the small air-conditioning unit from the wall above the sliding door. A big rectangular hole that allows me to see the blue sky outside is all that remains. It was my father who ripped it out, of course, and probably sold it for a few pesos the way he'd done with other appliances when he needed money. Often he'd sell stuff from the house. He'd spend months at a time paying off a TV or DVD player only to sell it for less than half of what he'd eventually end up paying for it. Once when I asked him why he'd do this, he said, "Because we don't need all these material things. You think you need them when you buy them, and then when you have them you realize that you don't really need them. Luxuries are for the rich, hijo, and we're not rich. Besides, I need the money. Are you going to give me money?" Pause. "Then?"

Then? Then how 'bout you work and stop feeling sorry about your sorry ass?

I said nothing.

But the worst was when my father almost sold off ten original Piña Moras for a mere one thousand dollars. Had I not arrived when I did, the paintings, which are worth thousands, would've been sold to a government representative—one of those people he considered crooks and so despised—and long gone. I'd always admired these paintings, which are mostly of Tarahumara people and landscapes of Chihuahua's Sierra Madre where they reside. Each is of a different size, with the smallest being 16 by 12 inches and the largest 3 by 4 feet. This largest one has always been my favorite. No matter where it hangs it always commands attention. It's of four Tarahumara men, who, if not for their dark skin and headwear, could easily be confused for fifth-century Roman senators, each seated and draped in a long white robe with a brightly colored sash. The one at the fore and the one right behind him each have on their head a basket with stacks of bread in it, while the two behind them don traditional Tarahumara headbands. And each bears the face of resilience, of loss and antiquity. But it's the one at the fore who's the most striking. Sitting majestically like a king on his throne, with his hands resting at his side, his stare is grave and unapologetic, like Geronimo's in the famous photo of him snapped by Ben Wittick in the 1800s, where he's kneeling and holding a rifle, looking like he's ready to kill a white man. Certainly the two share a similar history. Currently this painting hangs on the wall at my mother's house right above the dining room table. Around it hang other Piña Mora paintings. Most of them are of Tarahumara women and children. The others are of some of Chihuahua's Sierra Madre's scenic panoramas. My father's painting of the fruits and samovars hangs there, too: the work of the student beside the work of the master.

But this painting and all the others that today hang all over my mother's house almost never made it there. If I hadn't arrived in Chihuahua when I did that summer, a government lawyer would've made off with some of the most beautiful paintings Chihuahua has ever known for almost nothing. But if anybody was going to rob my father for these paintings, it was going to be me, and not some uppity lawyer lady with dollar signs in her eyes. So when he told me what he'd done, I told him that he had to get those paintings back by any means necessary, because if he didn't, I would never forgive him. I also added that I would gladly pay him the thousand dollars the lawyer had paid him for them. This made my father very happy, because as it turned out he had yet to receive any payment from the lawyer; when he'd brought the paintings to her office he'd been met by a young female secretary who'd told him that the lawyer had taken an early vacation and that she'd be gone for two weeks. This meant that the paintings were leaning against a wall in a bland government office being watched over by a clueless twenty-something-year-old. But what surprised me more was that my father was ready to go retrieve the paintings almost instantly. "Vamos pues," he said with excitement, "before they close. ¡Ándale!"

"Really, right now?" I said, not believing him.

"Pues sí. Don't you want the paintings?"

"Claro que sí."

"Pues vamos. ¡Anda! Let's get there before they close, because then we're going to have to wait until Monday when they open again."

Fuck that! I wanted those paintings.

My father and I hopped into the cabin of my uncle Chuy's truck and Aarón and Danny hopped in the back. And because only my father knew where we were headed, I let him drive. Within minutes we were parked in a yellow zone in front of a tall building right across from La Plaza Mayor, which is home to the statue of El Ángel de la Libertad, on the southeast corner of Calle Aldama and Avenida Venustiano Carranza, right in the heart of El Centro.

"I'll be back," my father said as he shut the door and walked away. Aarón and Danny jumped from the bed of the truck onto the sidewalk and came to the passenger-side window, where they met me with puzzled faces, as uncertain as I was about whether our father was actually going to return with the paintings. Silently the three of us stared at him as he disappeared into the tall building in front of us. It was ten minutes till five and I was hoping that we hadn't arrived too late. I didn't want to spend the rest of the day and night plus all of Saturday and Sunday wondering if I'd ever see the paintings again.

"Do you think he'll return with them?" I asked Aarón and Danny.

"Pues sí," said Danny in a quiet but certain tone. "If he says they're here, then they must be."

"Yeah, but will they give them back to him?" I added.

"Pues quien sabe," Aarón said, shrugging.

But before we could speculate any more, my father appeared holding the stack of paintings above his head. They were wrapped in a serape-like blanket and large black trash bags. Hunched over but steady, my father quickly made it to the truck, moving right past me to the back, where he carefully placed the works of art. I looked at them through the back window, wanting to see their condition, but all I could see were the dusty black bags and old blanket they were wrapped in. I hoped they were all there.

"Just like I said, hijo," my father said to me while standing over the paintings and dusting off his hands and forearms. He was happy and smiling, drips of sweat forming on his forehead.

"Are you sure they're all there?" I yelled to him.

"¡Todas! When we get home, you'll see. But first let's go get some sodas. I'm thirsty."

It was hot, and cold sodas sounded good.

In the living room of his house, my father carefully removed the blanket and trash bags. After, he carefully placed each painting against the room's walls. They were all there, all ten of them, still in their original frames and still in good condition.

"Eh, what did I tell you?" said my father as if showing off his own work. "You wanted them, you got them. Era chingón, Piña Mora. Do you notice the lines, his style? Look at this one here, of this Tarahumara woman. The strokes are strong, almost violent, but you can't see them from far away. She looks all smooth from back here. You like that?"

"Yes, of course, it's beautiful."

"Now look at this big one. The style is different. The lines are straight, more defined, sharp. Look at the men's robes, they look like they're from a Picasso painting. Están cuadradas las líneas, ¿qué no?"

"Sí."

"Nombre, hijo, if you would have seen these paintings

twenty years ago, you would have seen how much more beautiful they used to be, when the colors were still fresh and vibrant. They jumped out at you. But they're still beautiful— ¡hermosas! I still love them."

It amazed me to hear my father talk about these paintings in this way, like a curator at a museum, like a true lover of art, and not of any art, but of this particular art that was right in front of him, of an art he was so closely connected to. It was bewildering to think that only days earlier he'd made a deal with someone to sell this art to them for a mere thousand dollars. It pained me to know that although my father loved these paintings, he could so easily sell them off. Had my father really been that desperate for money? If he had, could he have done nothing else to attain it? Where was the love for the works there, the appreciation? Where was his dignity?

16

A pile of my father's clothes rests against the wall below the window, which tells me that this is where he'd been staying during the last days of his life. This room had become his sanctuary from the world outside. It's in the back, separated from the main house, and according to my father, he built it for me after I was shot, to accommodate me in my newly crippled condition and to give me privacy when I visited. But when I wasn't visiting, he could be alone in here and do as he pleased, including drink himself to oblivion without being judged. In here he could enjoy the company of his demons without having to put on airs for others—too much work. In here he could be Juan Silva the way Juan Silva was meant to be—no masks, no need to put on a show for anybody.

I search everywhere for signs of his blood. I'm convinced that he bled in here and I want to see it. I want to see a part of his suffering, touch it and rub it between my fingers; I want to put my tongue to it and taste it; because I hate that my father suffered, that he died a slow and agonizing death, that he could see the dark shadow coming upon him and was unable to do anything to save himself from it. I hate the hopelessness of it all, the suffocating feeling of drowning in our own creations; I hate that one man could do this to himself; I hate that no matter what, the time was marked, and it was just a matter of how much blood was left in him. My father's blood slowly dripping away—from here, from there—and leaving his body, is fucking with my head, and I wonder if there could've been a way to have put it all back. It was just blood after all—my father's blood.

Where's the blood, Pops, and why'd you have to go out this way? This is no way to die.

There's no blood though, not on the floor or on the walls or even on the bed or sheets, and from what I can tell from where I sit, there isn't any on his clothes either. Was it all a lie? Or did he bleed out somewhere else? Maybe in the main house or in the bathroom? Or maybe in the driveway or in the street? Or maybe, just maybe, he didn't die? But I saw him. I saw him dead.

I set my eyes on his shoes, which are placed carefully next to his clothes. The sunlight coming through the window splashes over them like a spotlight coming over an actor on a stage. They're black, dirty, and covered in scuffs and splotches of yeso, proof that my father, contrary to popular belief, had in fact worked. But when I think of this I instantly hear my mother's voice saying to me, "Yes, he worked, but only when he wanted to. Your father hated to work, he was lazy." I know, Mother, I know. But enough of that for now. I smile as I stare at the shoes, because they'd been my father's shoes, my father the drunk's shoes, shoes I'd given him the last time I'd been in Chihuahua.

"I like your shoes," he said to me on the night of my arrival, after all the welcoming hugs and hellos. "They'd be great for work." They were brand-new suede Stacy Adams with thick rubber soles that I wore as dress shoes. They looked fresh with blue 501s cuffed at the bottom, real cholo-like. "You like 'em, huh?" I said to him with a sense of guilt. "Well, if you want, you can have them. They're a little too small for me anyway." I took them off and handed them to my father, who lit up at the idea and just as instantly removed his own old and heavily worn shoes and tossed them aside. When they hit the wall and fell to the floor, I knew they would never be worn again. He shone as he put on the Stacys and walked around the living room in them. He jumped up and down a few times and even did a couple of squats. "Gracias, hijo," he kept saying. "Están chingones." And because I believe in living out books, in that moment, I remembered how Anton Chekhov had written this scene for my father and me long ago in his short story titled "A Father": Was I not Borenka, the son who loved his alcoholic father unconditionally and gave him all that he asked for and more, including his new boots? Was my father not Old Musatov, the abject father who preferred the drink over the love of his children? And were these shoes not a symbol of hope, of love, as were the boots that Borenka gave to his father?

The words came back to me like a river flowing backward. I'm in my room in my house back in California and they're jumping out at me from a yellow and cracking page glued to the spine of a worn hardcover. They are Musatov's words to Borenka after he realizes that the real reason Borenka offers him the boots is not because they were too small for him, but because upon seeing the condition of his father's old and tattered shoes, Borenka is moved by love and pity to give him his own boots. "I see through you! Your boots were too small, because your heart is too big. Ah, Borenka! I understand it all and feel it!" I begin to cry as I read Musatov's words to his son, my tears drowning the words on the page. Chekhov, how well do you tell my story! Had my father been in the room with me at this moment, I would've reached out and wrapped my arms around him. I would've kissed Juan Silva and told him that I loved him so. And like Borenka, I would've said to him, "It's okay, Papá! My heart is big for you!" But I can do no such thing. Because

I'm alone and wishing that he'd never died and that I was back in California despising my still-living father from a distance, sometimes hoping, and sometimes not, for him to call me. What, you need money? Sure, it's on its way. No, no, you don't have to explain. Yes, I love you, too. Goodbye.

After what happened with Piña Mora, my father would never again come across another opportunity to master his artistic talent. Yet he never did stop drawing. The last time I'd been in Chihuahua, during one of those peaceful moments that sometimes manifest during great storms, my father, while sitting next to his wife on the couch, drew a portrait of me with a number 2 pencil on a piece of white lined paper. "Toma, para tí, hijo," he said, holding it up for me to see. "So you can see that I can still draw."

I'm perfect. He'd drawn me exactly the way I was; there were no mistakes or eraser marks anywhere on the paper. Every line and shadow had purpose. El viejo still had it. And now that he's dead I'm looking at another portrait he'd also drawn with a number 2 pencil. This one isn't drawn on paper, nor canvas, but directly on the wall across from me in my father's room. And because I can't make it out completely from where I sit on the edge of the bed, I hop onto my wheelchair and roll over to it. The portrait, which is drawn within an oval shape no bigger than a football, is of a woman and two boys. All three have their eyes closed. The woman doesn't resemble anyone in particular and neither do the two boys. Yet it tells the story of a mother and her two sons. It evokes love and pain. The woman, one can see, is suffering, and so are her sons. But they're together and love one another. She has her sons and they have their mother. Each is a pillar that sustains the others' ability to endure. At the bottom right my father had signed it: *Dedicado a mis hijos. Juan Silva 2007.*

My father, I'm beginning to realize, was sometimes a sinner and sometimes a saint. My father loved us, but he loved us in the way that only a sick man can love anybody: indelicately. Because all my father's love did was drive us mad. He would kiss us one minute, and ridicule us the next. He would hand us a dream with one hand and crush it with the other. He'd kill our dreams and make us feel stupid for having dreamed them. "I love you," he'd say, "but you'll never amount to anything."

This was why my brothers stopped going to school. They believed him when he told them that it was a waste of time. "Estás loco, güey," I told him once when we argued over this. "That's not true, school's the best thing for them. They should stay in school until they graduate, and then they should go to college." But as my mother always says, there's no use in arguing with a drunk—and sometimes even when he's sober, because my father was set in his belief and didn't give a shit about what I had to say. To him, that I was working on a bachelor's degree in English at the time and finding success in my studies didn't mean anything when it came to my brothers. "It's true that you might be able to do something with an education over there, but here, all your brothers can look forward to with an education is hunger," he argued back. "An education in Mexico isn't the same as an education in los Estados Unidos. Here, in Mexico, all that really matters is hard work." And to support his argument he used my uncles Juan and Chuy (my mother's brothers who live in Chihuahua). "Look at your tío Juanito, he studied to be an engineer and never finished. Now what is he doing? Working in a maquiladora like the rest of the poor bastards around here. And your tío Chuy, have you asked him how much he makes as a schoolteacher?" It was true, my uncle Juan never graduated as an engineer and my uncle Chuy doesn't earn much as a schoolteacher; but both my uncles Juan and Chuy have never gone a day without being able to put food on their tables; more importantly, what my father overlooked is that both my uncles are men who, unlike himself, know what it means to be a decent and productive man, regardless of what the pay is at the end of the day.

When I was four, my father came to visit me at my grandmother's house in Westminster, California, where my mother and I were living at the time (with about twenty other family members). He came bearing gifts for his little boy: He-Man action figures that included Orko, Skeletor, He-Man himself, and his cowardly green tiger, Cringer; he even brought Castle Greyskull to close the deal and a BMX bicycle with training wheels for good measure. He was playing Santa in the middle of summer.

In the picture, I'm standing on the sidewalk next to my father behind all these gifts. The action figures and Castle Greyskull are still in their original packaging and some parts of the bicycle are still wrapped with plastic. Standing in my tight brown corduroy pants and red fake-leather Michael Jackson jacket with a thousand zippers, I barely come up to my father's waist. I'm a happy boy, and my father's a handsome and happy man. He's got a lot of hair, and it's as black as his youthful mustache. His smile shows off a full set of teeth. My father's a cool twenty-five here, healthy and strong, even a bit muscular in his red-and-green long-sleeve button-down shirt. He could still breeze through a couple twenty-four-packs of beer with no problem; could still drink himself an entire fifth of tequila without worrying about blood disgorging from his ass and mouth. His liver's still strong.

But in the same way that a picture can capture such happy moments, it can also hide horrific ones. My grandmother's house, which is the backdrop to our perfect father-and-son moment, for my mother and me can evoke painful memories. A lot of ugly things took place within one of its rooms.

I'm a child and I'm searching for a place to hide. The room is lit and I don't want to see what's taking place, what my father's doing to my mother. I grab for a blanket, but it's too thin. I can still hear the muffled sounds. I try to crawl beneath the bed, but that, too, doesn't work. My ears are too big. My mother's telling my father to get off of her and my father's telling her to shut up. I hear a slap and then my mother's cries. I'm crying now, too, but my father doesn't stop. I keep hearing the pushing and I want to run out, but I don't because then everyone else will hear and everyone else will know. So I cower into a ball on the floor with my blanket over my head and press my hands against my ears. "Please stop, please stop, please stop," I keep saying to myself. But time is too slow and the ugly sounds only seem to get louder. *Somebody save this boy from his father, somebody save this woman from her husband.* But salvation never comes, and the moment lasts forever.

What was it that I was hearing? What was it that my father had been doing to my mother that I couldn't see? I know now what I didn't know then. Just like I know now that—while we lived in this house, in this room—the reason my mother often wore sunglasses was because behind them was a pair of black eyes. I know now what everybody who also lived in this house with us knew then: that my father often brutally beat and abused my mother during the time he lived there with us.

So the picture's a fraud, another way by which my father, to this day, is able to bring me joy one minute, and suffering the next.

I don't know from where my father had come when he appeared with these gifts. All I know is that he didn't stay for long. The last picture we'd ever take together this side of El Rio Bravo would be taken later that evening at LAX by my mother: my father is squatting next to my mother's brown '67 Nova and a portable stereo that almost comes up to his knees. On my feet, I'm leaning into his chest and facing the camera. His left hand is gently on my back while his right sustains my head like a pillow. It's dark now and in a few moments my father will kiss me on the cheek, gather his things, then walk away to catch a plane to El Paso, Texas, from where he'll cross the border into Juárez, Chihuahua, and never come back, at least not to California.

Months later my mother would bring me with her to Chihuahua to formally divorce him. After that, I'd be the only link between them, and all of the memories of their relationship would become me.

Sitting on the edge of the bed reliving these painful memories, I recall the previous day's drive to the Tijuana airport. My girlfriend Shirin is behind the wheel and my sister Samantha is sitting in the back seat. Little is said during the two-hour drive.

I rest my head against the passenger door's window and stare out at the world I'm leaving behind. It all seems unimportant, and all of it is moving away from me faster than I can hold on to; but I can't help looking out at it as it rushes by and turns into a blur. It's better than looking at Shirin or my sister. Shirin is one of those women with an amazingly beautiful face that most can't resist staring at. It's achingly captivating, and her eyes are like two golden suns set next to each other. They can hypnotize any man and turn him into melted wax in an instant. I've been that wax many times, and I've loved it every time: being their victim, the flesh and spirit they burn right through. They're eyes that know me, eyes that have seen me cry and have seen me laugh, eyes that have seen me strong and have seen me weak—but not this weak, not this pitiful, and not this vulnerable to their compassion. So for fear of breaking out in tears at their sight, I prefer to curl up in the coldness of my own heart and to focus my eyes on the meaningless: on the cars with faceless people in them, on the trees, the buildings, the homes, fences, churches, bridges, posts, signs, and all the things that make up a civilization, on all the things that never last. And suddenly I'm asking myself, "Why, Papá, why'd you hit my mother? Why'd you hit your wife? Why'd you go?" Then Lennon reaches my ears and I see my father walking away from me:

> Father, you left me but I never left you
> I needed you, you didn't need me
> So I, I just got to tell you
> Goodbye, goodbye . . .

I'm singing in silence, but what I really want to do is scream. I want to sing the song the way Lennon did, like someone was ripping his heart out of his chest.

17

When I get out of the shower, Aarón is the only one in the house; everyone else has already left to go to the funeral parlor. It's already nine a.m.

I put on black jeans and a sprightly white T-shirt. I'd brought a black suit and tie to wear, but as I sit on the edge of the bed and stare at it in the suitcase, I think about how it isn't even worth the trouble. No one had worn a suit the day before, and I'm certain that no one will wear one this day either. It's Juan Silva for God's sake, who the fuck cares? Besides, my father had never worn a suit in his life. Suits were for *those* people, not for him; he was an honest man, not some crook ready to swindle you for your hard-earned money as soon as you let your guard down. Suits, to my father, represented el gobierno—the government—all the fat-bellied bastards who lived grandiose lives off the backs of the poor and hardworking people of all the world. To him, a suit in China or Russia or in the United States was no different from a suit in Mexico. "Son una bola de rateros," he'd say whenever the conversation turned to politics. "¡Nomás saben chingar al pobre! There is no place in this world where the government is not fucking the workingman. Te chingan aquí y te chingan allá. En todos lados te chingan." He especially felt this way about the suit-wearing government engineers who overlooked his work when he'd work on government projects. He'd call them imbeciles and good-for-nothings. Every time he'd spot one walking down the street of a neighborhood being developed as a government project he'd yell out to him from the car to get to work, to do a man's job, to get dirty. One morning, as I drove him and my brothers to work, my father, upon seeing one of these engineers walking in his black suit, holding a clipboard and shaded by a black umbrella that was being held over his head by the man next to him—who was wearing not a suit but old ripped-up jeans and a dirty white T-shirt—stuck his head and arms out of the car window and yelled: "¡Pinche ingeniero mamón! ¡Porque mejor no le dices que te detenga los huevos!" My brothers and I all laughed. And when he brought himself back in he looked at the three of us with a triumphant expression, like he'd just led a Marxist revolution through all of Mexico. Pancho Villa and Emiliano Zapata had nothing on Juan Silva. "Estos güeyes no hacen nada, nomás se la pasan caminando con su trajecito haciéndose pendejos," he said to us like a general relaying to his soldiers the ways of their enemy. "¿Y cómo la ven con el güey ese que le carga el paraguas? Ni que 'stuviera lloviendo. Y mira nomás que clase de casas diseñan. Ni talento tienen los güeyes. ¡Que se vayan a la chingada!"

That's right, you tell him, Dad! Tell him how useless and stupid they all are. Tell him who's the real man! Juan Silva is the real man!

When we arrive at the parlor, the casket is already outside. The lid is open and there are people standing around it. "What time is it?" I ask Aarón, thinking we had made everyone wait for us—for me—again. But this isn't the case. It's barely 9:45 a.m.

and my father still has fifteen minutes before he has to be completely removed from the premises. Someone must've been in a
hurry though, and that's why the casket's outside. Someone had
made the call to push my father out early. Not even in death
could people stand him in their homes for very long. As I think
this, I'm reminded of the Mexican saying my mother loves to
repeat when she gets tired of a houseguest: "Despues del tercer
día el muerto y el invitado ya empiezan a apestar"—After the
third day, the corpse and the guest alike begin to stink. I find
amusement in the fact that my father has managed to become
the real-life example of this maxim. Here he is on the third day
getting rolled out of the parlor before he could stink up the
place. "That's it, Juan, your time is up," I imagine the director
of the parlor saying to my father as he hurryingly pushed him
out. And I imagine my father saying back to him, "But I got
fifteen more minutes, hold on, why the hurry?" And the director replying, "No, no, that's it, you gotta go. Now hurry up
and have your people roll your ass out of here—apurale, que ya
estás empezando a apestar!" And as I laugh at this scene I'm
constructing in my head, I feel glad, because in a way, I'm in a
hurry, too. It's already too fucking hot out and the truck we're
in doesn't have air-conditioning. I'm beginning to sweat.

The people standing around the casket are mostly the
same people from the night before, and most of them, I notice, are still wearing the same clothes they had on the night
before, too. This makes me wonder whether they even went
home, or was it possible that they'd slept with a dead man?
I ask Aarón this question and he tells me that some of them
had in fact slept on the concrete benches outside the parlor.
"Víctor-Manuel, Veronica, Timbi (all siblings), and three of my
friends slept here last night," he says, pointing them all out to

me. At first I'm surprised by the idea, but when I factor in that the people he mentioned were people who'd also joined me in my drunken revelry the night before, it all made perfect sense: when fucked-up enough, drunks will sleep anywhere, even on a pile of shit, and even next to a dead man. Yet I couldn't help but think of the devotion such an act—whether done sober or inebriated—revealed; because after all, had they really wanted to, they could've gone to any of my father's relatives' or friends' homes and slept warmly within walls and under a roof. That's impressive, viejo, I think to myself, people did love you after all, at least enough to keep vigil over you while you peacefully wait to be buried.

I don't get off the truck. From the passenger seat I look out at the crowd and they look back at me, perhaps wondering if I'm going to get off before the casket is shut and my father is stuffed into the hearse. And when Aarón asks me if I want to see him one last time before we leave to the cemetery, I refuse. "Chale," I say. "Vámonos. Let's get out of here and bury this motherfucker. This scene's getting old and it's hitting ninety degrees already." I run the back of my hand over my forehead and wipe the sweat away. The day isn't looking too good. And to make matters worse, I can't stop thinking about my stomach, about my intestines. I hadn't been able to take a shit after waking up. I tried. I pushed. But nothing came out. It was official: I was—I am—constipated.

Months earlier I'd had a resectioning of my small intestine. One whole foot of it had been removed because it was gangrenous, and I was dying. In the months leading up to the surgery, I'd been heavily addicted to painkillers and cocaine. Neither of the two even alone is good. But there I was, easing both the physical and spiritual pain that comes with my disability with

Vicodins, alcohol, and cocaine, and though I was succeeding in killing the pain, I'd also been succeeding in killing myself. If not for a cocaine overdose that sent me to the hospital the night before the surgery, I never would have found out about the gangrene and I would be dead. According to my short Korean doctor, the Vicodins had constipated me and the impurities in the cocaine had been the cause of the infection that eventually turned to gangrene. I suppose he was right. For over a week before the overdose I hadn't been able to take a shit, but I never stopped to think that it was because of the Vicodins, so I just kept on popping them, and drinking, and snorting cocaine.

But the real lifesaver in that story is my sister Samantha. That night, I'd been at a friend's house drinking heavily and snorting cocaine. When I came home, I was completely wired and out of my mind, but I kept snorting. And at some point it just became too much and it was time to go to the hospital. From the downstairs living room I yelled for my sister who was asleep in her upstairs room; it was way past midnight. When she heard me and saw me in my pale skin and wide-eyed condition, she hurriedly came down the stairs and asked me what was wrong. I told her. So she threw on some decent clothes and her shoes and pushed me to her car. Within minutes we were at La Palma Hospital, where my face was not a new one. As with my first overdose, the doctor injected me with Ativan to reverse the effects of the cocaine, and it worked, but this time something was different. I felt a pain in my lower abdomen that I had never felt before, and it was unbearable. Yet the doctor wanted to discharge me and almost pushed me out of the hospital herself, believing that I was not telling the truth and was only faking the pain in hopes of being prescribed more pain medicine. My sister, however, always at my side, stood between me and the doctor and told her that she was not taking me home until they checked my stomach. The doctor finally obliged. She asked me to raise my shirt. I did. While a nurse stood by, she placed her hand over my lower abdomen and found it swollen and hard. I was taken in for X-rays, and before I knew it, Dr. Kim was there telling me that I needed an emergency surgery immediately, that if they didn't operate I could die. Within a couple of hours I was being prepped for surgery. By that time my sister had called my mother and the two were now at my side, seeing me to the operating room. The last thing I remember about that night is my mother telling me that I was going to be just fine, and Dr. Kim telling me that when I woke up I was going to have a shit bag attached to my belly. That was the last thing I wanted to hear.

When I woke up the next day, the first thing I did was check for the shit bag—nothing there, only a stitched-up incision from my chest to my pubic line, right over the incision that had been made on the night I'd been shot. Now I would have two zippers, one right over the other, but at least no shit bag, and more importantly, I was alive to tell another fantastic story about the time my sister Samantha saved my life.

My father is finally pushed into the hearse and everybody jumps into their vehicles. Some of our cousins and some friends of my father jump into the bed of the truck Aarón and I are in. The last time I rode in a truck with people riding in its bed with no camper was as a teenager, when—while (coincidentally) in Chihuahua—I was on my way to the river for a day of camping with my cousins los cuates and their friends. It was a happy time then. We'd been on our way to play with nature, to celebrate youth and to be the masters of our lives. This time, however, the bed is carrying a pack of lowly faces who signed up for a funeral. There is no celebration of any kind this time, only a soundless cry for mercy for one of our own. Our collective heart sings:

> For whom do the bells toll?
> For the dead man!
> And amongst whom will he be buried?
> The low and wretched!
> And shall he spend eternity with the saved,
> Or with the damned?
> That is a question for God!
> So we shall say a prayer for him,
> In which case, God might be merciful in all his glory.

Poverty, like expendios and liquor stores, is everywhere in Chihuahua. For although since the early 2000s a lot of narcos and rich people from other states have started to buy land on both sides of el periferico [Chihuahua's version of a freeway], on which they've built United States–style homes adjacent to United States–brand stores like Walmart and Home Depot and fast food restaurants like McDonald's and Wendy's, Chihuahua remains mostly a poor city. The poor are everywhere, whether on the streets begging for money or in United States–owned maquiladoras working their lives away for "una mierda," as my father would say. And as much as the government would like to put a happy gringo face on it by letting a lot of United States businesses set up all over the city, the fact of the matter is that there is no salvation in sight for Chihuahua's lowest class. The rich are getting richer and the poor are getting poorer. And unlike in the United States, where the lines between the lower, middle, and upper classes are seemingly blurred by endless credit and just as endless debt at every level, in Chihuahua, like in most, if not all of Mexico's states, the gap between the poor and the rich is as wide as the Grand fucking Canyon. The fact that it's there is as evident as its drug and cartel problem. Part of why it's so evident is because in Chihuahua, there's no real middle class, no bridge between the rich and poor. People either have or they don't.

We begin the procession from the parlor to the cemetery at ten a.m. Driving behind the hearse are Aarón, myself, and everybody else we're carrying in the bed of the truck. Chihuahua's hot and dusty and I'm already sweating profusely. What a fucked-up day to have a funeral, especially in a sad town like this, I complain to myself. There are no green trees anywhere, only dry roods with bullet holes and the names of lovers etched into them. And in Chihuahua, especially in barrios like the one where my father lived, grass is rare. There are no green lawns for Pedro's or Juan's landscaping crew from Anaheim Hills or Santa Ana to mow here. ¡No, señor! Here one must make do with dirt. Every yard is made of dirt and so are many of the streets; and what is not made of dirt has dirt on it: dirt, dirt, dirt. This is why I hate wearing good or clean clothes when I'm in Chihuahua, because by the end of the day my clothes, especially my shoes (which I don't even walk in because I just can't fucking walk) and even my face are flecked with dirt.

The hearse is white, the color of purity and one that is usually reserved for children. But not on this day. On this day this white hearse carries a sinner who never got to know redemption, a sinner who ráised hell to the end.

"Why white?" I ask Aarón.

"I don't know, maybe that's the only one they had."

Yes. Or like my father, the organizers of the funeral, too, wanted to fool the world, hoping that the people would say: "Look! There goes Juanito in that white hearse, on his way to heaven, I'm sure!"

Or not.

～

"Le tengo miedo a mi jefe, / Deseando que nunca regrese . . ." I'm startled by the music. I hadn't realized Aarón had pushed a CD into the stereo. I recognize the beat and the lyrics; they're from "La Novela" by Akwid, an L.A.-based Chicano rap duo who rap mostly in Spanish.

"This was my dad's song," Aarón tells me, looking at me curiously to see if I recognize the irony. "He used to say that it was about him." The volume is turned all the way up and I can barely hear what Aarón's saying.

"I know," I yell back at him. "I remember him playing it the last time I was here."

Aarón nods and we both fall silent to listen to the rest of the song. I look back at the people in the bed of the truck and their quiet and seemingly motionless dispositions tell me that they're doing the same. It's as if we're all in agreement that the song should be played and that its lyrics deserve uninterrupted attention.

The song is a riff on "Dos Monedas." Sampling its original instrumentals and chorus, the rappers describe how a family is forced to live at the mercy of an alcoholic patriarch. Singing it through the perspective of a son, the rappers describe the world my father created within the walls of his home. There's no peace for the son and his brothers, who are constantly walking on eggshells to avoid a beating from their father. The son notes how his mother cries when she sees how her kids suffer. The glow in her eyes is the only life she has left. On Sundays when they go to church, he watches as she prays, knowing what she's praying for. There's something there that they all know but that none have the courage to speak of. May God help them because their faith is running out. Their father, instead of helping, is out getting drunk. Monday through Friday, it's always the same shit; it's always them having to face the enemy. And so the son spends his days in the street to avoid "todo lo malo." He hangs with his friends who he believes might be suffering the same fate in their own homes; but afraid they might laugh at him, he doesn't let them know anything.

The song's uncanny affinity to the way my father had been gives me the chills. And as we drive behind the hearse through the dry streets of Chihuahua, we play it full blast. "That's right," I'm saying to myself, "let the world hear the truth about our father; let them know what kind of man we're burying today." "Mi jefe convirtió el canton en un infierno," the duo sings and I think of poets: The drunk man is the story that never was; a poem without meter; prose without punctuation; a dead world; a sea of tears; rage in a sunflower; darkness in a star; the bitter taste of surrender. The drunk man *is* a father.

I had it in me once to hurt my father, to break his face and to inflict upon him as much bodily pain as possible without killing him, and I acted on it. I'd been playing it out all day in my head. When he comes home drunk, I'm going to take him for a ride. I'm going to tell him that I know a place with the best tortas and ask him to come with me, that it'll be my treat. I waited outside the house and told no one about my intentions, not even my brothers. I was determined and didn't want anyone talking me out of it. It had to be done. It was time. The Devil was stirring inside of me and I couldn't shake him. I drank a couple caguamas while I replayed the scene over and over in my head. It'll work. He'll never see it coming: le voy a partir su puta madre.

He was walking down the slope, happily singing along to a ballad playing in his head—and he was completely drunk. Looked like a little boy the way he kicked stones as he walked toward me. I could've decided right then not to go through with my plan. It was like looking at innocence. But my boiling blood didn't allow me to forgive. I felt hot seeing him take wonder in the sport of children. Adrenaline moved through me like electricity. I ground my teeth, shook my shoulders and tightened my chest; I brought my hands together and clasped them in front of me. I felt like a criminal all over again. I could see the violence ahead, and I laughed at my stupid father who had no clue what awaited him. "Look at you, you fucking fool kicking rocks," the Devil whispered in the wind. "Hope you've had a good night so far because the rest of it is going to hurt, and bad. Come, Father. Come toward me."

"Qué onda, hijo, were you waiting for me?" he asked me when he got close. The tone of his voice was low, and sad, like someone had already hurt him. I didn't respond.

He leaned in and wrapped his arms around me tightly. He smelled of drink and dirt, of pure misery. He kissed me at the base of my head, then moved his hand over it as if dusting away all prints of his kiss. Then he placed his hand on my shoulder and let it rest there for a moment. Every second it was there weighed on me like a lifetime. I couldn't bring myself to embrace the tenderness this action attempted to convey. Under the dark sky and brilliance of the moon, I envisioned the claw of a dragon that could rip me apart at any moment.

"Well, were you or not?" he then said to me, taking a step back and looking into my eyes, his voice slightly elevated this time.

"Yes, I was," I said to him in a vapid tone.

"You were, really?" he said to me with a clumsy show of surprise.

And surprised by his surprise, I was moved to take the Devil by the tail and swing him around: "Yes. I couldn't wait to see you."

"You see. I knew you loved me."

"I always have."

"Because you're a good son, and a good son always loves his father."

"Sure."

"And a good son never judges his father, right?"

"Right."

"And you're a good son, right?"

"Get the fuck out of here!" I told him, having swung the Devil long enough. "What do you think I am? You're drunk and you don't know what the fuck you're talking about!"

His face turned to stone. Then his eyelids dropped and his body began to palpitate and totter as if something fought to escape him. This sudden change in my disposition had startled him, and he was having difficulty keeping his composure. The scene evoked sympathy. I was looking at a man who resembled a dying animal. But I fought it off. On this night there could be no room in my heart. I had to stand firm and stick to my plan. My heart had to remain cold—a mold of ice; so I reminded myself that no war had ever been won by one side being sympathetic. The enemy had to be looked upon as other than human. So I told myself that my father was not a man, but a rabid dog that needed to be put down.

My father, taking two steps back, brought his arms up high at his sides, the streetlight glowing behind him: The image of the crucifixion. In that position, with both hands dangling at his wrists, he said: "You crucify me, son. Your words are the nails that pierce my hands and the dagger that cuts into me." Then, unable to hold that position for any longer than it took for him to utter those words, he stumbled to one side and almost fell before catching his footing again.

"You see, what'd I tell you—you're drunk!" I said to him, watching him bring himself up. And instantly my father went from playing Jesus on the cross to the monster he was more familiar as.

"¡Y qué, güey?" he screamed at me with rage. "¿Qué te importa?" I could feel the anger in his words, and it made me happy, glad that I hadn't given in to sympathy earlier. I'd been right all along: he wasn't worth it, and here he was proving it to me. "What's it to you what I do?" he continued. "This is me. Don't act like you don't know. There's nothing new here. Or what, you think just because you come here things are going to be different? Well they're not. Because *I* live here—*we* live here. When you go back to California, everything's going to go back to the way it's always been. La misma mierda seguirá y yo seguiré siendo *el rey*."

My father laughed and foamed at the mouth, showed off his repugnance with pride. The man I'd been waiting for all day was now clumsily stumbling before me in the light of the moon. So I laughed with him and said, "That's right, that's how I like you—ugly. And that's how I love you, even uglier. But come now, güey, let's not fight. Let's be happy and enjoy this night under this dark sky. Are you hungry?"

I was quick to defuse the situation, and he was quick to fall into my trap.

"Eres cabrón, hijo, como tu papá. And I know that when you say that you love me, you really mean it. You just like to hurt me. Pero esta suave, bien suave, because I love you, too—y un chingo!" And again my father, no longer on the defensive, placed his arm around me. And again for the few seconds that I let him stand there with his arm hanging from my shoulder, all I could think about was my plan. The more I smelled him and the more I felt his oppressive breath on my face, the more I wanted to hurt him, the more I wanted him to feel pain, real pain, like the pain I was feeling and that was causing me to want to rip him apart.

"So, ¿qué? Are you hungry?" I eventually said to him again while slowly releasing myself from his grasp.

"Sí, hijo, I am."

"Then let's go eat. I know where they sell the best tortas in

Chihuahua, better than the ones they sell at El Cubano. But it's pretty far, en La Infona. You mind the drive?"

"Claro que no, hijo. I'll go wherever you take me. You're my son, and what pleases you, pleases me. I have faith in you."

La Infona is short for La Infonavit Libertad, a colonia on the other side of the city. It's where my tía Lupe (my mother's sister) once lived and where I'd stay for part of the summers when I'd come to Chihuahua as a child and teenager. And because there wasn't a moment that I didn't spend with my cousins Uriel and Ulises (the twins) running around this colonia during these summers, I was familiar with all its ins and outs. Knew every block and corner and the types of people I could expect to find there. Because although La Infona, during the '80s and '90s, was made up of mostly honest, hardworking, lower-middle-class people—by Mexico's standards—it was also known to have its bad elements, and unfortunately, my cousins comprised a large part of those elements. Since an early age they'd been known to be troublemakers. And as leaders of one of the neighborhood gangs, los cuates—as they were known—had quite a following. Their gang had over fifty members and I knew every single one of them by name. And although los cuates had long ago moved to the States, I knew that in La Infona I could still find some of their old associates who'd be willing to break a face for me if I asked them to. It'd be simply a matter of doing me a favor.

I hopped into the driver side of the Jeep and my father, after putting my wheelchair in the back, hopped into the passenger side. We were ready to go. But before we began our journey across town we stopped at an expendio right when it was about to close at ten and picked up two caguamas for the road. My father popped the two open and handed me one. It was going to be a twenty-minute drive and I needed something to keep me from going back on what I'd already set into motion. It often happens that too much thought deters the mind from action. A lot never gets done because of this. And I needed to act, to stay in character, and only another caguama was going to allow me to do this. To stop now would've meant surrendering to the enemy. At this moment every sympathetic thought and feeling I could have had for the man sitting next to me on this drive to madness was no good to me. Fuck what's rational and fuck everything that ends in love! Beer and violence are the only answers tonight. An eye for an eye and a fist for a fist. So I drank my caguama and I drank it quickly. By the time we arrived at La Infona, I was at the end of my caguama. I took the last swig and tossed the empty bottle over my shoulder onto the back seat. My father still had half of his left; I guess he didn't realize it would be his last for the night.

"We're almost there," I said to my father as I turned into one of the colonia's tight streets. The street was dark, but there were still groups of people communing outside their homes. I made a few turns here and there, looking for familiar faces. At one point, upon noticing how intently I was looking at the faces we were driving past, my father asked if I knew where I was going. "Yes," I assured him. "It's on one of these streets, you'll see." I was right. Because after a couple more turns, I came across four recognizable faces. The four young men were sitting on the tailgate of a small white pickup truck with a couple of young women. They were all drinking and having a good time. Empty caguama bottles rested at their feet and two of the men had one in their hand. This is going to be easy, I was thinking at this point, they're already drunk and won't have a problem doing me this favor. That there was a taco and torta stand with all its lights lit up right across from where they were having their celebration also made me think that my plan couldn't be coming together any more perfectly. There was an old woman and two young men working the stand asando carne, toasting bolillos and heating up tortillas. I could see the smoke pouring out from inside and filling the air. Perfect.

"Orale, güey, we're here," I said to my father, who was sucking down the rest of his caguama, as I drove past the tailgate party and the taco stand. Then, after making a U-turn a few yards away, I drove back and parked the Jeep next to the stand. "Time to eat," I said to him as I shut off the ignition and looked toward the faces I recognized to see if they recognized me. They didn't. At least not while I was still in the car. They kept drinking, talking, laughing, and paying no mind to the persons who'd just parked opposite them on the other side of the street.

When my father got my chair out from the back of the Jeep and brought it to me, I told him to go order while I said hi to some old friends I'd just recognized. "Get me a carne asada torta with everything," I told him, handing him money. And without showing any interest in what I'd just said to him, he took the pesos from my hand, crumpled them in his fist, and without a care in the world walked over to the stand while I rolled toward the tailgate party. Knowing that I'd spent a lot of time in this area with my cousins during earlier years, my father had no reason to question me. For all he knew I was just going to say hi to some old friends I'd only recognized from long ago and then meet back up with him at the stand.

But what my father was not aware of was that, at that moment, his life as my father was about to change forever. Because after he'd be bleeding from every part of his face on this grainy street on this pleasant night, he'd no longer be able to see me as the son who, no matter how much he pushed, would always show him unconditional love; instead, he'd see me as the son who once had a group of men break his face; he'd see the face of the son who hated him; he'd see the face of the son who was no longer willing to stand aside while he destroyed the lives of his brothers and sisters. What my father was not aware of was that at the moment when I said to him that I was just going to say hi to some old friends, I had disavowed him as my father.

"¿Qué onda?" I said to the men at the truck as I approached them.

"¿Qué onda, Obed, qué haces por aquí?" one of them said to me, putting down his caguama and walking toward me to shake my hand and give me a hug. "What a surprise," he said. "It's been a long time." This was a guy I'll call Javi, the same guy who'd given me my first tattoo many years ago. One of the others was my cousin Uriel's closest friend, who I'll call Rosendo. Though I didn't remember the names of the other two, I remembered their faces and I knew they remembered mine because, like Javi and Rosendo, they greeted me with a handshake and a hug. And though the last time any of them had seen me I still had a pair of strong legs to carry me, none of them asked me why I was now in a wheelchair, which was good because I didn't feel like getting into details about the past or about how fucked-up life can be. I hadn't come here to reminisce. And when they did ask me questions about where I'd been all this time and where my cousins Uriel and Ulises were now living, I simply told them that I'd been around and that my cousins were now living in the States. That was all. I told them nothing more because all I wanted to do was continue with my plan and see my father bleed. So I went straight to the bone with them.

"Look," I told them, "I'm here because I want to ask you guys for a favor."

"Of course, anything," said Javi, looking, indeed, ready to do anything for me that I asked. Rosendo and the other two looked at me in the same way. Brave they appeared, with raised shoulders and tightly closed fists. The girls, on the other hand, just stared at me with confusion, as if hoping that someone would tell them who I was and where I'd come from. But again I didn't care to reflect on the past, so I paid them no mind. There wasn't anything I needed from them in that moment.

"Well," I continued, "you see that man over there ordering tortas? I want you guys to fuck him up for me."

This was the last thing they'd been expecting me to say, because as soon as I said it all of their happy guises turned to blank expressions. Their raised shoulders dropped and their tightly closed fists opened up. They no longer seemed the willing comrades. The favor I was asking them to do for me had caught them by surprise. They stood silently and looked at one another with their mouths open, confused, now more so than the girls, who oddly enough now seemed more excited than anything. While the guys took a step back and seemed to shut down, the girls perked up like daisies in the sun and moved in close, giddy and seemingly eager to hear their male companions' response to my most unexpected request. I noticed one grab the other's hand and squeeze it with intensity. Yet like their male counterparts, the two didn't say a word.

"Are you serious?" Javi finally said, breaking the silence.

"Dead serious," I said, looking him straight in the eyes. But again there was silence. All four looked at one another once again and exchanged body language that said, *Don't look at me. I don't know what the fuck he's talking about.*

But all this silence and back and forth with their bodies was only making me impatient. I'd been expecting them to give me a straight "Yes, let's do it" right away, but this was not happening. Time was passing, the tortas would soon be served, and I'd be on my way back to El Cerro with my father's face still intact and with my dignity destroyed. I would have failed. And all because the little hoodlums who'd once been willing to commit violence on other people for no other reason than to feel powerful were quickly morphing into altar boys before my eyes.

"So, ¿qué? ¿Sí o no?" I pressed them for an answer, annoyed.

Javi, continuing to speak for the four, placidly and apologetically, and to my own misfortune, finally said: "Pues no, Obed. It's not like that around here anymore, we just don't do that." When he said this, I turned to the others to see if, in maybe one of them, I could find the slightest willingness to be his own man, and with a little bit more pressing, move him to step forward and tell me that he'd be more than happy to do me this favor. But all I got from each of them, as I looked directly into their eyes, was the same meek and apologetic expression with which Javi had given me his answer—what, after all, had been their collective answer all along. And though, just minutes earlier, the girls had seemed in favor of an ass-kicking, when I turned to them now to see if I could say anything to them that would make them talk their male counterparts into doing my bidding, they, too, looked at me with apologetic faces that, even worse than the men's, appeared to convey pity toward me.

I'd come all this way to get nowhere. And every time I

looked at my father, who was waiting patiently for our tortas, I got angrier. He seemed so relaxed standing with his back to me and his arms resting on the stand's ledge. And though I couldn't hear what he was saying, I knew that he was having a conversation with the ladies making our tortas by the way they smiled and looked at him as they cooked. He was being the charming man he was known to be when not on a rampage— and I hated it. He was getting exactly what I'd told him he'd get if he came with me, and I was getting nothing.

"What about for a hundred dollars?" I said to Javi as I turned my attention back to him. It was the only card I had left, and I figured they couldn't say no to it. After all, it's not every day that in Chihuahua someone offers up a hundred dollars in return for a simple favor like the one I was asking for. How could they possibly say no to me now? They just couldn't. But they did. And firmly.

"No, Obed, keep your money," Javi said to me. "We don't need it." He didn't even take a moment to think about it. And when I pulled out the hundred-dollar bill and hung it out in front of me so that the others could see that I was serious, all I got from them as well were blank stares. They shook their heads and closed their eyes as if embarrassed, and not for themselves but for me. I felt it and it hurt. How could I have stooped so low as to offer money to other men, honest, moral men, to commit violence against my father? It was at this moment that I finally felt the defeat of my own intentions. I remained still and said nothing, ashamed of my actions. And before I could put the money back into my pocket and apologize to Javi and the others for what I'd just asked them to do, I heard my father's voice call out to me. He was still by the stand. Only now he was facing me with a bag with our tortas in it at his side. I figured he was about to call me over to pay, so I pushed the bill back into my pocket and slowly began to roll his way. But like someone who'd suddenly been stricken by a grand realization, my father stood still for a moment without saying another word and then slowly started walking in the direction of the Jeep. When I yelled out to him to stop, to wait for me, he picked up his step and eventually started running. I yelled, "Hey, wait! Come back!" and I tried to chase after him, but to no avail. He started sprinting past the Jeep and eventually down the street from where we'd come. Only once did he turn back to look at me. And when he did, he yelled, "I know what you're up to, son! I'm sorry! I'm sorry!" I didn't get my torta that night, and my father didn't have his face broken.

Chihuahua's getting hotter by the minute and the people are coming out to watch the parade. "There goes the Prince of Fools!—the buffoon!" they're yelling as they point at the white hearse. "And listen, they're playing his song!" We're moving at five miles per hour, and we're wallowing in our pain, or lack thereof; at least for me this is the case. The thought of being constipated is beginning to fuck up my day even more than it already is. I can't stop worrying about the possibility of the constipation leading to gangrene again. Then it will be me on the verge of dying again. "Chihuahua's a good town to die in!" an old woman holding a child at her breasts yells from her front door to us and then quickly disappears back into her house. "There goes Juan Silva!" another man yells from the curb; he's tapping his feet and drinking a caguama. He laughs wildly toward the sky and adds, "Hear me, San Pedro, and open your

doors for this man!" Another chimes in as he stumbles by: "¡Por
que era cabrón el hombre!" Then he drops to the ground on his
back and a pint of tequila falls out of one of his pant pockets.
There's nobody there to help him up. Then, suddenly, another
wino comes running out from one of the homes we've just
passed and he's yelling for us to stop. "¡Paren! ¡Paren!" cries the
scraggly man. He's running out of his yard holding a caguama
in front of him. "I want to go to the funeral of the man who
once gave me a drink and sang me a song. ¡Ese hombre era mi
amigo!"

Aarón stops the truck and the happy wino joins the other
mourners in the back. I watch him through the back window
as he climbs onto the bed and eagerly offers his hand and a
drink from his caguama to everyone. And before he sits, he
gratefully thanks Aarón for having stopped for him. "Gracias,
peloncito, por parar para que este pobre borracho los acom-
pañe." But his happiness doesn't last long. As he takes a seat
and the truck begins to move again, he becomes overwhelmed
with sadness. Holding his caguama close to his chest he looks
around at all the faces he's just joined and begins to weep. "My
friend," I hear him say, "my friend is dead." He's crying heavily
into his bottle now and everyone's looking at him with com-
passionate eyes, even me. "I'm going to miss him, you know?"
he says, and then he takes a drink. As he does so, the others
respond with:

"Sí."

"Claro."

"Sí."

"Sí."

"We're all going to miss him."

"Todos."

We all understand the wino. We all know where he's coming from. He's one of *us*; not a Silva, but an "alcoholic who still suffers."

"He was one of my best friends, a good man. ¡Ah, que pinche Juanito! ¿Por qué? ¿Por qué? ¡Subanle a la música! ¡Ah, como le gustaba esta pinche canción a Juanito!"

The old wino continues to cry for his dead friend like a child cries for his absent mother. If only I could be doing the same for my father.

I'd met this wino once before on one of my trips to Chihuahua after I'd been shot and gotten off probation in 2006. My father and I had still been on fairly good terms then. There'd been an exhibition of some of Piña Mora's paintings at the historic Quinta Gameros mansion.

"Hijo, I want to take you somewhere," my father said that morning without telling me anything else.

"Where?" I asked him.

"You'll see. It's a surprise. Te va a gustar."

We were on our way. But before we could make it to the car, a man I didn't recognize met us in the driveway. It was the wino who was now joining us to bury my father. "¡Q-vole, Coruco!" my father said loudly, opening up his arms when he saw him, and the man, who was known as Coruco, smiled and walked into my father's open arms. "Look, Coruco," my father said to him, "this is my son Obed from el otro lado." My father said it like that, as if "from el otro lado" was a part of my name. But it also implied that my father had told his friend about me before this moment. Coruco extended his hand to me and I extended mine to him. "It's great to finally meet you," he said. "Jaunito has told me a lot about you. Me da mucho gusto conocerte."

Coruco went on and told me that it was such an honor to meet me, that he'd never met anyone from el otro lado before, and that he hoped to drink a beer with me. I told him that that would be great, that I'd like that, and apparently this would happen sooner rather than later because my father would invite Coruco along on our little trip and he would gladly accept.

Coruco was drunk. In fact, I'd later learn, he was drunk every day. He was a terrible alcoholic. He was one of those alcoholics who roam the streets all day looking for a way to get their next beer. He had a melancholy face most of the time, one that made you feel pity for him, which is why it wasn't too difficult for people to hand over their pesos to him so that he could keep drinking. It's also why my father cared for him so much. He felt bad for the guy. My father would later tell me that the reason Coruco drank so much was because his wife had left him for another man and that she'd also taken their children from him. "After she left, he started drinking and hasn't stopped since," my father said. "You have to feel sad for a man like that," he added.

"I can't even imagine his pain," I said, in agreement. "Must be something almost unbearable."

Something else about Coruco that evoked sadness was his own name. Coruco wasn't his real name. It was one that the people in the neighborhood had given him because of his seemingly meaningless existence. "Un coruco," my father told me, "es un piojo de gallina." "That's fucked-up," I said to my father, "why would anybody call him a chicken louse?" "Because," he said to me, "in the same way that a chicken louse is a pest to the chicken, people feel that he's a pest to society."

My father never told me his real name, and I never asked for it. Everyone called him Coruco, so I called him Coruco.

At the exhibition, my father and I walked around and stared at the paintings in awe, but Coruco looked confused, and finally, as my father and I discussed one of the paintings, he interrupted and asked, "Juanito, what are we looking at?" And my father, rather cruelly, said to him, "¡Ah que Coruco, no sea pendejo! These are paintings by our very own Aarón Piña Mora, Chihuahua's greatest painter." "Ahhh, okay," Coruco responded, as if he now knew exactly everything about the paintings and their painter, and for the rest of our time there, every time my father and I would stop in front of a painting and discuss it, Coruco would stand behind us and nod in agreement. We stayed for no longer than thirty minutes. There were other exhibits in other rooms, but we were not interested in them. My father had brought me there only for Piña Mora and nothing else.

Our first stop on our way home: the first expendio we saw—three caguamas, please!

Corucos are everywhere.

Ralph spends his days wandering the streets and drinking on curbs and bus stop benches around my mother's house in Buena Park, California. I met him many years ago when she first moved to that area. I was living there with her and my brother and sister at the time. Ralph had been sitting on the asphalt between two parked cars in front of a bar called the Town Tavern that was on the corner of Knott and La Palma. He was drinking a beer and looked like shit. I noticed him as I rolled by, and I asked him if he needed help. I thought he'd fallen and had been unable to get back on his feet. But no: "If you really want to help me," he said, slurring his words and looking up at me with yellow eyes, "then you can get me another beer. Any kind you want." Say no more. I bought him a six-pack of Budweiser from the liquor store next to the Town Tavern. "Wow! You're a really swell guy," Ralph told me as he took the six-pack from me with both hands while not making any effort to get up off the ground.

After, I'd often see Ralph dragging his shaky body through the streets of Buena Park day and night. And every time I'd see him I'd buy him a beer or two. And every time I would, he'd remind me that I was a swell guy.

Back then, Ralph was in his late forties, had a family that consisted of a mother and a few brothers and sisters. His father was already dead. Ralph was also an uncle. He'd told me this during many of our conversations after I'd buy him beers. I also know that on many occasions every one of his family members had tried to help him. But Ralph had refused the help every time. He'd told me this, too.

"They want to help me by not letting me drink," he'd said to me once, and added: "I don't want that kind of help. I'd rather sleep under a bridge and drink a beer."

That was it. That's all Ralph ever wanted: a beer. Ralph didn't want a home with a warm bed and blankets and pillows to sleep with, and he didn't want a car to drive to and from work every day; and he didn't want a wife and children either. Hell!—Ralph didn't even want to have sex.

"This is my woman," he'd say, raising up a tall can of

Budweiser. "She's all I need to keep me happy. And she doesn't even cook."

Lost. Free. Lost. Free. Lost. Free. Lost. Free. Lost. Free. Lost. Free. Lost. Free in the fire.

After a time, I never saw or heard from Ralph again. My best guess is that like every alcoholic, he finally found his peace in heaven.

18

I was in Chihuahua the first time I ever got drunk. I was thirteen and had been staying at my tía Lupe's house with my cousins Uriel and Ulises during one of my summer visits. One day my cousins asked me if I wanted to drink and get a tattoo. I said yes. Seemed like a good idea at the time: my first beer and my first tattoo with two of my favorite cousins. If only I could've known what a not-so-promising future drinking has to offer—no, I don't think knowing this would've made much of a difference. I still would've done it: A boy can't say no among friends. Because drinking's a man thing to do, at least that's what boys are always being told: "You can't drink. You're just a kid." Well, what a boy wants to be least is "just a kid," and what he wants to be most is a man. It should be no surprise then that the boy dreams of drinking.

It's common in my family (on both sides) for the grown-ups to allow their children to have a sip from their beers. At times it's even cute, a perfect moment for a picture. The child can barely walk and the entire family's gathered around him, or her, to watch him be propped up in front of a camera with a beer between his stubby little hands. "Look! Look how he holds the bottle! Isn't he cute?" Sure he is. Just the cutest little thing the world has ever seen. Now just wait until he's all grown up and having trouble putting that bottle down. Let's see how cute he is then.

In my family, almost all of my cousins have had their picture taken while posing with a beer bottle or can. My cousin Claudia (on my mother's side), for instance, who's now a grown woman with a child of her own, in one picture, is holding a Budweiser beer to her mouth with her head tilted back while sitting on her father's lap on their living room couch. In another, I'm standing next to my grandpa Charlie with a can of Budweiser in my left hand. I'm raising it to the camera. Surely the adult behind the camera was instructing me on how to hold the can. And while I look happy, my grandpa Charlie has his head on his lap, looking like he's had enough. All you can see of his head is his silver hair. I, like Claudia in her picture, am no older than four. Take a picture, kid, your future begins here.

I ended up drunk and with a fucked-up quarter-size tattoo of the Old English letter *O* on my right thigh where no one could see it. "Drink a beer," my cousins and their friends told me, "and you won't feel a thing." I did and it tasted like shit. But at thirteen I was too cool to say no and the sharpened guitar string on the homemade tattoo gun digging into my skin hurt something crazy. I had to drink. But every time after I took a sip from the twelve-ounce Carta Blanca bottle, I popped a chili-sprinkled pork rind with lemon into my mouth to kill the taste. And before I knew it, I had gone through at least four bags of pork rinds and a six-pack of beer. I was buzzed and felt the needle a lot less. At some point it stopped hurting altogether. When Javi, the tattooist, was done I didn't realize that instead of having tattooed me, he'd simply scarred me for life. He'd been digging the needle too deep all along and my

Old English O that I thought was going to look fresh ended up looking like a burn from a cigarette lighter from an old car. But fuck the tattoo. When all was said and done I no longer cared about what it looked like. I'd tasted beer and now knew how good being drunk felt. Because after that sixth beer, I didn't need any more rinds, hell, I don't think I needed them after the third. The beers went down easily after that, like water, as they say.

It began to rain later that day, and I ended up sleeping off my drunkenness under a commuter bus that was parked on the street next to the basketball courts down the street from my cousins' house. And if my tía Lupe hadn't come to get me, I probably would've slept there through the entire night like some homeless vagabond.

19

When I was shot, on October 25, 1996, I spent almost a week in intensive care, about a month healing in the hospital, and about another month in rehab, and my father never showed. At the time, I guess I would've liked for him to come see me. I mean, I had almost died. But he never did.

"Does my dad know?" This was one of the first questions I asked my mother after I woke up from my surgery.

"Sí, hijo," my mother said, sitting at my bedside caressing my face and head. "I called him as soon as I could."

"Is he coming?"

"Yes. He said he was going to leave right away. He said he was going to call you within the next couple of days to tell you himself."

The next day my father did call, and said he would be coming soon. "No matter what," he said, "I will be there."

The thought of seeing my father was comforting. I hadn't seen him in almost two years, with me constantly getting into trouble and spending more time on the streets with my friends and in juvenile detention centers. The thought of having my father at my side consumed me. I expected him to show up at any moment. When I'd hear footsteps coming to the door I'd turn to it and anticipate my father's body walking into the room. I could see him smiling at me, and then crying while telling me how much he loved me. But as the days passed and there was no father of mine walking in, I began to lose hope. Eventually I stopped turning to the door every time I heard someone approaching; most times when I was alone I just kept my eyes fixated on the TV or my dead legs, at my dead feet that seemed so distanced from me. Not that I wasn't grateful when other members of my family would come visit me, but I hadn't seen my father in so long, and if there was a time when I needed him most it was now. I found solace in the idea of having him there at my side and helping me to get well. But he never came. A few days after he'd called to tell me he was coming, he called again, this time to tell me that he was still in Chihuahua and wasn't sure if he was going to be able to make it after all.

"How are you, son?"

"Good. Still here. When are you coming?"

"Well, that's the thing. You see, I tried, but I couldn't make it. I was caught at the border trying to enter illegally, and I was turned back to Mexico. They said that if I was caught again I would be arrested and taken to jail."

I was saddened and disappointed. When we'd first spoken, he'd told me that he'd be here "no matter what," and now it was obvious that he'd given up; "no matter what" actually didn't mean what I'd thought it meant. "It's okay, Pa', you don't have to come. I understand," I told him.

"I love you, hijo."

"I know."

I hung up, and for the next couple of months that I was in the hospital and rehab I pushed him out of my head. I needed to get better, and thinking about him wasn't going to help the process. About every two weeks he'd call to see how I was doing, and I'd tell him that I was doing just fine. I'd keep the conversations short, not wanting to break down and cry because he'd given up on seeing me at this critical time in my life.

Four months after I got out of rehabilitation, my mom bought me a 1991 Acura Integra so that I could drive myself to Palomar College, where she had enrolled me in a reading course. Around this time my father called me and asked me to meet him in Tijuana, Mexico; said he'd be there with my little brother Danny.

At the time, we were living in Fallbrook, a small rural town in north San Diego, best known for its most famous resident: Ku Klux Klan leader David Duke. My mom had moved all of us out there a couple of months before I was shot to keep me away from my friends and out of trouble. That plan didn't pan out too well, and soon things would get worse before they'd get better. Later that year I'd be charged with attempted murder for the shooting of a rival gang member at an Anaheim house party, another crucial moment in my life that my father would not be a part of; but for now things were as they were and I was doing my best to learn how to live in a wheelchair.

I wasn't eager to go to Tijuana, though I *did* want to see my father. I was afraid that Tijuana wouldn't be wheelchair friendly. But my father pleaded with me, telling me that it was the best way to see each other. I was close to the border, he couldn't cross it, and my little brother Danny really wanted to see me. My father said Danny had been saddened by the news of my disability. It was to this last tidbit that I couldn't say no.

Danny was ten years old at the time, just a boy, and I didn't want him to think that I didn't want to see him.

A few days later I was on my way to Tijuana. I met my father and Danny at a small shopping center near the border. The two had been standing in front of an ice cream store sucking on paletas de fruta when I arrived. They didn't notice me in the car when I parked in front of them. It wasn't until I honked that they turned toward me. I could tell that my father was happy. As soon as he saw me, he smiled, tossed his paleta into a trash bin, and pulled Danny toward me. The two walked up to my window and greeted me. My father leaned in first to hug me and kiss me on the head, and then he lifted Danny so that he could hug me, too. It felt good to see my father, exciting. The moment reminded me of the times I'd visit him in Chihuahua as a child. Seeing Danny, whom I hadn't seen since he was seven, also brought me joy.

They hadn't brought much with them, just a plastic bag with a change of socks and underwear. Because I was driving on my own, I had my wheelchair frame on the passenger seat and the wheels in the back seat. I told my dad to put both the frame and wheels in the trunk. He grabbed the frame, lifted it, and said, "It's light. That's good." Then he ducked and brought his head into the car and looked right at my face and then at my legs. "You look good, son," he said, "and I'm glad you're here." For a moment, as he said this, it appeared a tear was going to drop from his eyes, but before it could he stepped back, took a deep breath, and walked to the trunk. Through the window I could see him wipe away the tear. "Los hombres no lloran," I recalled him saying to me many times when I was a child. I popped open the trunk and he placed the frame inside and then the wheels. Danny, in the meantime, stood by the passenger-side door staring at me. He was in awe of me. I was his older brother from el otro lado, from the United States, that big country of magic where Disneyland exists. He probably saw me as a giant, who brought magic with him, but the only magic I had was the capability of driving without using my feet.

We drove to Ensenada, and the whole way there we talked of the past and of the future, but never about the present, never about my legs or how I was dealing with my disability. Not that it wasn't on his mind or that he didn't care. I know he cared and I know it was consuming his thoughts. I could tell by the way his eyes would give way to my legs and my left hand, which I was using to work the hand controls attached to the gas and brake pedals. There was a sense of mystery there, of loss, of confusion, of helplessness. Nothing he could do or say could change what now was. It was a matter too difficult for my father to address. Maybe, even, he felt guilty, like somehow, had he been a better father, a better husband, a better man, he could have prevented it. Whatever the reason, I was glad he didn't bring it up. Like my father, I've never been good at talking about the things that most affect me emotionally. I wouldn't have been able to handle crying. Danny certainly wouldn't have wanted to see that. He wanted to see his amazing big brother from Washeenton!

We found a hotel made up of small bungalows close to the beach. By the time we arrived, however, it was dark and cold out, so we opted to stay in our hotel room for the rest of the night; but my dad couldn't just stay in without having his beer, so he went out to the store and came back with a six-pack of canned Tecates in one hand and a bag full of snacks and a couple of sodas for me and Danny in the other. "Do you want a beer?" he asked me as he opened one. "No," I said. "I'll just take one of those Cokes." "But you *can* drink, can't you?" he added, as if I might not be able to because of my disability, which to him, perhaps, would have been the greatest tragedy. Relationships change when one person drinks and the other doesn't. There's a big disconnect. The drinker feels as if he's constantly being judged by the nondrinker and the nondrinker *is* constantly judging the drinker. On the other hand, when the two parties drink, life is good—seemingly. I wanted life with my father to be "good," so I changed my mind. "Of course I can drink," I told him, "and you know what, give me a beer instead. I'll drink a couple with you."

My father smiled, tossed me a beer, and said, "¡Ese es mijo!"— That's my boy! We were on an equal playing field now, could let our guard down and just be, without having to check ourselves or our emotions.

I drank only two beers, and my father the rest. Danny drank his Coke and ate his chips, and eventually we all fell asleep. The next morning we woke up to a beautiful sunrise.

My father and Danny went to the beach while I stayed behind and got dressed. Danny had never been to the beach before, so he'd been overwhelmed with excitement since he'd opened his eyes that morning. For me, the beach was like just another Southern California freeway, so when they asked me to come with them, I respectfully said no. "You guys go ahead. I'm going to stay behind and get dressed." "¿Seguro?" my dad said. "Seguro," I told him. So they left. I watched them as the two set out: father and son walking side by side toward the sunrise. It was then that I also noticed that with his cutoff-jeans shorts, my father was also wearing big ugly brown work boots, probably steel-toed. I couldn't believe the man, or actually I could. My ridiculous father didn't care. Life was not about things or looks to him. It was about simple pleasures, the small things: it was about moments like these, where he wasn't burdened by work or a wife telling him what to do; it was about the freedom to do as he pleased; it was about existing to be happy. And today, he was happy. Throughout the entire day he was happy. Sure, he'd come to see me after I'd come out of such a tragic event, but this was also like a mini-vacation for him, where I drove him and Danny up and down the coast of Baja and took care of the bill. I was fine with it, too.

"What's with the boots and the shorts?" I asked when he and Danny returned from the beach. "What's up with them?" he remarked. "Well," I told him, "you look like a fool. I mean, you got work boots on with cutoff jeans. You look ridiculous." When I said this he looked down at his shorts and boots and laughed. Then he said, "Well, you got something better for me to wear?" I did. I'd brought an extra pair of tennis shoes and shorts. "Here," I told him, tossing him my backpack. "There's a pair of shorts and some tennis shoes in there. Put them on." He grabbed the bag, opened it, and pulled out the shorts and shoes. "Órale," he said, holding up the shoes. "These are nice, and so are the shorts." The shoes were a semi-new pair of white FILAs and the shorts were brown Dickies. My father changed into them right then and there in front of me and Danny, and when he was done he looked at us with a smile and said, "So, how do I look?" Danny nodded in approval and I told him that he looked much better. Then my father said, "I look like you, hijo, bien cholo!" We both laughed and then he thanked me a couple of times. And once he put his boots and cutoff jeans into his plastic bag, we headed out to the port.

At the port we had mariscos in a cup and watched white tourists disembark from cruise ships and swarm the food and crafts vendors who set up shop all along the port. My father spent a lot of time criticizing them, saying that they were the most entitled and greedy people on the planet. "They never want to pay the actual value of things, and they look down on you even in your own country," he said. "Just watch how they demand a lower price for everything and then attack the seller with angry expressions when they refuse." I listened to my father and so did Danny, and the three of us looked out in disgust at the sea of whiteness as it swallowed up the entire port. We dug into our plastic cups with our forks for mariscos and shoved them into our mouths, all the while tracing white bodies decked out in Hawaiian shirts and Dockers shorts and short floral sundresses and sandals and colorful visors and straw hats. When our cups were empty, my father said, "Let's get out of Washeenton," and led us to the boat docks.

I ate shit there. Like at most ports, there were long ramps leading to the docks, and because the tide was low on this particular day, the ramps were steep. I would never have been able to go down any of them on my own. Since I was still new to the wheelchair life, I was well aware of my limitations, so when my father asked me if I could make it down on my own, I firmly said no. "Then I will help you," he said. "Just tell me what to do." I thought about it for a minute. I kept looking at the ramp and calculated the best way to go down it. It looked too steep, so I told my father that it was probably best I didn't even make an attempt, even with his help.

But he persisted. Said I needed to experience it with them, that I'd enjoy it; and though I told him I didn't much care to go down to the docks because I'd already been to many docks on many other occasions, he still insisted that I go. Fine. I gave in. "Okay," I told him. "Then just grab my chair by this bar right here that runs across the backrest, and hold it tightly as you push me down on an incline." "I got it," he said. Down we went. Danny followed close behind. As we moved down the ramp, I glided my hands over the side rails. We were doing fine, moving slowly, for about the first few feet, then all of a sudden I felt a slight push downward from behind, and although I tried to grab on to the rails, down I went. Bam! I fell straight back and my father came crashing over me. My wheelchair, because of the incline, rolled away from under me and then tumbled down to the bottom of the steel ramp, eventually crashing into a wooden post. People were looking at us and I was embarrassed, even angry, because this was exactly what I didn't want to happen. Here I was, crippled and on the floor of a ramp, clinging to its side rails wishing I hadn't come all this fucking way to be made a fool of by my father, who quickly jumped up, frightened, and saying, "¡Hijo! ¡Hijo! ¿Estás bien? Here, let me get you up!" His face appeared between my eyes and the sky, and it looked confused, devastated. It was the face of a man who didn't know what to do. And as he wedged his hands within my armpits he cried out to Danny to get the chair. I tried to calm him down, telling him that I was fine, not to panic. "Estoy bien. Estoy bien," I kept repeating, but he kept yelling for Danny to get the chair. So Danny ran down to the bottom of the ramp, but once down there he was unable to flip it over onto its wheels. It was too heavy for his little body. Luckily, a number of people who'd seen the entire incident quickly came to assist us. Wrapped in my father's arms, dangling like a rag doll, I could see a couple helping Danny with my chair, and two boys who'd been selling chicharrones and candies on the port came to help my father. "Las piernas," my father said to the boys. "Grab his legs." The boys pulled my legs up from behind, bending my back upward. I was in the most awkward position I had ever been in since my injury, and the worst part was that all of this was happening in front of dozens of people. It felt like the entire world was watching this moment unfurl and I wanted to bury myself inside of my father's chest. But at the same time I wanted to get as far away from him as possible. If only he'd listened to me when I first told him I didn't want to come down to the docks. If only he hadn't persisted.

With my body bent like a crescent moon, the boys and my father rushed me to the bottom of the ramp, where Danny and the couple were holding on to my wheelchair. "Okay, okay, turn him over," my father said to the boys when we came to my chair, and gently the three turned me over and placed me on it. I grabbed on to the wheels and pulled myself firmly on to the frame, and then I put the brakes on. Everyone stood around me in a circle, hovering, concerned that I might fall again. "I'm okay," I told them. "Thank you." But they still stood there like idiots, not knowing what to do, so I turned toward the boats and rolled myself away from them to the end of the docks. I didn't say a word. I wanted to move on.

"¡Hijo! ¡Espera!" my father yelled, but I ignored him and kept rolling. He could catch up. Eventually he did and so did Danny. I turned back toward the ramp and noticed that the people who'd helped me were no longer there. I hoped they didn't think I was ungrateful for their help. "Are you okay?" my father asked me again as Danny stood beside him, blankly staring at my face. "Yes, I'm fine," I assured him. "Just forget about it. It's over. Let's just enjoy the rest of the day."

I don't recall much of what we did for the rest of the day, but the pictures say that we went on to pose in front of multiple docked boats. They say that the three of us were happy and enjoying ourselves. Later in the afternoon, I drove us back to Tijuana, where I dropped off my father and Danny at the bus station. And after hugs, kisses, and goodbyes, I watched them walk onto a bus and make their way to their seats, my father holding one plastic bag with his things in it, and Danny another with his. They found a seat somewhere in the middle, and from there they continued to wave bye to me through the window until the bus drove away. I wouldn't see my father again for over seven years after that, for my life would get even more complicated. In less than a year, I'd be charged with attempted murder and wouldn't be allowed to leave the country until first the case and then the sentence were completed.

It happened at a house party in Anaheim, California. We'd come to see the Mike Tyson fight where he bites Holyfield's ear. I was with my younger cousin Chucky and my homeboys

Cricket and Wino. I'd also brought along my girlfriend Angela, who, less than a year later, would become my wife. This
was our second date.

A friend of Wino's had invited him, and Wino had invited
us. So we went. Didn't think much of it. If Wino's friend said it
was cool that we come, then it was cool. But it wasn't cool. At
the party, we were confronted by a rival gang, and they outnumbered us. At the time I'd been carrying a gun with me everywhere I went because I was still an active gang member, or
at least was still trying to be. I'd come to the conclusion early
on after getting out of the hospital that I needed a gun on me at
all times in case I was ever "caught slippin'" by a rival gang. I
couldn't run or fight anymore, but I certainly could still shoot
a gun. So a gun it was. And not just any gun, but a TEC-9.
I drove around with it underneath my car's driver seat. And
that's where it was on this night.

The guys from the rival gang had been eyeing us all throughout the Tyson fight, and I knew it'd be only a matter of time
before they made their move on us, so before the fight ended,
I leaned in to Wino and whispered into his ear to take care of
Angela, and, as inconspicuously as possible, rolled out of the
party as fast as I could to retrieve my gun from the car, which
I'd parked in the alley around the corner. Once the gun was in
my hands, I cocked it, placed it on my lap with a sweater over it,
and rolled back to the party. But when I turned onto the street
from the alley, the party had already spilled out onto the street.
People were out on the sidewalk watching a large group that
had formed a semicircle around another smaller group. I knew
right away what was going on, so I pushed as fast as I could.

Before I knew it, I was in front of my homeboys and girlfriend
telling the others to back off. But they wouldn't listen. They

were too drunk and eager to do us harm. So after the last time I told them to back off, one of them, the one that was leading them, looked right at me and said, "What are you gonna do?" Then, in less than a second after saying this, he took the beer bottle he was holding, broke it on a concrete pole, and charged right by me at my cousin Chucky with the jagged edges of what remained of the bottle leading the way. It was then that I pulled my gun from under the sweater and let off a shot. Everything happened in the blink of an eye. And just like that, my life once again took a turn for the worse. I was arrested that night and charged with attempted murder. And again, it was not my father to the rescue, but my mother, who bailed me out of the county jail before I could spend another night there. It was also my mother who found two great lawyers to fight the charges. For two years I fought the case, showing up to different hearings every few months with my mother at my side.

It was during this time that my mother also enrolled me in college again, which at the end of the case was a big part of the reason that I wouldn't go to prison and would instead be sentenced to five years on gang-terms probation. Taking it upon himself, the judge, recognizing the progress I was making in college and the changes I was making in my life, put aside the deal that I had already agreed to with the prosecutor, which entailed me serving twelve years in prison in exchange for pleading guilty to three charges: reckless discharge of a firearm, causing great bodily injury, and being a gang member.

During those five years on probation, I wouldn't be allowed to leave the country; thus for those five years I would also not see my father. I couldn't go to Mexico, and he couldn't come to the United States. During this time, however, things weren't all bad. For although I was unable to see my father, I managed to graduate from community college, transfer to California State University, Los Angeles, and at the end of spring 2005 graduate with a bachelor's degree in creative writing. The future was looking promising, except for two things: Angela and I would separate at the end of 2004, and as a way of dealing with the depression over losing her, I'd submerge myself in various political movements, one of which had been formed to protest the anti-immigrant vigilante organization called the Minuteman Project. Like many university students, I'd become an idealist, a believer in revolutions, a wannabe Che Guevara, and the Minuteman Project had become my Cuba. I needed to free my people from the oppressive and discriminatory views and actions of these paddy bigots who were gung ho to capture immigrants crossing over into the country illegally.

My gang-terms probation ended on May 25, 2005, and the very next day I joined a group of students at a protest against the Minutemen in the city of Garden Grove at the Garden Grove Women's Club. Things turned terrible quick. Minutemen supporters taunted protesters from behind yellow police tape and the protesters shouted back. This would go on until the sun set. It was then that sheriffs on horseback began to arrive, forming a line on one end of the street. This agitated the protesters, and to make matters worse, this was around the same time that a Minutemen supporter would drive his van into the protesters who were blocking the entrance into the Women's Club property. The protesters, over a hundred of them, moved in and many began to yell obscenities at the Minutemen, the driver of the van, and even the sheriffs. Eventually many of us began to throw water bottles and rocks at the Minutemen. I was one of them. In the mix of the milieu I felt the overpowering urge to participate in this moment of revolution, in this fight for my people. Like the others, I was driven by anger toward these paddies who demeaned and used violence toward my people at the border and who here at this moment were being protected by the sheriffs. I had to do my part. I had to hurt them as much as they hurt us. But alas—the joke was on me, because by the time it was all over the only ones who were going to hurt more than anyone else, even more than the people who'd been hit by the van, were myself and four other students. We'd be arrested and hauled off to the county jail. And the next day the newspaper would dub us the Garden Grove Five. I was now a political prisoner.

My mother would bail me out, again, and I would fight the case throughout the rest of the year. The outcome would be another three years' probation, but this time informal, which meant that, with permission from my probation officer, I would be allowed to travel. The following year I finally got to go to Mexico for the first time in over seven years and see my father.

20

Every December 1 she awakes at dawn. Before the cock crows three, she's well on her way. In the same clothes she slept in, she rises from her bundle of blankets and makes her way through her dark and cold home to the bathroom sink, where she washes her hands and splashes cold water on her face. Cold, everything's cold; but nothing more than her heart. Love moves her. Death moves her. There's a memory in her mind that she can't shake. Her bare toes and fingertips are nearly freezing. Already she's beginning to cry, but her children and grandchildren are still asleep, so she represses the sorrow stirring inside and wipes away her tears. Everything is slow, even the way she looks at herself in the mirror. She could stay there a lifetime and wonder if she'd ever been happy. She knows something in her eyes has died, and that what has been set to time cannot be left for tomorrow.

Her double-layered socks, her shoes, her two sweaters and jacket help only a little, so she crosses her arms, rubs herself, and then blows hot breath into her cupped hands. After, she grabs her hand-stitched satchel and walks over to the refrigerator, opens it, reaches for the two caguamas she stowed there the night before, and carefully places them inside her bag. When the two bottles meet they clink and she remembers the way they once shared a glass together. "Te llevo una," she says to her memory and drapes the straps of the satchel over her shoulder. The cock crows three and she shivers from sadness.

"Jesus was supposed to die," she says to herself. "Dying was his purpose, not yours." With her satchel at her hip and her heart leading the way, she walks into the living room, kisses every one of her children and grandchildren on their foreheads as they silently sleep on their beds and the floor. None of them feel her kisses, and when they awaken only the youngest of her granddaughters will ask for her abuela.

She's walking up an empty street. She's waiting at a lonely bus stop. She's riding on a hollow bus. She's walking down a lifeless dirt road. Ten miles of emptiness. Twenty-five years of terror. This is love. This is the picture that it leaves behind. She remembers him every step of the way, up every street, at every bus stop, on every bus, down every dirt road. "I'll never forget you," she says to her memory, "and I'll never stop coming to be with you." She's close now and can see the sun beginning to show itself on the other side of the mountain. Behind her, her footprints mark her journey. She passed through here, they say, on her way to be with her beloved. But this is a journey that no one will ever value, an event in history that one day will never have happened. This is the march of the sorrowful, the march of the ones who can't free themselves of the dead.

> My lonely widow,
> My lonely black heart,
> Why do you come to the grave?
> Why do you bring life to the dead?
> Turn 'round and go whence you came,
> Turn 'round and go away.

But on this December 1 this dead man was born, on this December 1 many, many years ago. So on this day she's come to his grave to cry and to bring life to his memory.

She's standing at the gates, peering through its decaying bars at the valley of death. She's cold and tired. The sun is gaining strength, but it's still no match against the winter morning that envelops her world. "¿Dónde estás, Pedro? Abreme aquí," she yells out to the gatekeeper. And from the other side of the adobe wall adjacent to the gate a voice responds, "¿Eres tu, la viuda del primero de Diciembre?"

"Sí, yo soy. Abreme por favor."

"¡Ya voy! ¡Ya voy!"

Pedro's old and crippled. Drags his right leg when he walks as if pulling an iron anchor. He's the keeper of graves at this cemetery, and he calls it his home. "Yo vivo con los muertos," he says. And every morning before opening the gates to the living he recites a dozen Our Fathers and Hail Marys in front of his altar of saints for his "muertitos," as he likes to call them, while drinking a pajarete (mixture of warm cow's milk, chocolate, and tequila). This is what he was doing on the other side of the wall when he heard the widow's voice. "¡Aquí estoy! ¡Aquí estoy!" he says to the widow while searching his pockets for his keys. "¡Es que estaba resandole a los santitos para que cuiden a mis muertitos!"

"Pues ojala y lo escuchen, Don Pedro," the widow tells him, watching him insert the key into the lock. "Que frío," she adds, folding her arms.

"Sí, tremendo."

The two shiver at the same time and he offers her a drink from his pajarete, but she refuses, telling him that she brought something to drink of her own: "No, gracias. Yo aquí también traigo que tomar." And, bowing to her the way subjects bow to their queen, he says to her, "Pues pásele, mi borrachita. Pásele que allá la espera su muertito."

She's on her knees, weeping before a weathered and crooked white cross with the name of her beloved written across it, barely noticeable now, erased by the elements. She has one hand on top of it and the other at her side over her satchel, pressing it against her body. Her head is lowered and her tears sadly fall to the earth. Nothing's changed here; the scene remains as always. A thousand sad stories with a thousand sad endings, but hers is the only one worth a thousand tears. She'll sing it and no one will hear: "Te amo. Te amo. Te amo."

> Why did you go, my Beloved,
> And why didn't you take me with you?
> There is something terrible about your hands that I miss,
> The way they would make me feel alive
> When they crashed with my flesh,
> The way they pounded my breasts,
> The way they beat my spirit.
> Why don't you scream,
> Why don't you yell my name?
> I love you so much less when you are silent.
> Awake, my Beloved!
> Awake thine fury!

She reaches inside her satchel and brings out one of the caguamas. "Mira lo que te traje," she says to the cross. "Vamos a tomar, mi amor, por que es tu cumpleaños."

One drink.

Two drinks.

Three drinks.

Four drinks.

Five drinks.

The tears turn to laughter. Vicente Fernández sings in her head and she cries out to the cross with a smile on her face: "¡El Rey! ¡El Rey! ¡El Rey! ¡Siempre serás mi Rey!" Three-quarters through the bottle she pours the rest onto the dirt and watches as it bubbles up and seeps into the ground. "Para ti," she says. She reaches into her satchel for the second caguama and just as soon as she pops it open she puts it to her lips and begins to drink. There's a shouting match inside of her now and she's weeping again, and laughing. And soon she'll be curled up on the dirt, tasting its grains and shivering from the cold. Next to her, two caguamas will lay sadly spent like neglected children. This is love. This is sorrow. This is misery.

Chihuahua, like many states in Mexico, is in constant mourning. It has been ever since the war between the cartels and the government broke out. Death is everywhere, from the narcos who fill the streets with blood every day to the women who continue to disappear off the streets of Juárez. This is why the city of Chihuahua, which once had been peaceful and quiet, is now anything but. Not a day goes by that the sound of a gun or machine gun being fired doesn't fill the air in some parts of the city. Bullet-riddled homes are no longer uncommon, as well as makeshift altars that decorate the streets to memorialize the dead. Candles and calaveras reveal the deceased's last moment alive on this earth: *Someone died here—here is where their spirit left them.* Everyone knows where the hearse is going; and the sympathy from those who follow it has vanished. Because everyone is certain that another hearse is coming shortly after this one. The dead, now, have become to the people as un-intriguing as the living. Every new dead man, woman, or child, is just that: only another dead man, woman, or child, a lifeless body being carried to its final resting spot.

As in Juárez—the epicenter of the narco war in the state of Chihuahua—La Santa Muerte has begun to reign all over the city of Chihuahua. Of the thousands of cartel-related deaths that have occurred throughout the state since the beginning of 2007, many have occurred in this once-peaceful capital of no more than a million people. Death's shadow looms over the whole city, and one can't help but feel the piercing eeriness that comes with it, especially when you're slowly creeping behind a hearse. Chihuahua's under siege. Handfuls of young masked soldiers in military fatigues ride on the beds of trucks, clenching M16s. Death is on their minds. They fear it because they know it's on the face and heart of every Mexican citizen they have sworn to protect. They've been called to arms, to fight the cartels gun to gun. They've pledged allegiance to the flag of their great country, and are now in the hands of Fate. Fatum. Wyrd. Anatkha. That mighty force that has been the topic of much debate among philosophers, men of God, and men of letters ever since the beginning of thought: What of life if man must die? "I cannot suffer what is not my fate," cried Antigone. To Boethius, man was subordinate to Fatum and Fatum subordinate to divine Providentia. To King Alfred the Great, Fate *was* God. To the Old English poet of "The Wanderer" and "The Seafarer," all of man's journeys are set by Fate. Fate! Fate! Fate! Every man must die. Man has no say in the matter. He can seek, hoard, build and destroy, love and hate, and drink and drink, but in the end, there's something he will never do again: live.

In 2011 my cousins the twins—Uriel and Ulises—were both assassinated in Chihuahua five months apart: Ulises on

April 29 and Uriel on September 18. Like many young men, they had gotten pulled into the drug business, joining one of Mexico's more dangerous cartels. Ulises's death was pretty straightforward: while protecting a part of his "plaza," members of a rival cartel drove up on him and his bodyguard and started shooting at them from inside a truck with assault rifles. Ulises was hit in one ankle and managed to get away with his bodyguard, who led him to a safe location. Story goes that after the ambulance picked him up, he called his brother Uriel and told him what had happened, and upon hearing about the incident, Uriel, able to foresee that things were going to get worse, urged Ulises to get out of the ambulance and instead find a safe place to hide. Ulises, however, didn't listen and let himself be taken to the hospital, where only a few minutes after being admitted, two masked men entered and found him hiding in a bathroom. There, as he huddled in the corner of a bathroom stall, they shot him multiple times. He never had a chance.

Uriel, only a few months after burying his twin brother, would be shot multiple times as well while working the expendio he owned. Why he was murdered remains unclear. Some say that it was related to his brother's death, while others believe he was simply a victim of a robbery gone wrong, which is hard to believe considering that no money was taken from his person or the cash register. Whatever the case, like his brother, he became just another victim of Mexico's gun violence. The two are buried side by side in a small rancho two hours away from the city. A headstone in the shape of a flame marks each of their graves.

21

Chihuahua is one huge desert, and its summers are hot and dry. We've been driving now for an hour, and the heat is starting to get to me. "Where's this fucking cemetery?" I ask Aarón in frustration. "Can't this motherfucker go any faster?" But Aarón remains calm and laughs it off. The kid's cool cruising with his big brother and happy to be listening to music that reminds him of his dead father. He smiles at me and says, "Ya mero llegamos."

I wonder about him, about what he's feeling. Is he sad? Is he angry? Does he miss his father? I haven't seen him cry, and he has a gorgeous smile. He seems happy, strong. But how happy, and how strong? I see him so focused on what's in front of him and I wonder: Who is this kid? How does he suffer so gallantly? I'm a rock, a stone, I can't suffer for my father; but he, does he not have the right to weep publicly for his father? Why must he be a gentleman? Why must he swallow his sorrow? "Los hombres no lloran," was one of my father's favorite things to say. "Don't cry, don't cry, don't cry," he'd impress upon us. Tears were not his style, and he didn't want them to be our style either. Is this what Aarón remembers?

At eighteen he looks like a fully grown man. A short and very thin one, but nevertheless—a man. He does everything every grown man in Mexico is expected to do: work, drive, drink, have sex, and now he's burying his father. On top of that, he's leading the pack of mourners. He's a spotless boy, a loyal son! And he's *it* now. He's the one. Fate's choice. The youngest of all of our father's children. Through him, the memory of Juan Silva will live on most. He knows what to do. He won't disappoint.

"I'm going to stop and get some beer," he says, veering off the highway and away from the procession. We pull into an expendio. Danny pulls in next to us. The procession continues on its five-miles-per-hour course to the cemetery. "¿Quieres algo?" Aarón asks me.

"Just water," I tell him. He walks into the store and Danny walks in behind him. Nobody else follows. I take this opportunity to look out at the procession as it continues to move past us. I notice that every vehicle in the line is old and busted in more ways than one. They're all dirty and have fucked-up paint jobs. There are cars, trucks, vans, and they're all from the last century—literally. But I'm impressed by the number of them. I count twenty-two vehicles in all, and in every one of them a band of wretched spirits. "There goes my father's world, his tribe, the miserable folk, the rabble, los pobres he always proudly talked about."

In Chihuahua, such a scene has become the norm, part of the everyday of things. The extraordinary occurs only when a rich person dies or a big narco. Only then is there something to see: all-new cars with their dark-tinted windows rolled all the way up, some even bulletproof. Only if my father had been rich—only then, his people wouldn't have to sweat so much and hang their babies out of their cars' windows. The last vehicle in the procession is a blue early '90s Chrysler minivan. Its paint's peeling and most of the body's covered in dirt. Both the front windows are rolled down and the sliding side door is completely open. There's about ten people bunched up inside: men, women, and children. A little boy and girl are sitting on the edge of the open space with their little legs and feet dangling in the air. They look right at me as they go by. I smile and wave at them and they return the gesture.

Aarón walks out of the store clutching two Carta Blanca caguamas and Danny a couple of large paper bags and sodas. I wonder what Aarón plans on doing with the caguamas. Is he going to open them now or are they for later? I hope they're for later because I don't feel like drinking this early. Before walking to his car, Danny walks up to my window, hands me a bottle of water and offers me a bag of chips. "No, thanks," I tell him. "Water's good for now." Meanwhile, Aarón's placing the two caguamas behind his side of the seat. I don't ask him anything about them and he says nothing about them to me. No one in the back asks either, which only makes me more curious about when he plans on drinking them. Still, I avoid the topic. As far as I'm concerned, he could leave them back there forever, because I really have no desire to even taste a beer in this moment—*or* to drink one later in the day, either. I'm constipated and beginning to feel discomfort in my stomach. Aarón gets in the truck, cranks the ignition, and within seconds we're back behind the white hearse, once again leading the procession. I open my water and take a drink. Its coldness moves down my throat and into my stomach. It's refreshing, but I'm still hating the day.

Eventually we turn off the highway and onto a long stretch of dirt road. It's dusty and bumpy. And though we're moving even slower than before, nothing prevents the dust from kicking up and getting all over us. I'd roll up my window but it's just too damn hot. I imagine myself being back home and driving around Orange County streets in my semi-new, air-conditioned car. But because this isn't Kansas anymore, dirt and dust it will be until we reach the cemetery, which, as my bad luck would have it, is at the very end of the road, and it will be at least another twenty minutes before we reach it. It's far, seemingly endless. An endless fucking road of dirt, rocks, and large holes. My pretty Mexico, when will you pave all your roads? Can't you see the inconvenience they cause to visitors from el otro lado like me? And why does this fucking cemetery have to be so far? I ask Aarón this last question. "Was there no other cemetery that was closer?"

"No, this is it," he says, unmoved by my complaining. "This is where my grandma's buried, too."

Of course this is it. Where else would anyone put a cemetery for people like my father and his mother if not as far as possible from the main populated areas of Chihuahua? The poor and the destitute are always pushed to the margins of every society, and Chihuahuense society is no exception.

We finally come up to a steel gate between two long adobe walls splattered with white paint and the word CEMENTERIO painted on them in large black letters. On one side of the gate there's also a small kiosk-looking room from which an old man comes out, dragging his right leg and cheerfully saying to the driver of the hearse, "Hola, ¿cómo están?" He uses the plural form of the Spanish "you," which makes me wonder to whom else besides the driver he could be talking to. As far as I know, it's only him inside of the hearse, him and of course my father. But my father's dead and I figure he must know this. Funny how so many times the wrong way we use words goes unnoticed. But I digress. Because after greeting the driver of the hearse, the man walks up to Aarón's window to tell us that we can't bring the cars into the cemetery.

Fuck that, I immediately think to myself, I ain't pushing over all that dirt. And I'm about to tell the man this, but before I say anything Aarón informs him about my situation. "But my brother's in a wheelchair. He can't go over all that dirt."

The old man ducks and looks observingly at me through the window. "Really?" he says. "He looks fine."

"Really," Aarón assures him. "Look, his chair's in the back."

The old man takes a step back, sees the chair among the passengers, and says, "Okay, then go ahead. Come right in, but only this car. Everyone else has to park their cars out here and walk in." Fuck it. Cool with me. The old man opens the gate and waves us in, and as we follow closely behind the hearse the rest of the mourners walk beside and behind us.

Cemeteries are always creepy, at least to me, but nowhere are they creepier than in Mexico. In this one, for example, there are stone and wooden crosses everywhere, and concrete slabs of various sizes. Dried-up flowers and decaying statues of saints adorn almost every grave, from La Virgen María—the general favorite—to San Martín de Porres (my personal favorite because he's a negrito like me) and San Judas Tadeo and even La Santa Muerte (which is the favorite among the narcos). There are no manicured lawns in this cemetery, only dirt and weeds. And no trees, only an endless view of erected crosses and slabs of concrete with the names of the dead either painted or engraved on them, and most of them in bad condition.

We stop before two freshly dug grave sites; a mound of dirt lies next to each one. Everyone gathers around the hearse and Aarón asks me if I want to get out. "Yes," I say to him, though I really just want to stay in the car—hell, I really just want to be somewhere else. It's already too hot and there's dirt everywhere, and I hate having to push my wheelchair over dirt. It gets all over my hands and eventually all over my clothes. And when I wear black the dirt stands out. And on this day I'm wearing black jeans. And I still can't get the fact that I'm constipated out of my head. But who would understand my plight? So while my father's getting pulled out of the hearse, Aarón is setting my wheelchair between me and the open passenger door.

There's a quiet storm. People are once again beginning to cry as they gather around the coffin. I don't get close to it. I stay by the truck and look on. "You don't want to see him?" Aarón says to me. "They're going to open the casket again so we can see him."

No, I don't want to see him again. What for? In what way could my father have changed since the night before or since earlier that morning at the funeral home? He's still dead and in the same position with the same fucking face, and he's still going to the same fucking place.

I shake my head.

"You sure?" Aarón asks me again.

"I'm fine here," I say. "You go." He does. He walks away and disappears into the crowd. A few times I'm able to see his little dark brown bald head pop up and glance at me as if to make sure that I'm still here. He isn't the only one who does this. Others look up or back at me and stare with wonder, each one seemingly wanting to ask me the same question: "Don't you want to see your father one last time?"

NO!

Time is dragging and the heat is doing a number on me and my black jeans are getting covered in dust, just as I'd predicted. I want my father to be buried already. I see no sense in prolonging the inevitable, plus, still feeling the effects of the hangover from the night before and worrying about my guts, I want nothing more than to return to the house, make an attempt at taking a shit again, and then go back to sleep. Be done with it already, I keep wanting to tell everybody, bury him already and wipe your fucking tears!

It's something like a dream, like a surreal world in which I don't belong. The cemetery's playing tricks on me and the people are putting on a spectacle. I've never seen anything like it before. What is this place and why does it feel so normal? My father has walked me through it before, shown me how life can be ridiculous, shown me how even a moment like this can be meaningless, how empty even cries can be, even for a dead man. "From the moment you take your first breath, you're already dying," my father used to say, "and life isn't all it's cut out to be." And after taking a deep breath, he'd sing: "No vale nada la vida, / La vida no vale nada," one of his favorites by José Alfredo Jiménez. Something that had always sounded like gibberish when coming from the mouth of a drunk is now making all the sense in the world to me. I understand it all now.

I keep looking at the trash that's everywhere and wondering where it comes from and why no one bothers to pick it up. Wrappers of every kind, empty potato chip bags, pieces of paper and plastic bags, empty soda cans and beer bottles and even dirty diapers are scattered all over the place. Not one tomb is too sacred not to be marked by trash.

And as I continue to scan the cemetery with my eyes, I come across the unexpected: Rocío. There she is again, looking more beautiful and more out of place than yesterday. In her aqua top and light-brown sandals, she looks more like she should be at the beach. She's among the crowd, next to my sister Axcel and Danny's wife, Lucy, and when I spot her I realize that she's looking right at me. The sun is in her eyes and she's squinting, and when she sees me look at her, she smiles. Then I smile. Then I wave from my chest, then she waves from her waist. And behind her, far back away from where we all are, another woman catches my attention. She's tall, slender, and beautiful. And she's dressed the way one expects people to dress at a funeral, and not like any of us are dressed now. She has on a long, fitted black dress that comes down to her calves, and she's wearing black high heels. I wonder if dirt has gotten into them. Can't be comfortable, I think, and she's got it worse than I do with my black pants. She also has on dark black sunglasses and her hair is done up in a stylish bun. I don't remember her being at the wake. I'm certain I would have seen her, and I'm certain I would have remembered her. Because I appreciate her, the respect she brings to my father's funeral, the elegance and formality she evokes, even as a yellow plastic bag blows right by her. I'd later learn, from Aarón, that the woman was our uncle Trini's ex-wife. And while the ex- would make sense to me, the ever-having-been-his-wife part would not.

There is no priest and there are no prayers, just final goodbyes and glances. This is where it all ends for my father, and soon the casket will shut for the last time. Like the shadow that casts itself over the city as the sun begins to set, a shadow is cast over my father's face before the lid completely shuts. To the side, my brothers, sister Axcel, and Cokis wrap themselves in each other's arms. My sister Cecilia, on the other side, stands alone with her hands clutched in front of her and her white skin turning red in the sun. All this time she's been unwanted by this side of her family for something she had no fault in, and now here she is, wanting to share in their misery. She stands like a lonesome dove in the desert, thirsty and eager to fly with a murder of crows. I wonder what must be going through her head, seeing what's all around her. It's a thing of beauty, ain't it, sis, this creation of our father's? It's all his doing, his work, his magnum opus. Your father was the pope, didn't you know, and everything he did was holy. This is why they cry for him, this is why they mourn his death.

One boy in particular is crying more than anyone else. He's one of my uncle Trini's sons, David. "¡Tio! ¡Tio! ¡Por qué? Why?" he keeps shouting while sprawling his upper body over the casket. It's a sad and terrible thing to see, and to hear his cries is even worse, like fingernails scratching on a chalkboard. They make me cringe. But the whole thing confuses me. I question his outpouring of painful sentiments. Not even my brothers are expressing their pain the way he is. Had he really been that close to my father that he'd suffer so much for his passing? David, I knew, had in fact crossed with the Devil and made tracks beneath a poisoned moon. He'd drunk from the fountain of sorrows and partaken in the dark celebrations of my father and uncle—his father. I witnessed it once, and it felt like I was seeing one of the worst sins committed by men.

My father had purchased a small adobe shack only a few blocks from the house where he lived with his family. This, I was told by Cokis, he'd done so that he could have somewhere to go when she'd kicked him out for any of the many reasons she'd become accustomed to kicking him out for. This was to be his doghouse, a place for him to dwell in his misery alone. I was surprised when I first heard about this "otra casa," as my brothers, sister Axcel, and Cokis came to call it.

From the outside, the house looked like a shithole. It was

built in what seemed like a sinkhole on a dirt street on the side of a hill. Only the top part above its one front window and its roof were visible from the street. You had to walk down a number of steps and past a huge tree, whose branches and leaves helped conceal most of it, to get to it. This being the case, I never got closer than the street. It wasn't ADA approved. But I pulled up in front of it a couple times with Aarón to look for our father. Aarón would get out and go to the door to call for him while I waited patiently in the car. And every time our father would come out looking like shit from head to toe. His pupils would be dilated, his skin would be pale and thin, and his breath would reek of alcohol. He'd look like a fucking zombie coming out of a cave, and I'd tell him this to his face, after which he'd laugh uncomfortably and tell me that I was crazy, that I didn't know what the fuck I was talking about. "Estás loco," he'd say. "I'm no zombie. I'm your father, tu papá." Then he'd reach in through the window, wrap his arms around my neck, and kiss me on the forehead. And in case I misunderstood what it was he did in that house, he'd make it clear to me that he and his friends were only there drinking and playing poker, and that was all. But that was never all. Something else was always going on, and that something else was cocaine and other drugs. "So you mean to tell me that with only beer you're able to stay up and play poker all night, and with nothing else?" I'd ask him. And "¡Sí, sí, sí!" he'd assure me over and over. But my father hadn't been fooling anybody, especially his sons who'd come to know him too well, who'd come to recognize all of his lies. Alcohol alone doesn't dilate your pupils or weaken you and turn your flesh pale, nor does it make you grind your teeth obsessively and lick and bite your lips just the same. I've seen this man before. Hell, I've been this man before; but in darkness where no one could see me, and in silence where no one could hear me. I'd been my father's son. I knew what went on in that shitty house: junkies dressed as relics turned in there to tune out the world outside.

Here my father was able to truly be himself and do as he wanted. There were always at least three other men, aside from my father, in this house. And aside from them, there were always your endless bottles of caguamas, cheap tequila, cans of beer, and of course—seemingly endless lines of cocaine and sometimes methamphetamine. The place, even from the street, smelled of old beer, sweat, and urine. There was nothing home-like about it; there was no kitchen, only a small restroom with a dirty toilet to shit and piss in and a sink to wash your hands and face. There was also no bed, no television, no couch to sit on, only a bar-style aluminum table with the Carta Blanca logo painted on it, with matching aluminum chairs. Beds, couches, kitchens, and televisions are material things that would be difficult to accommodate in such a small place like this, where what was most important was the drink and the drugs.

This "cueva," as I came to call it, served only one purpose, and that purpose was to provide a place where my father and his friends could drink and sniff or shoot up cocaine or meth all day and night for as many days and nights as their bodies could take without having to do it out in the open where everyone could see. This was a place where these men could practice discretion. This was a cave for men who wished to waste away slowly out of view of the rest of the world. This was the house of the rising sun.

I saw David come out from it once, behind his father and mine. He looked like a nightmare, like a mother's broken heart, thin and sickly, with pupils the size of quarters. Standing next to his father, Trini, he looked like a boy who'd just been introduced to the Devil, helpless and blue, high on the drugs that had been given to him by his own father and uncle (my father). He said hi to me and I said hi to him, and we both said that we were happy to see one another. But there was nothing happy about anything in that moment. My father was high, his father was high, he was high, and the world seemed like shit to everybody, including to me and Aarón, who was still in the car with me. The sun was hurting all of us, fathers and sons, high and not high. We were all feasting from the same pile of shit. The elephant was crushing us, and the silence that we'd swallowed felt like acid flushing down our throats, dissolving our souls. Something like a dark secret that that house quietly had been keeping was erupting like a volcano. A father had betrayed his son because he could no longer restrain the Devil. And this was the result: the son would do what the father did, but every time with a little less pain and a more empty heart. No big deal: a father has passed on his addiction to his son—he's taught him how to be a man.

What I didn't know was this: that my father had been almost a better father to David than my tío Trini. On our way home after the funeral, Aarón would tell me that even though our tío Trini was clean and sober now, when he was drinking and doing drugs, he was much worse than our father. "At least our dad always had food for us and a place for us to live. When our tío Trini drank and did drugs, there were times when he wouldn't return home for many days and his kids would be left with nothing to eat. Our dad never did that. There was always food, even if just beans and tortillas. And sometimes, all of

Trini's kids, including David, would come over to our house to eat. All of them loved our dad, but especially David. Because he said that he cared about him more than his own dad, Trini."

Love is strange. Fathers and sons are strange. Love between fathers and sons is even stranger. Our fathers can damage us forever and we will still love them forever. David wasn't crying over the death of his uncle; he was crying over the death of a man that to him had become a father, even if he'd once let him inside the house of the rising sun to do the things of beasts.

Being so far away from my father after he and my mother divorced, I would cry when I didn't hear from him for a long time. And when he'd finally call and I'd hear his voice I'd cry even more. Couldn't help it—I loved him, and hearing his voice come through the speaker was overwhelming. Because although the sound of his voice meant a lot to me, I always wanted more. I wanted to see my father, so that I could touch him and wrap my arms around him so tight as to never let him go. And through the phone my father would always tell me to not cry. "No llores, hijo. Los hombres no lloran," he'd say, pushing me to man up. But I'd continue to pour out my tears for him throughout the entire call, because I was not a man. I was a little boy who wanted to be close to his father. I needed to cry. My father was far away in Mexico and I was over here in California and a phone call was never going to fill a young boy's heart. I needed my father then.

Fathers were all around me, and none of them were ever Juan Silva.

At thirteen I did the worst thing I've ever done in my life. My father drove me to my tía Lupe's house where my mother was waiting for me so that we could return to the United States. Our two-week summer vacation in Chihuahua had come to an end. When my father and I arrived at my tía's house, my mother was in the driveway loading up the car with our suitcases. My father pulled right up to the front of the house next to the driveway, and I got out of the car and walked up to my mother, who was organizing our luggage in the trunk of the car. It was a small blue 1992 Ford Escort sedan. It was also the first car she'd ever purchased new from an actual car dealership. She was proud of this car because it was a symbol of all her hard work in the United States. She was proud of being able to return to her homeland in this symbol of success.

On our way to Chihuahua she and I had listened to tapes of Juan Gabriel, ABBA, Michael Jackson, Madonna, and even Run-DMC, which she'd purchased for me at a gas station somewhere right before exiting California. The drive had been filled with excitement and lots of talk about what the future held for us and what we were going to do once we got to Chihuahua. She was most excited to see her father, sister, and brothers, and I was most excited to see my cousins the twins and of course my father.

"Go say bye to your tía and tío and your cousins. ¡Apurale!" my mom said to me. I quickly ran into the house and said goodbye to everyone, but when I came out they all followed me to say their final goodbyes to my mother, who was already sitting in the car. She was in a hurry to leave, which seemed odd to me; the day before she'd talked about how terribly sad she was over having to leave. If not for the roots we'd already established in the United States and for the economic opportunities it had to offer to a single mother like herself, she would've preferred Chihuahua any day. Yet here she was urging me to hurry.

Upon seeing my tía and tío and cousins come out of the house behind me, my father stepped out of his car to greet them. They were surprised by his presence; they hadn't expected him to still be out there. "Hola, Juan," my tío and tía said to him, and he returned the greeting while walking up to them. He shook my tío's hand and gave my tía a hug, and then he nodded at my cousins. There were a couple of minutes of small talk between my tío and my dad, but my tía quickly turned to my mom inside the car and said goodbye and wished her a safe trip, after which my mom called out to me to hurry up and get in the car. I hugged everyone really quick one last time, including my father, and then I jumped in the car. My mom turned the ignition, put the car in reverse, and everyone moved out of the way. My father walked out of the driveway and to his car, but he didn't get in. He stood next to the driver-side door and watched as we pulled out. He had a modest smile. My mother angled the car toward him. There was no way around it; we were headed in the direction where he was parked. And when she stopped to change the gear from reverse to drive, my father took the opportunity to walk up to her window and say hello.

"Hola, Marcela, ¿cómo estás?" he asked, as if he and my mother were good friends who hadn't seen each other in a long time. The only thing true about this statement, of course, was that they hadn't seen each other in a long time, and this was not because of missed opportunities; no, my mother had always made an effort to avoid seeing my father. When he'd pick me up from my tía's house, she'd go out of her way to be as far deep in the house as she could. She didn't even want to accidentally get a glimpse of him through the door or a window, but more importantly, she didn't want him to get a glimpse of her. I knew this, but I didn't understand the depth of it, I didn't understand the reasons for it. And because of this ignorance, I blamed my mother—she was the bad one here, always wanting nothing to do with my father, with the man who showed me love and took me everywhere with him every time I came to Chihuahua.

And here they now were, after many years, in this moment that only I am to blame for, coming into contact once again. I look at my mom and await her response. My father's at the window, smiling, being kind, extending an olive branch, and my mother not once turns to look at him, but she does respond with a cold and solid "Bien. Gracias." Nothing more. Not even a "How about you." Just "Bien. Gracias." Like that. With the firmly placed period separating the two. Makes a lot of sense to me now. But it didn't then.

"Bueno," my father finally said after a long and awkward silence, "que les vaya bien." And then he lowered his head to look at me around my mother's statuesque face and said, "Adios, hijo—te quiero." My mother's profile was prominent in my sight. It raged with an emotion that has no name. It wasn't anger and it wasn't fear. Disgust? Repulsion? Close. But I don't think that even those words capture it entirely. Whatever the word, she was fully consumed by it, paralyzed. She didn't blink or flex a muscle, not on her face or on her body. This was my mother exuding her power, knowing that my father couldn't touch her or make her say anything she didn't want to say—she'd been done with that many years ago. And if my father had to suffer the consequence of looking like a fool for it, then so be it. And so it was. On the other side of my mother's profile, my father's pathetic face pulled back and quickly disappeared from my view. All that was there was the right side of my mother's face. And I hated it!

She let her foot off the brake and slowly we drove away. I turned back and watched as my father looked on at us as we made it to the corner. My tía, tío, and cousins had come out from the driveway and stood behind him. My cousins waved and I waved back, but my main focus was my father, the lowly man whom I was leaving behind and had been unable to stand up for. And as we came to a stop at the corner, I turned to my mother and said, "Why did you do that? Why did you have to be so mean to him? He was being nice to you." Then my mother said, "Son, I'm sorry, but I—I . . ." She struggled to speak, to articulate her reason, and in this moment of her loss for words my anger grew into rage and everything went out of control and I clenched my right fist and I pulled back my arm and then I punched her. As hard as I could. She'd been wearing a blue sleeveless top, so when I pulled back I could clearly see a big baseball-size red mark on her right arm, below her shoulder. She didn't cry. She didn't even yell at me. She just looked at me with sadness. Looked both ways, and then made a left turn.

There was no Juan Gabriel or ABBA or Michael Jackson or Madonna or Run-DMC music the entire way home. But worst of all—my mother did not say one word to me for the entire eighteen hours that we would be in the car together. She just drove with a red mark on her arm that would eventually turn into a dark purple-and-black bruise that would remain there for almost two weeks. And people would ask and my mother would say . . . anything but the truth.

Before my father's lowered into the earth and dirt is dropped on him, Aarón takes the two caguamas he'd purchased earlier out from the truck and places one on each side of the casket. This is the ultimate gesture, the ultimate goodbye from my brother to his dead father who'd been an alcoholic. There are no falsehoods here, no apologies. In the face of the world Aarón is doing exactly what his father would have wanted him to do: bury him with what killed him. Thus his will had been done.

Some of my father's brothers shovel dirt into the hole while some of the other mourners push piles of it in with the inner sides of their feet. A cloud of dust rises from the hole every time the dirt hits the casket, making the sound of crashing raindrops. My father's finally being put away forever; there will be no more viewing him, no more parading him around. Adiós, Juan Silva, adiós, viejo triste.

I wish that I could hug him,
I wish that I could feel the stubble on his cheeks
And smell the scent of drink on his breath!

Here he is, coming 'round the corner
Draggin' a Beast behind him!
Stumbling!

Falling!

Rising with fire in his eyes!

Loud he roars!

Hard he thunders!

Kicking the wind and stomping the earth!

"Te quiero vida!" he screams,

"Te quiero! Te quiero!—y te mato."

"How 'bout it, son, we die together,

And we die today?"

"You first, Dad, you first."

Only his children and wife remain. They stand by one another, and, with vacant eyes, each stares at the grave. Soon they will all go, too, and leave him behind. Soon life will have to go on without him, and all of them know this. One walks toward the cross, another kneels at the edge of the mound, and the others remain still, like statues untouched by the apocalypse. A small gust of wind blows through, whirling dust into the air. The wife looks down, one of the daughters cries, and the other shuts her eyes. This one wants to know more about the father she's just buried; she's been wondering for so long about the man who helped create her and now there is nothing more to say. Meanwhile, the one in the wheelchair still can't see how things would have been better for any of them if the patriarch hadn't died: he knows there's a dream in the rood that is better kept secret; he sees solace in its silence; finds grace in the quiet heat, in the piled dirt, in the jagged rock he holds in his hand that cuts through his skin when he makes a fist. He'd love to chuck it to do his part. There is life in the desert, and a future in the crown of flowers. Time is ticking, and there is no more to do here; the will that governs commands that everybody must rot and be left to bloom again within minds that suffer from never forgetting. But there is too much silence, and now it's becoming difficult to bear. Somebody must say something. How about the boy by the cross, or the one on his knees now playing with the dirt, watching it cascade from his palm onto the earth like sand flows downward in an hourglass? Or how about one of the daughters, are they lost for words as well? The wife isn't speaking. She's been dying for far too long; now she's enjoying the moment, embracing the thought of peaceful nights to come, or maybe she's thinking about finally having a drink all by herself. Certainly the one in the wheelchair isn't going to say anything; he loves his thoughts too much, the way he's able to mold the past, present, and future into one fucking senseless story never worth telling. All seems too much like a sad tale sprinkled with a bunch of funny moments to him. Like who really gives a fuck, really? This moment had been played out in all of their dreams for so long; someone had plastered it on a wall. Scene by scene, every act had been meticulously rehearsed, and so had every cry—every tear counted long ago. And now the curtains were coming down.

Here come the músicos, a pair of jolly men who've come to serenade the dead. Each one is holding a guitar up to his chest. Where did they come from and who invited them? They walk up to the mound of dirt and without instruction start strumming their guitars and singing "Una Cruz de Madera." I stare at them and think, Oh, but of course, how fitting. ¡Canten, caballeros, cantenle al muerto!

Too perfect! Too beautiful! Can I die, too, so that you may sing to me as well? My father's living out the song. Instead of holy water, he'd been buried with two caguamas, and instead of luxuries all that was placed at the head of his tomb was a wooden cross "de la mas corriente," and now, though not in the wee hours of the morning, he's being serenaded by a pair of músicos. They play enchantingly. This is the magic of live music! It can turn a smile into a tear and a tear into a smile, and even make a poem out of death. This is the moment for which you die, the moment you wish you could be alive to see. With a song everything comes full circle, and like the cross, it marks the absolute end of your life while acknowledging that you had one to begin with, and it pushes the memory of you forth into the world. Remember me, is what it always says.

22

I turned thirty-one today, and I didn't receive a phone call from my father to wish me a happy birthday, something he'd done ever since I can remember. Year after year it was certain that my father, at one point or another, on my birthday, would call to wish me a happy day and to tell me that he loved me: "I'm calling to wish you a happy birthday, son, and to tell you that I love you." Not once did he ever miss one of my birthdays. He was always there.

But February 3 has come again and there is no phone call from my father, nor will there be, ever. I'm awake early in the morning and staring at the ceiling from my bed, realizing that something will be missing today. "Such is life," I say, "and life is sad as such." I take my cell phone off the charger and I hold it in my hand. It's cold. He isn't going to call today, I remind myself, he's dead, my father's dead. In this moment, however, I can't kick him out of my head. Right now I love him more than ever. He's there and he's playing. He's there and he's smiling at me. He's there and he's not drunk. "Happy birthday, hijo," he's saying. "Te quiero." I wish I could cry, but I don't; I remind myself that everything that happens is a result of something else. And still, in this moment, right now, I love him more than ever.

I raise my phone and I go through my contacts: Pops—this is the name I have for my father's number. It's still there. I haven't changed it.

I called my father a lot during the last five to six years of his life, and most times I'd be drunk. I'd be at bars, clubs, parties, or just drinking with friends at random places, and as soon as I'd be drunk, I'd get this melancholy urge to call my father. "¡Qué onda, jefe?" I'd yell into the phone. "Do you miss me?"

"Claro que sí," he'd say, often shaking off his sleep.

"Yeah, me too, and guess what, viejo?"

"What?"

"I'm drunk."

"Yo se."

Of course he knew. Why else would I be calling him at one, two, three, and sometimes even four in the morning if not to share with him my joy of being drunk. Our conversations almost never went on for much longer than this; he'd have to go back to sleep and I'd have to go back to getting more drunk. Sometimes, however, before hanging up, I'd pass the phone to some of those around me and say, "Here, it's my dad on the phone, say hi to him, he's a great man!" I'd take a lot of pleasure in having my drunk friends talk to my father on my phone. "¡Q-vole!" they'd say. "Yeah, I'm your son's friend. He's a helluva guy, and he's told us a lot about you." Then there'd be a pause, and then: "Okay, it was nice talking to you, too. We're going to drink some more and get real fucked-up before the night ends, and don't worry about Obed, we'll take care of him. Okay, bye-bye!"

I take it death can't be so bad, on account that we all must die. So why is it that we make such a fuss over life? Don't know. Seven times I've almost died, and I'll probably have a few more encounters with death by the time I finish telling this story. The first on account of me crawling through the rails of a second-floor balcony and almost falling to my death at the age of one. Would've made the trip down had my mother not leaned over the railing and snatched me up. The second on account of me being in a car with a bunch of other kids that my cousin Armando drove off a cliff at Big Bear Mountain after the car's brakes went out—I was eight then. The third on account of me getting shot for being a jackass—seventeen then. I'll include here the other numerous times I was shot at but never hit. The fourth on account of a meth overdose—was old enough to know better. The fifth on account of a cocaine overdose, which led to the discovery of gangrene on my small intestine, which led to the removal of a foot of my small intestine—again was old enough to know better. The sixth time again on account of an overdose, of a mixture of cocaine and meth—again was old enough to know better. The seventh time on account of choking on a dry and stale McDonald's fry. My brother Roberto performed the Heimlich maneuver on me and the grain-size piece of fry came rocketing out. Would have been a most embarrassing death. Really glad I didn't go that way. Seven times—and probably other times that I just don't remember on account I've been jumped and had my head pounded on with fists and stomped on with boots on more than one occasion. I almost became nothing more than a tiny memory in the minds of a certain few. But here I am still, for now.

But even after so many close encounters with the reaper, I still don't know how to go about accepting it, accepting that we all must die, and that death can come at any moment. People die doing ordinary, everyday activities, like riding their bikes on the street, or making a wrong turn during a blizzard, or marrying the wrong person, or getting on a roller coaster, or eating too much or smoking too much or drinking too much or doing stupid shit like jumping off cliffs with a parachute or fake wings too much or wanting to know too much about nature too much, shit, you can even up and die for drinking too much water. You can just die. That's it. It's the law of life. All that lives must die and there is no telling when your day is going to come. But wouldn't it be so serene, so peaceful, so out of this world to just stop living? Victor Hugo once wrote: "All men are condemned to death." Not one person has ever been granted a reprieve from death, nor will one person *ever* be granted one. Straight to death we're all heading, to that most perfect state from which there is no return. So why such sorrow over such beauty?

No matter how much I try,
I keep returning to the Beast!
Drink after drink and piss after piss.
Life becomes easier—
Hurrah! Hurrah! Hail to the Beast!
And ajajaaaiiii! I'm loving it—
    Father, I miss you, and so much more do I yearn for
      death

It's a Beast, it's a monster, it's the Devil in disguise—
I dance and laugh,
I do the waltz with Vicente Fernández.
Candles for friends and tequila for lovers—
I imagine myself surrounded by mariachi

Drinking and dying too slow
With a cigarette and a drink.
Father, do you remember
How life was beautiful
        Before you made it ugly,
                A spell and a curse?

I have to write this down, record it—
Who else will tell our story, yours and mine?
Drunk father
Drunk son
The leaf follows the leaf—and so it goes.
The pain too real, the pain too good
Bukowski was no genius,
Just a drunk—
He would've had fun with us,
With you,
With me,
Would've screamed his guts out
At the cry of Vicente—
        "Volver, volver . . . vooooolveeeerrrrr!" the drunk
            would've sung;
                "Me canse de rogarle," he would've shouted to
                    the world;
                        And "El hijo del pueblo," he would've
                            proclaimed to be, just like us.

I once heard a scholar ask why Bukowski was relevant,
And I told her that only a scholar would ask such an
    irrelevant question.

"How so?" she asked.

"Because the scholar doesn't know shit about shit," I told
her.

And she cried and felt stupid,

Inadequate and unworthy of being in my presence.

Then she smoked a cigarette and smirked at my misery.

I'm drunk,

Can you tell?

A mess,

A hurricane!

Destruction is my goal.

Destruction of myself.

No one cries

No one laughs

No one loves

Like me.

Victor Hugo was my friend,

Knew me like a spell.

Wrote about me—*The Condemned Man.*

And he wrote and he wrote and he died!

Boy! do I miss you! and my father—

Do you drink with him?

23

"¡Impresionante—*punto*!"

We made this exclamation our inside joke every time either of us saw or heard something worth noting. Didn't have to be anything too amazing; the simplest things sufficed. Even watching Aarón and Danny bounce a soccer ball off of each other's knees was enough to set us off. If my father saw them doing it before I did, he'd turn to me and say, "¡Impresionante—*punto*!" And I'd echo the expression, putting as much weight on each syllable as my father had done when he'd said it. Then we'd both turn to each other and smile at our own little secret, our own little joke. For more than a week, whenever we saw something that made an impression on us, we'd say this. From a kid hopping off a curb on his bike to a good-looking woman with big breasts and a big behind on a telenovela or an incredible Mexican shoot-out on a low-budget narco movie with the brothers Almada to a street dog taking a shit would inspire us to remark: "¡Impresionante—*punto*!" We worked as a team and we liked it.

We started saying this after watching the Italian film *Le Chiavi di Casa* (*The Keys to the House*). Because in Chihuahua, if you don't have a steady job, hobby, or anything productive to do to help you escape the mundane and drab redundancies of life, watching rented movies at home becomes somewhat of a great substitute. (Alcohol, though, is the preferred choice.)

On one particular night, while everyone else in the house was asleep, my father and I decided to watch a movie we had rented earlier in the day.

It was about the complicated reunion between a father and son—just perfect for us. From an old blanket and sheetless mattress on the living room floor, my father and I watched as the father in the film, after having abandoned his son at birth because of his mental and physical disability, returns to reunite with him, which, on account of the son's disabilities, is difficult to do, but that in the end, because of love, becomes easier. Father and son eventually bond over what had initially separated them. It is love that triumphs.

"¡Punto!" the son keeps repeating in one scene in the film as he dictates a love letter, meant for a girl he likes, to his father, who is typing it out on a laptop.

"¡Punto!" I begin to say after my father says it.

"¡Punto!"

"¡Punto!"

"¡Punto!"

We both laugh at ourselves without looking at each other. We've found something that is equally amusing to the two of us and we play with it like children play with new toys. "¡Punto!" We can't stop saying it even as the movie continues. We go back and forth as if passing a ball to each other. "¡Punto!" he says. "¡Punto!" I say. "¡Punto!" we both say. And we continue to laugh at ourselves.

What a moment. How beautiful it must have been to a stranger's eyes: a father and son making fun of life, having fun with life, having fun with one word. Wish I could've been those eyes. But who would've known it would end so quickly?

Van a decir que ese güey es un sabio bien hecho—
Como un Shakespeare o un Cervantes,
    Pero, ¿quién se la cree? Ni el mismo.
    Pura locura. ¡Punto!
    Lo bueno es que el es el que cuanta el cuento,
        Porque si fuera otro el que lo contara—
            ¡Puta! ¡Que gran abuso de la verdad
            sería!

I prayed he would die. I wanted him gone, completely out of our lives, mine more than anything. I wanted peace. Silence. Moments of tranquility. I wanted a new beginning: "Die! Die! Die, good father—be gone forever! Disappear from this world!"

But I was only angry.

I couldn't take the fights anymore, the hurt and the crying. I could no longer bear the image of the drunk. I'd see him coming and already I wanted him to be leaving. My father, a lonely shadow, depleted of all hope, walking toward me in the light of the moon provoked in me feelings of resentment. Here he comes, I'd think when he'd appear in the distance, *and I wish he wasn't.*

"¿Qué, hijo, no me quieres?"

"Yes, of course I love you. But . . ."

"But what? I'm drunk? I know I'm drunk. I was there, or didn't you know?"

My father would gather my head in his arms and kiss me, and then he would say, "This is how I am, son, this is how your father is—tu papá. I can't hide it from you any longer."

This was life made simple, broken down to its most basic element: LA PURA VERDAD in capital letters so that there could be no misunderstanding.

There's a knife on the table and the thought crosses my mind: I should kill this motherfucker right now, stick him right in the fucking heart and put him out, just like that. I can't stand the way he's looking at me, laughing at me. I should just kill this motherfucker!

We've been drinking sotol and tequila all day, and now we're challenging each other from across the table. He's already beaten me twice, sending me to the ground each time: "You can't do it, son. You're never going to beat me!" But I want to. I want to show him that *he's* the weak one. So I place my elbow again at the center of the table and bring my arm up. "¡A la chingada, qué no?" I tell him with rage and hate in my eyes. "Let's do it again!"

"Bueno," he says calmly, taking on the challenge. "If you want to, I want to." He places his elbow next to mine in the center of the table and faces the palm of his hand toward mine.

"Ya no," Cokis says with concern. She's sitting at one end of the table with us with a cup of beer in her hand. "I don't like this," she continues. "Somebody can get hurt." But son and father don't listen to the drunk woman. This is about manhood, and she doesn't understand.

My father clasps my hand with his. Our hands are firmly

gripping each other. Mine thin and soft: young. His thick and rough: old. "Listo," he says, squeezing my hand tightly. He's looking into my eyes, smiling. He knows I can't beat him. And he's right. He's too strong. His arms and hands are three times the size of mine, plus arm-wrestling's something he's had much experience in as a barroom sport. The last time I arm-wrestled someone was over a decade ago as a teen while serving time in juvenile hall. Plus my wrists are thin, like my fingers, meant more for typing than for a bout like this. But I'm drunk, and I don't give a fuck. There's no courage greater than a drunk's. I fear nothing, and I hate this man across from me; I hate his fucking laugh and I hate the way he drinks. Maybe I'll beat him this time and will be able to laugh at *him* in *his* fucking ugly face, to tell *him* that *he* ain't shit, that *he* can't fuck with me because *I'm* the stronger one.

"¡Que no!" Cokis cautions again before we start. But no one hears her.

"¡Vamos!" my father yells, and our hands stiffen up against each other. We're looking into each other's eyes, piercing each other's spirits with fiery hostility. He never blinks. The fucker makes it all seem so easy. I'm giving it all I've got and he can't hold back a smile. He's smirking at me, at my vain determination, at the reason why I'm drinking even as I write this. I lose my eyes. I want to cry. I know it's coming. I can't win. *Bam!* The back of my hand hits the table and again I hit the floor; my legs are tangled up between the side bars of my wheelchair's footrest. I'm broken, shattered, realizing the extent of my disability. My dignity is destroyed. I have none. I'm no man. I'm a thing. A broken fucking thing. And my father's standing over me with his hand extended to me. I hear Cokis say, "Help him up, Juan. I told you this was a bad idea." I want to kill her, too.

It all makes sense to me:

My father, my beautiful padre. I can see him right in front of me, and he's happy. He's the man I love. He's the one I cry for when he's not around. And here he is, right in front of me. He's on his knees with one hand on my shoulder and the other in his pocket. He's digging for something, a few pesos. "Here, son," he says, handing me a couple of crumpled bills. "Take this, it's for you, for a couple sodas." He leans in to hug me and he gives me a kiss on the cheek. The rough stubble on his face scratches against mine. Doesn't hurt, just feels funny. "Te quiero," he says to me in a soft voice, his eyes never turning away from mine. "You're my son and I love you."

"You see, Juan, I told you not to," I hear Cokis saying again. "¡Ya no! ¡No mas!"

He's walking away now, becoming nothing in the distance. "Papá! Papá!" The little boy is crying out but no one hears him. "Don't go, please!" The little boy opens his hands and two crumpled bills fall to the ground.

"He's a man," I hear my father say to Cokis. "We're both men."

The lights, the music, are each much brighter and louder when drunk. Even the beating of your heart is louder. It beats like a war cry. Beat after beat becomes pound after pound. The Beast is awakened and it wants more. From my chair I let out a loud roar: "Fuck you, puto! I could kill you if I want to. But I won't, and do you know why? Because you're already dead!"

I reach for the knife and hold it in my hand by its wooden handle. I point with it at my father and I say one word: "¡Muerto!"

"Do you want another drink?" Cokis says to me.

"Yes," I tell her while reaching across the table for a lime, "and get one for him, too." While she pours, I cut the lime right down the middle as my father looks on.

"Here," Cokis says, handing us each a shot glass filled with sotol, "drink and forget."

But there is no forgetting, at least for me. I can never forget this—never. It's become part of me, much like my wheelchair. I can never say that it's not there. This is Saturn eating his son.

My father walked out of the house and I rolled after him.

"Where you going?" I asked him from the door.

"Somewhere," he replied without looking back at me.

I hopped down the step and rolled down to the end of the

driveway and told him that I was coming with him. By this time he'd made it to the front of the neighbor's house where he stopped, turned to me, and said, "To where?"

"To wherever the fuck you're going."

"But you don't even know where I'm going."

"I know where you're going. Don't try to pretend like you're not going where we both know you're going."

He laughed. Under the illumination of the streetlight he boomed with laughter. When he was done laughing, he stood silent for a moment while staring at me, contemplating whether to bring me along or not.

"You really want to go?" he asked.

The way I saw it, I was already in hell.

"Yes."

Cokis came out of the house and asked where we were going. We both ignored her.

We took off in my mother's Jeep, in which I'd come to Chihuahua. He drove. It was close to midnight and people were still out. We passed groups of men drinking from the hoods of their cars and tailgates of their trucks and women chatting on concrete steps while their teenage sons and daughters hung out on the street corners talking about sex, drugs, alcohol, love, death, and other adult themes. For the first hour all we did was cruise familiar territory—we went up and down the dirt and asphalt streets of El Cerro de la Cruz. Then my father asked me again, "Do you really want to go?"

"¡Chingado! Aren't you my father, mi papá, el pinchi papá?"

"Pues sí."

"Then let's fucking go! ¡Vamos pues!" He was beginning to piss me off.

We drove out of El Cerro de la Cruz and onto the main highway in the direction of the airport, which was about fifteen minutes away this time of night. A couple of miles before reaching it, we turned onto a dirt road that led into a dark neighborhood. It was so dark that I could barely make out the houses on either side of us. We drove slowly to prevent stirring up too much dust or hitting a large rock or sticking one of our tires into a large pothole.

"It's around here?" I asked my father, looking ahead and to the sides of us.

"Yes," he replied, pointing forward with his right index finger. "It's right there where the car with its lights on is parked."

All I could see were brake lights; I couldn't see the car. It was not until we pulled up right behind it that I was able to see its shape and that there were two persons inside. For a few seconds, as I analyzed the car and our surroundings, I was at a loss as to what was going on. I had no clue about where my father had brought me. Everywhere around us was dark and dusty, and silent. I rolled down my window and aside from the motor of our Jeep, I didn't hear anything—no voices, crickets, cars, nothing. It was quiet all over—scary quiet, the type of quiet that makes you nervous; the type of quiet that always leads to a crime; the someone's-going-to-be-murdered-tonight type of quiet. Finally, a hand came out through the chain-link fence that the car in front of us was parked next to and handed something to the hand sticking out from its passenger side. Cocaine.

When we drove up to the fence after the car in front of us slowly drove off, I noticed there was a young man on the other side of it sitting still on something, and I could barely make him out in the darkness. "What's it gonna be?" he asked me as he brought his face forward. I turned to my father for the answer; and leaning into my side and projecting his voice out the window to the dark figure on the other side of the fence, my father said, "Dos tostones." Toston is slang for fifty pesos, so what my father had just asked for was a hundred pesos' (about ten U.S. dollars') worth of coke. The figure heard the order, pulled two small rectangular envelope-looking folds, no bigger than the top end of my index finger, and held them up close to the fence to show us that he had them ready to go.

"Well, pay the man," my father ordered me. Motherfucker!

"Right. Hold on," I said to my father, and then to the figure. I'd been buying drugs from dealers ever since I was thirteen and all of a sudden I was forgetting how it all worked. I should've had the money in my hand ready to go way before turning into the fucking street. So after fidgeting through my pockets, I finally pulled out a crumbled-up hundred-peso bill and handed it to the figure through the baseball-size hole in the fence, just like the person in the passenger seat of the car that had been in front of us had done only moments earlier. Once the figure had the money secure in his hands and had checked it to make sure it was the correct amount, he pushed his hand through the same hole and dropped the two small envelopes in my hand.

"There you go," the figure quietly and calmly said. "Enjoy."

"Gracias," I courteously replied, clutching tightly to the two envelopes.

Again I turned to look at my father. This is it, I thought, staring deeply into his glossy eyes, there's only one way to go from here. My father released his foot from the brake, softly stepped on the gas, and off we went into the night.

Once on the main road, we headed back toward El Cerro. I didn't say anything. Just thought about what the moment when we opened up the envelopes was going to be like. My father, on the other hand, didn't seem to be having the same thoughts as me. In fact, he'd become more talkative. He began to talk so much you would've thought he'd already done a line. As soon as we drove away from the hole, he began to go on about how it all worked. "This is all one big mafia," he said. "There's a shitload of places like this one all over Chihuahua. Day or night, it doesn't matter. Estos cabrones are always selling. But they only sell tostones, that's it—nothing under and nothing over fifty pesos. No, here it isn't like in the U.S., where you can buy a gram or an eight ball or whatever you want. No, here only tostones, and no discounts. And a toston isn't a lot, maybe like a little under a twenty in the U.S. And don't think it's a lot for less than what you'd pay in the U.S. It's just that over here people are poor, so the dealers adjust their prices to what they know people can pay. Imagine if we had to pay twenty dollars for a toston, we wouldn't be able to support our habit. Fifty pesos ain't bad, about ten American dollars. But tostones is all there is. So if you want to buy more, then you have to buy more tostones, which sucks because after you finish one toston you quickly want another one and then you have to come back, and everybody usually always comes back, which is what they want. They want you to keep coming back, como en el Micdonas [McDonald's]. It's good soda though. It gets you going right away. As soon as you sniff it, you can feel it all over your body and face. Esta a toda madre. We should be able to get at least four good lines out of each toston, you'll see. Do you have them?" He stops talking and turns to me with a serious look.

"Yes, they're in my pocket."

I'd been holding the two envelopes in my clenched fist inside my pocket. I kept thinking about them and about how fucked-up the place we were headed was going to be. We were headed nowhere good; but just like my father, I, too, was itching to get there fast. I wanted a line just as much as he did. I wanted the high, the fuck-everything feeling. I didn't care anymore. Didn't care that it was my father sitting next to me, that we'd just scored coke together and that we were now going to do it together, too. Fuck it! I quickly changed my reality to where I'm cruising with one of my homeboys back in California after having just scored and we're on our way to get loaded. There's no remorse, nothing to be ashamed of. This is the journey of the wounded heart. Cocaine is nothing new to me, I'm thinking. Just do it.

"Pues saca uno," my father says. "What are you waiting for?"

As I reached into my pocket for the tostones, my father pulled to the side of the road and there, on this warm summer night in Chihuahua, as most of the city slept, my father and I committed ourselves to a part of hell from whence we could never return. He took one of the envelopes from my unfurled fist and eagerly opened it. On a blank CD case he let a small pile of white powder fall and quickly cut it up with a pocket knife he'd been carrying.

"You have a bill?" he said.

I dug into my pockets and pulled out the first three bills I felt: two American five-dollar bills and a ten. I handed him one of the fives and shoved the other two bills back into my pocket, along with the other envelope. My father rolled up the five, put it to his nose, brought his head down to the CD case, which he was holding up in front of him close to the steering wheel, and inhaled. Then it was my turn.

There is nothing like a cocaine high. The world looks and feels prettier, and there's no reason to cry. The euphoria takes over and the first thing you want to do is open your mouth and say how good it feels, or how good it feels to not feel. You're numb, alive, and cold all over. You're something excited. You want to talk and you want to love. You want to tell someone that you love them. All is good. All couldn't be better.

"Is it good?" my father asks.

"Yes, real good," I tell him, tilting my head back against the headrest, allowing the powder to make its way down my throat—this is what we call the drips.

My father looks at me, laughs, and says, "That's it, hijo, that's the way you do it."

We ended up at a strip-club-slash-whorehouse close to where we'd scored the coke. There we salivated over the naked putas and drank more beers—all paid for from my pocket. We also smoked a shitload of cigarettes and talked about a whole lot of nothing—a common side effect of cocaine. Besides, what could a son possibly talk to his father about at a whorehouse? The whores, I suppose. The music was too loud and the whores too fucking beautiful. I wanted to escape with one. I wanted to leave the side of this man and plunge my happiness into pussy. I wanted to share my high with a woman, especially the one who'd brought us the beers. She was special gorgeous: tall and big breasted with the face of a telenovela actress. I told her this as she popped open our beers and she smiled. She told me that

I was handsome, too, muy guapo, and I believed her. I tipped her a five-dollar bill, and she kissed me on the cheek. She also whispered into my ear that if I needed *anything* to just ask her. "*Lo que sea*," she said seductively, and again I believed her. She seemed like a woman I could trust. "Claro," I told her, grinding my teeth like a crackhead. "Come back in a few minutes and I'll have a list for you." She smiled, turned, and walked away, dripping sex all over.

Noticing that I couldn't take my eyes off the telenovela whore's ass, my father placed his hand on my shoulder and said, "You like that? You could have her, you know, for as little as fifty dollars." I thought for a second: Fifty dollars? I have fifty dollars. There was a motel next door, a place meant only for fucking putas, rented only by the hour. That's where we went.

We hopped into the truck and my father drove the puta and me a few yards to the motel. I suppose we could've just walked there, but the dirt ground was too much for me, and the cold too much for the puta, who was only wearing a bright pink bikini top and a matching thong. She was also wearing cheap stiletto heels.

The motel was as shady as they get. We drove into a U-shape structure of small rooms that each had their own carport. A figure came out of a small kiosk to the left of the entrance and walked up to the driver-side window. "What will it be?" he asked. "My son and this bella mujer need a room," my father replied. He had said "my son" with emphasis, as if with pride, as if we were in a coming-of-age story where the father takes the son to have his first sexual experience with a prostitute. "One hundred pesos," the man said. I couldn't see his face clearly. He was short and barely reached the window. All I could see were his eyes and the top of his head, which didn't reveal much. "There it is, hijo, cien pesos," my father said as he dropped his arm across the puta's lap, who was sitting snuggly between us, and waved his open palm in front of me. I didn't say anything, just reached into my pocket, took out a roll of bills, peeled off a ten, and dropped it in my father's palm. The puta watched it go from my hand to his and then to the attendant's. I couldn't stop staring at her legs, pussy, and tits. She in her thong and me loaded as fuck, and we were about to go fuck. She loved my American dollars and I loved her Mexican everything.

But something strange happened, something unexpectedly magical. Something quick. My telenovela actress morphed into something amazingly other than a prostitute. In the light of the motel room she became just another simple woman with stretch marks on her big breasts and stomach and a face with way too much makeup: a lie, nothing more than a damsel in distress, a poor soul in need of a muchacho with gringo bills. That was me, the horny American-wannabe with coke up his nose and the crazy father pushing the issue.

And I had lost the desire to fuck. I was too drunk and high, and in the light of that motel room, the puta just didn't seem so pretty anymore. All her defects had come to light, and I became disappointed. I just couldn't get past all of the stretch marks on her breasts and stomach and all the makeup on her face. She was a grown woman after all, and I, still relatively young and shallow. This was a good thing, though, because what happened in that motel room after I'd done away with the "fucking" option turned out to be all the more wonderful. We talked. She fondled my penis and we talked. But what could a young man with a college degree talk to a prostitute about? "Do you know who Henri de Toulouse-Lautrec is?" I asked her as she gently stroked my penis. We were both on the bed. I was lying on my back with my shirt off, my pants and underwear pulled down to my knees, and she was on her knees next to my legs. "No, who's that?" she replied, looking at me, her hand still moving slowly up and down.

"He was a famous painter from France, a great one."

"Oh yeah? And what did he paint?"

"Prostitutes. Well, he painted other things, too, but mostly prostitutes. Lots and lots of prostitutes. He loved to paint them."

"Is that all he did?"

"Well, no. I told you, he painted other things, too."

"No, that's not what I mean. I mean, did he do other things with the prostitutes besides paint them, like, would he fuck them?"

"Oh, I'm sorry. I didn't realize that that's what you were talking about. But yes, he did. He fucked them often, probably more than he painted them."

This is where I first buried my father, in this shitty motel room where this wicked conversation took place. I buried him here, where I found solace in a conversation with a prostitute. Here is where the funeral took place; here is where I laid him to rest—yo y mi puta lo enterramos.

And I loved it. All of it. Loved the scene: something dirty and immoral, something you could never turn back from. I'd landed on Mars and loved it more than earth. My puta was like a lonely cactus in the desert, existing only as a form of resistance against the elements that every day worked to destroy her, and I was like the happiest boy ever, slowly coming apart inside. I stared at her thick thighs and the cellulite that marked their thickest areas, looked like moon craters, like dimpled white cheese, and I stared at the stretch marks on her belly, marks left after having given life. I was beginning to appreciate something ugly, something often disguised. She was nice, kind to me, didn't care that my dick remained limp like a dead fish. She played with it regardless, smacking it against my leg like a whip, and I smiled and she smiled back. We were both broken, and we understood each other's pain.

"So this Toulouse," I continued, "he loved prostitutes—las amaba! To him they were the most beautiful type of women to paint, and the saddest. Are you sad?"

But whether she was sad or not, I would never know because she never answered that question. She just continued to love me, to do her job. She rubbed my chest and her hands felt good, soft and firm, like a heavy breeze on a hot summer night—all was good, all felt good. And I wanted to touch her breasts, too, but I kept talking. "María Magdalena was a prostitute, too, you know, and Jesus loved her." And I wanted more cocaine, but it was too far at the other end of the room on the table, next to my wallet and my green card.

After I stopped talking about prostitutes and of the historical men who came to appreciate them, this woman began to tell me about her children, and of how if she didn't do what she did, they'd probably go hungry and not have a roof over their heads. She had two young sons and a daughter, all not yet teenagers. She spoke endearingly about them, telling me that she hoped they would never find out about what she did because it would kill her. I asked her about their father, and right when she was about to tell me there was a knock on the door. "¡Hijo! ¡Hijo!" It was my father. "Open the door!"

"This motherfucker," I said aloud to myself. I couldn't believe that he was already at the door. It hadn't even been fifteen minutes, and I'd told him to return in half an hour. "Espera," I said to the woman. "Let me go see what he wants." I pulled up my underwear and pants, quickly zipped up, and jumped on my chair.

"¡Hijo!" my father yelled again before I got to the door.

"Hold on!" I yelled back. When I unlocked the door, he quickly turned the knob and pushed his way in. "¿Qué paso?" I said, but he ignored me and walked right into the room, looked at the woman on the bed, and said to her, "Are you done? Did he perform well?"

"Yeah, we're done," I said before the woman could say anything.

"All right then," he said, turning to me, "where's the coke?"

That's why he'd come so soon. He wanted more coke. He couldn't wait, as junkies never can.

"It's right there, on the counter," I said, pointing at the paper next to my wallet in which it was folded. He quickly walked over to it, unfolded it, and let some of the white powder fall onto the counter.

"¿Quieres?" he said to me.

"Sí."

Then he looked at the woman, who was now standing up next to the bed with her little purse in her hand, and asked her if she, too, wanted a line, but she quietly said no. As I counted off fifty dollars, my father cut up a couple of lines. I rolled over to the woman and handed her the money. I heard my father snort behind me. I thanked her for everything and told her that she was a beautiful mujer. My father called me and I went to snort my line.

After we dropped the woman off back at the club, my father and I went back into the night and let it swallow us. It was more cocaine and alcohol until the sun came up.

I woke up with shortness of breath and I felt really dizzy. My heart was racing. I thought I was overdosing again, but I hadn't done any drugs. My sight was going black. Oh shit! Oh shit! I think I need to go to the hospital. I woke up my sister Samantha, told her what was wrong, and just as she had done before, she quickly drove me to the hospital, all the while reminding me of how I need to stop drinking and doing drugs, that I'm going to die one day if I don't. And though I'm hearing her, I'm not really listening, because in that moment all I care about is getting to the hospital and making this terrible feeling go away.

"What's bothering you?" the nurse asks.

"I'm having trouble breathing," I tell her.

"Do you have any pain?"

"Yes."

"Where?"

"In my chest, but it's more like tightness."

"Do you have asthma?"

"No."

"Do you smoke or drink?"

"Yes."

"Do you do drugs?"

"Sometimes."

"What kind?"

"The good kind."

"Be specific."

"Cocaine."

"Not good."

"I know."

"When was the last time you smoke or drink or do drugs?"

"Last night."

"Last night?"

"Yes. But I only smoke and drink. No cocaine."

"No cocaine? Are you sure?"

"I'm sure."

I hadn't been lying. I'd checked myself into the emergency room that day over what I thought was the world's worst hangover. I thought I was dying. I couldn't breathe and every light including the sun was going dark on me. But my nurse was sweet and understanding. My breath smelled of alcohol and cigarettes and I was trying not to point it at anybody, especially my nurses. There were two of them working on me now, both loud Filipinas, but lovable. They checked my vitals and admitted me into the hospital. When the ER doctor finally came to check my breathing and my heart, he was unable to find anything wrong, so he requested that I stay until the pulmonary specialists did further tests on my lungs and my blood had been checked. But the doctor was just following a hospital protocol that in the end wasn't going to bear any results. The nurses, on the other hand, had a better way of diagnosing my problem. When the doctor left, they continued to ask me questions about my drinking problem.

"So you drink last night," one asked as the two hooked me up to an IV.

"Yes."

"And what did you drink, and how much?"

"Tequila."

"Tequila!?" the two let out simultaneously as they turned to look at each other. They had arrived to the base of the problem.

"That's why," said nurse number one, bending down to look me straight in my eyes.

"How much did you drink?" asked nurse number two.

"I don't know. A lot."

"Wow!" they both said. Then nurse number one said, "You drink too much."

"Maybe," I said, though I knew she was right.

"Was it good?" nurse number two asked, cracking a smile. But before I could answer her, nurse number one jumped in and added, "Yeah, if it was good then you should have brought us some so we can all have a party, no?"

The three of us laughed. It was a joke, and I was the butt of it, because here I was chatting about tequila with two Filipina nurses after having checked myself into the ER because of a false near-death experience that had been brought on by a hangover. The absurdity of the whole thing was beginning to dawn on me. And even though I now realized it and was already feeling better, I couldn't just get up and say, "I feel better. Thank you. I will be leaving now." Nope. I had to wait and just play the whole thing out until the doctor properly discharged me. In the meantime, I'd have my two nurses to keep me company and to lift my spirits and to let me know that I was going to live to drink another day.

A breathing treatment, an X-ray of my lungs, an ultrasound of my heart, and a blood test later, the doctor was able to conclude that there was absolutely nothing wrong with me.

"Well, just as I had thought," he said as he walked into the room. "There is nothing wrong with you. You are too young to be having any heart problems or to have emphysema. I think that perhaps you just had a bad morning." My original nurse, nurse number one, who was in the room, upon hearing this, looked straight at me with a devious smile, as if the two of us knew something that the doctor didn't.

"I think you're right, Doc," I said, "because I feel much better. So what do you say I go home now?"

"Sure thing. We'll have you out of here in a couple of hours. We just need to do some paperwork."

"Please, do hurry. I have a date tonight. It would be terrible if I stood her up!"

"We'll do our best."

"Thank you."

My mother, who'd come with my brother to pick me up after my sister had left while I was being checked in, stood at the side of my hospital bed with my brother and looked on me with chastising pity.

"Son, when are you going to learn, when are you going to realize that you need to stop drinking?"

"Today, Ma, today. That's it. That's it. I'm not going to do it anymore. So no more drinking and no more smoking either. None of that shit. I'm too crippled for it." I said this with a sense of determination and authority, like I was really foreseeing my future and gaining full control of it. But my mother, being the shrewd woman that she is, reminded me of what I was apparently forgetting:

"That's what every borracho says, son, but he never does. That is his dilemma. Must I remind you of the words of the borracho in *El Principito*?"

"Yes, Ma, remind me."

"He says he drinks because he's ashamed, and he's ashamed because he drinks. It's a cycle, son. You are trapped in a cycle that only you can break."

Even so, I believed what I was telling myself and my mother. I'd had enough. These hospital visits for alcohol and drugs were getting old and I was tired. And this time it was different: I was dying. But I was always dying. And the Little Prince can't always be right; there's always an exception, isn't there?

"No, Ma, I'm serious!" I pleaded with her. "You have to believe me!"

But no, my mother didn't believe me. She trusted in the words of El Principito more than in those of her own son. And rightfully so because later on, when I was on my date, I ordered myself a Modelo Especial to go with my dinner. My date didn't want to drink alone. "Come on," she insisted after ordering her drink, "we have to toast together!"

I remembered the hospital, the nurses, my mother and her words, but then I saw across from me a face I couldn't say no to.

"One then, and only because you're so fucking beautiful!"

"Great!"

We toasted, we drank, and we both got wasted that night, and after that I never saw her again. And so goes the dilemma of el borracho. My mother, I've come to learn throughout my many years of life, is always right.

24

When you're writing a book, everyone wants to know two things: what the book's about, and the title. I give them both in the title: *My Father the Pope*. But it's never enough. They always want details. I understand why. I mean, why the pope?

My father was no pope, in any religious, moral, or idealistic sense. He was far from it. He did, however, consider himself a Jehovah's Witness, but that was only because my grandma, his mother, had been one, and a good one, too, very devout and holy, everything that my father was not. Only thing he was devout about was the bottle. The bottle was his higher power.

In Spanish pope translates to papa, which is the same word used for dad, which is less formal than padre, which in English translates to father. I never called my dad padre, and neither did any of my brothers or sisters. Most Spanish-speaking children don't call their fathers padre. Sounds too formal—a phrase reserved for a priest. And I never called him papá either, which is the most commonly used term in Spanish to refer to one's father; it's somewhat informal, but still carries reverence and respect. This is what my brothers and Axcel called our father: papá. I, however, simply called him pa'—that is, before I started calling him güey.

I felt weird calling him papá; didn't feel natural. There was a great chasm between us that had to be acknowledged, and the way I acknowledged it was by not giving myself completely over to him as a son. In a way, it was a defense mechanism, how I kept myself from being completely sucked into his world. It helped that I didn't live with him like my brothers and sister, but it was also a conscious decision that I'd made from an early age.

Maybe I'd called him papá when I was a child, early on in my life, but as far as I can recall, I always called him pa', even at seven and eight years of age. Pa' this, pa' that, and even that felt weird at times, and for both reasons: because I didn't feel that it was enough and because I felt that it was too much.

On the way to Cokis's house toward the airport, on the right side of the main road, painted upon a white stucco wall, is the image of Pope John Paul II, a favorite among the Mexican people. Only his head and upper body are painted; he's waving at the passersby on the road, as if wishing them a farewell on their way to the airport. We were never on our way to the airport unless it was my time to fly back to the United States; instead, we were on our way to Cokis's house, which we visited once or twice or three times a week, and every time on our way there, we came across the pope and his waving hand.

Usually I'd just say to myself, as we passed the pope, "Hi, Pope"; but on one particular occasion, as my father drove and I sat shotgun and Cokis and both of my brothers sat in the back, as we passed the pope, I said, out loud, "Pinche papa." Maybe I was angry because my father and I had been fighting the night before and I resented everything having to do with fathers, even the fucking pope, who, with his arm waving and his cynical smile mocked the collective misery riding inside our car.

Neither Cokis nor my brothers had been saying much

during the drive since we'd left El Cerro de la Cruz. Everyone was on edge since the previous night's fight. It felt easier today to just stay quiet. It took too much effort to speak, and we were all completely drained of emotion. We were all, even my father, damaged souls taking this time to convalesce.

But when I said "Pinche papa" out loud, everyone turned to look at me, wondering what I was going to say, especially my father who thought I'd been talking to him. He looked at me and squinted, probably thinking I was about to curse at him, but I just looked at him and said, "What? I wasn't talking to you. I was talking to the fucking pope! Are you the fucking pope?" Then, in a serious tone, he said to me, "Sí, I am El Papa, your papá," and then he turned to my brothers and said that he was their papá as well, so that made him El Papa: The Pope.

Shit was funny, and we all laughed quietly. El Papa kept driving with a sense of accomplishment, happy to have let us all know quite frankly that he was "our father the pope."

It was official: From then on our father was no longer just our pa' or papá; he was "El Papa." We all had elevated him, turned him into what he had always wanted to be: something grander than what he actually was. He loved it. Hearing us call him El Papa was like taking a drink through his ears; he became intoxicated by it. From that day on, he'd smile and put a bounce in his step every time he'd walk through the door into the house and I'd announce, "Ya llego El Papa." It was as if I'd led a line of trumpet players to mark his arrival. He'd turn to me and give me a look of approval, encouraging me to keep it coming.

"El Papa!" someone else would say, and applaud and cheer. And then laughter would follow, which at first my father wouldn't mind; but quickly the laughter would become too much and he would come to resent it. He would resent all of us. The joke was made evident, and he was the butt of it. He saw that we were laughing at him and not with him. El Papa was not something to cheer but something to laugh at. Because he was no El Papa. He was, instead, a caricature of El Papa, a caricature of a father, a caricature of a sick and dying alcoholic who just happened to be a father.

The damage had been done and there was no going back. Juan Jesús Silva Sánchez had gone from being Father, to being Dad, to being güey, to finally being El Papa—that cartoonish image of the pope on the side of a highway eternally waving, like a fool, at passersby. Making matters worse, a few days after christening him with this name, somebody wrote *Pecador* across the pope's image, perhaps in protest of his cover-up of the hundreds of child abuse cases that were coming out around this time. Only my father and I were in the truck that day, and though we both turned to the pope and clearly saw the word graffitied over him, neither of us said anything.

I almost felt sad for him, like I wanted to turn to him and tell him that I was sorry for making fun of him, like I wanted to tell him that he was a good dad and that he was better than the fucking pope and that the motherfucker who'd written that over the pope was a piece of shit. But wanting to do something and actually doing it are two different things, and I went with the former. I was too proud, too angry still. This man, after all, had threatened violence against me and my brothers. He had requested the assistance of other grown men, drug addicts, to help him beat us, and I'd firmly held a six-inch knife in preparation to stab anyone who attacked me or my brothers, even my own father. I would have stabbed him over and over, and I probably would have killed him, too. And the saddest part of all is that I probably wouldn't have felt any remorse afterward.

The person responsible for the graffiti over the pope's image was right; the pope, El Papa, was a sinner, responsible for countless crimes against humanity, from genocide to sexual abuse against children, guilty of every crime in history committed by the Catholic Church. And my father was guilty, too. He was a sinner; he was a terrible man, guilty of murdering dreams and terrorizing a family. But always, just like the pope, he was still papá, el papá, our papá. There was no undoing this reality. He would be our father until the day he died.

The fight had started as soon as he'd come home, drunk. Earlier in the day he'd asked to borrow my uncle Chuy's truck; said he'd be back in a few minutes, that he was only going to go inquire about a job. He returned seven hours later, drunk. There had been no job. He had used the truck to go drink and get high somewhere, but he wouldn't say where. Every time I asked him where he'd gone he'd say that it didn't matter, that he was back now, and that that was all that mattered. Angry and hurt, I went outside to calm myself down. My brothers followed. Outside they tried to console me, telling me to forget about everything, that the solution was to just never let him borrow the truck again. But to me it was more than that; it was just another betrayal by the man who was supposed to never betray you.

While my brothers kept trying to calm me down, an old white station wagon rolled up in front of the driveway, and inside of it were four grown men. My brothers and I were quiet and waited for them to say something. They talked to one another for a few seconds and then the one in the back closer to us popped his head out of the window and said, "¿Está Juan?"

"Yes," Aarón replied. "He's inside. I'll go get him." But before he could go inside our father came out. Instantly I sensed that something bad was going to happen, so I whispered to Aarón to go inside anyway and get a couple of big kitchen knives. He did. And as he walked in, our father walked up to the station wagon and greeted the men. "¿Qué onda, Juan?" they said to him, and he responded with the same phrase. At this point Aarón came out and handed me one of the knives, which was about eight inches long. I placed it on my lap and extended my shirt over it. I could see Aarón concealing his at his side. "What are you up to, Juan?" one of the men asked him, and he said to them, "Well, I'm here fighting with these three little fuckers. They like to gang up on me." As he said this, he looked back and pointed at us, and then he snickered as he moved out of their way so they could see us. Then the one in the back who had first asked for him said, "Do you need help? We'll help you take care of them right now." It was then that I reached beneath my shirt and clutched the knife's handle. "Órale," my father said, "let's do it." My brothers and I looked at each other for a second and then back at them, telling one another that we were ready for whatever was going to happen next. But as the man in the back was about to open his door, our father kept him from opening it all the way and told them that he had only been kidding. "Son mis hijos," he told them, "and I love them more than they know, and even though they don't love me." Again, he was the victim. Then he turned to us and said, "Órale, hijos, you want me gone, then I'm leaving." We didn't say anything. We were too angry and disappointed in him to even tell him to fuck off. We watched him get in that station wagon with those men who were just like him and drive away. He wouldn't return until the following morning, and he would act as if nothing had ever happened.

25

Leaning against the car on one elbow and holding a caguama, she's between tears and laughter. I can't make sense of her. I want to know how she feels and what she plans on doing with the rest of her life. Will she move on, remarry, learn to love again, and put her years with my father behind, or will she trade her "tomorrows to remain in yesterday" and remain in mourning forever? I hope she will love again, find her life again. My father had taken so much from her and caused her so much pain. Mourning him forever will only keep her in the shadow of his death, chained to a ghost, and she will die miserable. I don't want that for her. I want her to find a new path: to be free and see the world as a blank canvas waiting to be covered in colors, in images without lines; I want her to see the world as limitless, as a place where she can dream and make those dreams come true, something my father had always kept her from doing.

"For twenty years," she says after taking a drink from the caguama, "I lived with your father, and for those twenty years I never stopped loving him, even in the moments after he'd hit me. Because that's how your father was, a bad man, but *my* bad man, and I loved him, we all loved him—your brothers, your sister, your uncles, and even you. I know that you loved him even though you say you didn't, and you know what, he loved you, too. He would always talk about you, to me, to your brothers and sister, to everyone. He was proud of you for being so smart, for accomplishing all your goals. When you graduated the first time he celebrated for a week straight, drinking and listening to music. I know that is not a good thing, but he would say that he was celebrating his son graduating college, and he would play 'Hermoso Cariño' a thousand times a day, and sometimes he would cry like a little boy. You are lucky, Obed. You are lucky because you never had to live with him. You are lucky for having a strong mother and for being like she is. Sometimes I used to wish that I could have been more like your mother and left your father the way she did. But where would I have gone? Where would I have taken my kids? They would have hated me if I had left your father. They all loved him too much. Look at how sad they are. Look at me. I have nothing but my kids, and you, and this caguama."

She's crying now, tears flooding her face, and snot bubbling at her nostrils. No more an in-between. The laughter is completely gone. But I can see that she's happy, light and free. There's a realization in her words. Epiphany. She no longer has to leave, run away with her kids. She looks up toward the blue sky and her tears rush to her ears and her heart says goodbye to Juan, and she takes another drink from her caguama.

"Everything's going to be all right, Cokis," I say to her. "Juan Silva's not going to be coming home anymore."

"I know. I know."

～

I saw him hit her once. We were at a bar: me, my father, and her. We had gone there to see and hear Axcel sing. She was part of a small band and had been wanting me to come out and see her sing while I was in town. So here we were, drinking, smoking, and watching my sister perform in front of a small audience at a seedy bar on an otherwise uneventful Saturday night. There was a pool table there, and my father and I played a few games and drank and smoked while Cokis sat and drank at our table watching Axcel sing. We were having a great time, feeling merry. Then something changed. It came suddenly, like an unforeseen tsunami. My father and I had come back to the table to sit with Cokis and drink shots of tequila with her. Up to this point in the night we'd only been drinking beer, but I suggested we drink tequila to cheer and celebrate Axcel, who was doing a fine job of keeping the party going and everyone entertained with her lovely voice.

We have one round, then another, then another, then another, then another, all at my behest, then suddenly, as I was about to order another one from the waitress, I turn to my father and Cokis, and see my father's forehead connecting with hers. The shock of it all paralyzes me. I'm staring at Cokis as blood is running down her face from an open gash on her forehead. My father is casually sitting back and taking a drink from his beer. I can't hear anything even though I know Cokis is crying and Axcel is still singing, unaware of what has just happened. I'm now staring at my father, but he's looking ahead, knowing that my eyes are on him. "¡Hijo de su puta madre!" I yell at him, and then roll over to Cokis. I grab a napkin from the neighboring table and hand it to her; she receives it with her bloody hands and places it over the gash, but it's not enough. The blood keeps pouring out. I continue to yell at my father, asking him why he'd hit her, but he doesn't answer. He pushes over the table, stands up, and yells at Cokis to stop crying. Now everyone in the bar has taken notice of what's happening, even

Axcel, whose voice has gone silent—the band has stopped playing. Cokis is bleeding profusely, I'm cursing at my father who's
cursing at Cokis, and there's a flipped table on the floor. Three
men walk up to us, wanting to know what's going on. My father tells them to mind their business, and it escalates from
there. Suddenly my father is fighting with all three of them
and women are screaming. I see my father taking punches and
I become engulfed with rage. I'm punching away at the men
punching my father, while desperately trying to not fall out
of my wheelchair. But they're all too strong and I'm too disabled. They're dragging my father toward the entrance as they
continue pummeling him. I make one last attempt to defend
him. I grab a bottle from the nearest table and break it over the
back of the head of one of the men, at which point he turns to
me and punches me on the right side of my face, knocking me
out of my wheelchair. Cokis and Axcel run over to me and try
to help me up, but I'm too drunk, too wild. There's an uncontrollable blaze inside of me. Everything is out of my control.
From the floor, I watch as the three men continue to beat my
father and eventually drag him out of the bar. I shut my eyes
and wish that I could kill those men for what they're doing to
him. When I open my eyes, Cokis's blurry face is right there,
looking at me through a stream of blood.

"Obed, ¿estás bien?" she asks, and instead of answering her
question, I ask her, "Why did he hit you?"

"No se."

I'm drained from being in the sun all day and still feeling
hungover. Cokis offers me a drink from her caguama, but I say

no. Then my tío Polo, who's leaning against the hood of his car, offers me a drink from his pint of Hornitos tequila from which he's just taken a drink, and I say no to that, too. I'm still feeling discomfort in my stomach, and I want nothing more than to take a shit. My guts feel full and dry. I also need to sleep. So after a few more minutes of watching my brothers mope and Cokis and Polo disappear into their bottles, I excuse myself and go to my room. At first, Cokis tries to stop me, begging me to stay, to drink with her, and telling me that others are on their way with more beer, that this is where la fiesta will be taking place, that this is where my father will be receiving his final despedida. I still refuse. I'm too tired and my body hurts.

In the room, before falling asleep, I think about my father and of how he'd fucked everything up, and I think of how much I already miss him and of how it would be nice to take a shit. I think of going to the bathroom and making another attempt at moving my bowels, but in the end I'm just too tired. My body aches all over, well, the part of it that I can feel, especially my back. But it feels good to finally be out of the sun and to be able to lie down on the bed and stretch. Soon, I'm fast asleep.

I sleep for nearly four hours. It's dark out and not so fucking hot anymore when I wake up. And suddenly, I have the urge to do something, anything, to move around. I want to feel something pleasant. I think about Rocío and how nice it would be to see her. I also still want to take a shit, but I quickly decide to wait until morning to do that. I also want to change my clothes because my pants and shirt are wrinkled and shrouded in dust, but I also decide to do that in the morning. Fuck it, I'm already dressed. So when I get out of bed and into my wheelchair, all I do is take my shirt off, leaving on only my tank top.

Cokis was right, people were coming over. Almost every character that had stayed up drinking at the parlor the night before is now hanging out and drinking on the driveway and in front of the house. Music is playing loudly—rancheras and corridos. Seems more like a party for a birthday than a mournful gathering after a funeral. When I come out, everyone lets out a welcoming cheer. I smile and say hello. Quickly I'm offered a beer by my cousin Víctor-Manuel, who's closest to the door. "Toma, güey, una cerveza," he says, putting a beer in my hand. It's already open. Aarón, Danny, Cokis, and some of my other cousins come and cheer with me as I take my first drink, and then, for a moment, the scene from the day before, when I first arrived at the parlor, is replayed, with different people coming up to me and hugging me and saying hello. I don't like the attention, and once it's over I quickly integrate myself into the party and drink away with everyone else.

I find myself talking to Víctor-Manuel, my cousin Veronica, and my tía María. All three of them are sitting on the floor of the driveway with their backs against the house, and all three have a beer in their hand. I'm right across from them drinking my own beer. We're laughing and cracking jokes when something catches my attention: My tía María's two front top teeth are missing—eight and nine. What the fuck! I swear they were there last night. I'm squinting, looking closely at this black gap in her mouth, wondering if I'm already drunk. But I can't be. I've barely started drinking. Then my tía María, noticing my confused face, says, "¿Qué paso, mijo? ¿Por qué me ve así?" I'm embarrassed to ask, but I can't help it any longer, so after taking a moment to think of what to say, I come out with it. "Your top teeth," I tell her, "they're gone." "No," she says, "they're not gone," and in an instant, after she closes her mouth and opens it again, there they are, just like the night before. What the fuck! Now I'm really blown. And the three of them are laughing, holding up their beers. They're in on the joke, and I'm struggling to figure it out. Then my tía closes and opens her mouth again, and again the teeth are gone. More laughter. Then there they are again. More laughter. And I finally get it. And I'm laughing, too. The fucking things are fake. Her real teeth are gone. These are attached to a retainer and are a temporary replacement. Somehow she's been flipping them backward and then forward, making them disappear and then reappear. And all of a sudden I start thinking of my father and my tíos Mundo and Polo. I run my tongue over my own two front top teeth and think about the genetic possibilities, of the odds and where I fit in them.

The next day when I wake up with my front facing the ceiling, the first thing I do is run my tongue over my entire crown of upper teeth. Then I laugh at what I'm thinking. No, that shit'll never happen to me. I take care of mine. I see my dentist every six months. She always notifies me when it's time. The second thing I do is get up and go to the bathroom: *complete relief*! It is then that I know that all is going to be all right.

26

Ten years after my father's death and the day I wrote down the first word of this story in a journal, I come to the end of this tale as a forty-year-old man. In eight years I will be the exact age my father was when he died. It's taken me longer to write this book than it will take for me, from this moment on, to get to that point. And I have to ask myself: Am I the man that my father was? If I am, then I, too, will probably not make it past fifty; and if I am not, it won't be alcohol that kills me.

I am two people.

I am the man who is the smart college professor who wears a tie and inspires his students, who by his mere presence shows them that they, too, can aspire to complete their degrees and live out their career goals. I am the man who gives inspirational talks about redemption and overcoming obstacles to large groups of young people at different college campuses and other institutions. I am the man who was pardoned by an immigration judge and allowed to remain in the United States. I am the man who paints, the man who writes. I am the man who is always smiling and seems to be unaffected by stress or even sorrow. I am the man who can tell you a thousand stories and make you fall in love with him. I am the man who can love you back with everything that he has. I am the man who cries during sad movies and cries even more when reading sad books. I am the man who is sensitive and caring. I am the man who is a good friend. I am the man whose friends and family members ask to be their best man or the godfather of their child. I am the man who is a brother, a nephew, a grandson, a cousin, and most importantly—I am the man who is the son of his mother.

But if I am that man, then I am also this man: I am the man who rolls up to the bar, has four double shots of whiskey within a couple of hours and then begins to slur his language. I am the drunk man. I am the drunk man at the bar who spills food all over his shirt because he has no sense of being. I am the drunk man who falls off his wheelchair in the street at midnight and has to be helped up by a total stranger. I am the drunk man who wakes up on the kitchen floor with piss all over his pants. I am the drunk man who gets a DUI after his pardon and is afraid to return to Mexico to visit his brothers because of it. I am the drunk man who lost his wife because he couldn't stop drinking and betraying her love. I am the drunk man who has lost every woman he has ever loved because he loved drinking even more. I am the drunk man who drinks to not feel alone. I am the drunk man who drinks to not feel at all. I am the drunk man who drinks because he's ashamed and then drinks to mask that shame. I am the drunk man who is always dying, dying, dying. I am the drunk man who is the son of his father. I am the drunk man.

Act 3
THE BEGINNING

—

EVEN THE DARKEST NIGHT WILL END
AND THE SUN WILL RISE.

— *Les Misérables* (MUSICAL)

27

Around 9:30 p.m. she finished washing the last dish and told her brothers that it was time to go to sleep. Their father was in the bedroom and had gone to sleep an hour earlier. "Vamos," she said to them in a motherly voice as she set two large knitted blankets on the concrete floor. Since their mother had run off with another man to el otro lado a couple of years before and their eldest sister had recently married and moved in with her husband, it was now up to her to look after her brothers and father. In an instant, she had become the woman of the house. "It's time we all go to sleep," she told the boys. "We can't wake up our father. He's tired and has to be up early to go to work tomorrow."

For almost a year she had been committed to performing this nightly ritual: Once their father was sound asleep, she would clean the house with the help of her brothers, and then wash the dishes while the brothers talked among themselves by the living room window. And after she'd laid out the blankets and her brothers had sprawled out their skinny brown bodies over them, she'd walk to the restroom, which was located in the backyard away from the house. There she'd change into a long floral nightgown of different bright colors her mother had left behind. It meant a lot to her. Reminded her of her mother and of the urgency of the role she was now forced to fulfill. Once changed into the gown she would walk back to the living room to lie next to her brothers and finally go to sleep. This was what she was about to do when, on this night, at the moment that she was going to bend her knees to sit on the floor, there was a quiet tap on the window. Straightening herself back up, she paused for a second in the darkness of the room and wondered who it could be at the window at that time of night. There was another knock, and she thought about her father waking up. She'd grown protective of her father's sleep. She knew how hard he worked for them and how much he needed his rest. So, not wanting the tapping to continue, she walked to the window and slightly pulled the curtain aside.

It was Juan, the seventeen-year-old boy she had been seeing for the last couple of weeks but with whom she had also broken off their relationship because he'd been pressuring her to sleep with him.

"What do you want?" she asked him in a whisper.

"I want to talk to you. Come out," he said.

"No. I can't. My brothers are asleep right here and my dad is asleep in his room. I don't want to wake them."

But he persisted. "Please. I just want to talk to you for a little bit. I'll be quiet. I promise." He wasn't going to leave unless she did as he said, so she, very quietly, barefoot and in her mother's nightgown, walked to the door, slowly unlocked it, and pulled it open. Nothing could have prepared her for what came next. She felt it on her stomach before she saw it. It was a small black pistol with his finger on the trigger. She froze in the doorway as a slight breeze blew through her hair and ruffled her gown. The flowers shook and her bare feet rooted themselves into the concrete floor beneath her.

She had fallen for his charm and handsomeness. And he'd talked sweet to her. At seventeen she had never had a boyfriend and thought that it couldn't hurt to at least try him. So she accepted his invitations to the park, for a walk around the neighborhood, for a soda, an ice cream. She liked him. He was charismatic and joyful. Until he wasn't. A kiss led to another kiss and another kiss to a touch and a touch to more touching and more touching to him pressing his entire body on her and wrapping his hands tightly around her wrist while pressing his mouth on hers. He was suffocating her. Drowning her in his mad desire. She needed to breathe. She needed to free herself and run as far away as she could from him. And she did. She had seen him for who he really was, and she didn't like it.

But he'd returned, armed with an idea. It had been growing in him since she had escaped his grasp, telling him that she didn't want to see him again. Now it had taken full control of him and here he was, willing to pull the trigger if she didn't do what he asked.

"Cállate," he told her. "Don't say a word, or I will shoot you."

She didn't make a sound, just turned to look at her brothers as they slept, unstirred by what was happening at the door of their house. She wanted to scream for help, for her dad to wake up. But nothing came out, only short huffs of desperate breath. It was her fault. She was the reason he was here. And it would be her fault if her father's sleep was disrupted. He had to be up early for work.

"Come. Walk this way," he ordered her, pointing to the end of the side of her house.

She did as he said, carefully closing the door behind her. The gun always pointed at her. When they got to the side of her house, he directed her into a dark space between her house and the one behind it. It was too dark for her to see where she was stepping, but she stepped into this dark crevice without a challenge. She could feel the dirt and gravel press into her feet, and the barrel of the gun press into her lower back.

All she remembers is shutting her eyes and clutching on to her gown in front of her. She had always liked how it looked on her mother. Bright. And she had always liked how it felt on her. Soft. Once, she had tried to name all of the flowers, but she was unable to. In Chihuahua, flowers were rare. It was mostly dirt. But she knew the daisy, and she knew the sunflower; she knew the daffodil, and she knew the lily; she knew the orchid, and of course she knew the rose. One day her mother would come back, and she would return her gown to her, and she would not have to be the woman of the house anymore.

When the child was born, she refused to touch it or see it. On the day of his birth, one of the nurses brought him up to her chest as an offering, and she turned her face away, her jaw tilted upward. Her eyes were windows to the afterlife. Black and dead. She was soulless. The child had sucked it out of her. She was only a body that breathed and pumped blood and felt nothing.

Outside of her everything was distorted. Faces had no features and nothing was defined by lines or edges or colors. It was a reality where nothing made sense, where everything became part of the same nothingness. It all flowed, and slowed. Fragments of a past life she didn't recognize. And the child cried. Yearning for a purpose. Yearning to return into the womb of his mother. The lights were bright and his mother rejected him. There was no love, no touch. And he cried. And she turned away.

It was the same on the next day. The nurse brought him in. She came in with a different group of nurses at different times throughout the day. Some cared about the child. Others were only curious to see the woman who wouldn't hold or even see her baby. How could any mother reject her child? What was wrong with her? What was wrong with the child? They wondered, and they talked, and the word spread, and she became the crazy woman who didn't love her newborn baby, and he became the newborn baby that was unwanted by his crazy mother.

Her father, brothers, and sister visited and they, too, brought her the child. But it was the same. Not a glance, not a single touch. She looked away into her murky world. Sank there. No one could bring her out.

"Hija," her father said, "¿estás bien?" No response. But she remembered the day she told him that she had a boyfriend and that she was going to marry him and that she was with child. And she remembered that he was happy for her. They all were: her brothers and sister, too. She had wanted them all to be happy. She had wanted them all to never know the truth. Her father would have killed him and been sent to jail for a very long time. Or her brother José. He was only fifteen at the time, but he was hot-tempered and it didn't take much to set him off, especially since the day their mother left. If the father didn't kill him, José certainly would have. And she would be the cause of all of it, for having accepted the boy's advances in the first place. She should have known better.

And what of the child? How would they have looked at him, treated him? He was the stain, the thing that happened, the act, the night, the gun, the bare feet, the gown, the flowers hitting the floor.

Enfermera Luz, the head nurse of the hospital, however, would not give up. She was the one who had been walking into the room holding the child the last two days since he'd been born. She had been the one who brought the child to his mother's chest and pleaded with the mother to receive her son.

Now, on the third day, as she picked up the boy from his hospital bassinet, she looked into his little black eyes, and told him that today was going to be the day. "Mi niñito," she said to him, "I am not taking you out of that room until she has held you and sees how beautiful you are. Te lo prometo." And with that promise and a prayer she walked into the mother's room with the child in her arms.

"Mija," the nurse, walking into the room alone, said to the mother, "look, I've brought you your baby again so that you may hold him." But like on the previous days, the mother, without making a sound, looked away. The baby cried, and the nurse rocked him. "It's okay, it's okay, my little boy," the nurse said to him. "Look, this is your mommy, and she loves you very much." She turned the child to the mother but the mother remained immobile. "You have to see your son, mijita," the nurse said to the mother. "You can't keep pretending that he doesn't exist." As the nurse talked and rocked back and forth, the child grew silent. "He has all his little toes and all of his little fingers," the nurse continued, "and you should see his eyes. They're deep and dark. They look for you. Look, even now he opens them and they wander."

Then it happened. The mother broke and tears began to rush from her eyes. His eyes had come to her like two fireflies in a dream, and she had stared into them and seen the presence of love. So she turned, slowly, toward the nurse, who grew still and silent like the child. "That's it, mijita," she told the mother. "Turn to your child. Look how beautiful he is."

She looked on at the bundle in the nurse's arms. She saw his little brown face and his black hair, then she focused on those black eyes of his, those fireflies in a dream that had been wandering, looking for his mama. They wandered no more. He recognized her right away, and she him. "Toma, mija," the nurse said, handing the mother her baby. And she took him. And she brought him to her chest. And as she looked upon him and into his eyes, she continued to cry. But they were no longer tears of sadness or guilt or pain or sorrow. These were new tears. The mother was crying because she loved the boy, and she was happy. And the boy was happy, too, because he knew that his mother loved him.

Then the mother brought him up to her face and she smelled him, and she was full again, fully alive! Then she kissed him. And then she told him this: "You are my son, and I love you, and I will always love you, and I will always protect you. You are my son, my beautiful son. Eres mi hijo Obed."

ACKNOWLEDGMENTS

Dear reader, upon reading the pages within this book, you will notice that my mother, Marcela Mendoza, is absent from most of them. This is intentional. Per her request, I have made her presence minimal, writing her in only when absolutely necessary to maintain the integrity and flow of the story. Since he caused her much emotional anguish and physical pain throughout her early adult life, my mother would like little to do with anything involving my father. By the end of this book, you will fully comprehend why.

Nevertheless, it is my mother whom I would like to acknowledge first, to thank her for everything that she has done for me. For without her unwavering commitment to providing me with a promising and fulfilling life, I would either be dead or in prison serving a life sentence.

My mother was the first to introduce me to books, and she was the first to realize that the way to saving me from the streets and myself was for me to go to college and earn a degree. In short, my mother is the reason for everything good that has come about in my life, including this terrible book.

I also owe an abundance of gratitude to Christie Diep, my English professor at Cypress College. Before meeting her, I had failed various times at being a college student. But because of her strong belief in me, and her mentorship, I was able to graduate from community college and move on to a four-year university, where I would eventually earn a master's degree in English. It was Professor Diep with whom I first shared the early pages of this book, and it was also she who first encouraged me to keep writing and to turn those early pages into a book.

Lastly, I would like to thank my friend, mentor, and now writing brother Héctor Tobar, who guided me all along the way in the development of this book, reading and rereading many of its multiple drafts. His advice and notes have been invaluable.

THE SOLOPRENEUR'S
MONEY MANIFESTO

THE
SOLOPRENEUR'S
MONEY
MANIFESTO

HOW TO MASTER YOUR FINANCES AND
CREATE THE LIFE YOU WANT

GABE NELSON, CFP®

LIONCREST
PUBLISHING

The Solopreneur's Money Manifesto:
How to Master Your Finances and Create the Life You Want

Hardcover ISBN: 978-1-5445-2134-3
Paperback ISBN: 978-1-5445-2133-6
eBook ISBN: 978-1-5445-2132-9

To Melissa, Lauren, Avery, and Lydia.
You make me a better husband, father, and man every day.
I love you tons upon tons.

CONTENTS

INTRODUCTION

It was May of 2008, months before a global financial crisis that I did not see coming. I had a successful insurance and financial services practice with New York Life and more than a decade of experience behind me. But I had just gotten another email from the mothership, asking me one more time to explain the reasoning behind my approach in serving my clients and the fees I was charging.

It was the fourth or fifth email I'd gotten along those lines—I'd lost count, but it was one too many. "That's it," I said to myself. "I'm done. I'm starting my own firm."

I went home that day and told my wife, Melissa. We had three daughters under the age of nine, and I was acting on impulse. "I want to do things my way," I said, "and I'm going to figure it out."

She chose to trust, which is only one of the many reasons I love Melissa. "Okay," she said. "Go."

I was pumped—and I was setting myself and my family up for trouble.

I started my firm on August 1. The financial world fell apart about forty-five days later, plunging us into the Great Recession. I threw myself into flat-out, move-my-clients, build-my-business mode. I was either going to make it or not, and I was scared to death. I hung on for dear life for a year with my staff of two, people I'd brought with me to make the transition. Finally, I was forced to let them go.

It was a close call. I was lucky to survive.

Today, I am proud and thankful to say that I have achieved financial success as a solopreneur. It is a blessing, many times over. I have achieved the control I wanted and the freedom that comes with it—freedom of time, freedom of destiny, freedom of income. And I've now built my business around helping other solopreneurs like me.

If you're a solopreneur and you've picked up this book, regardless of your business and your stage in life, my guess is the same objectives in life animate you. I got there, but I made a ton of mistakes in my journey. The kinds of mistakes I see many of the people who come to me for help with their finances making too.

I wrote this book to help you avoid them.

STEP BY STEP

During my career as a solopreneur and financial planner, I've learned that success begins with developing a vision of where you're trying to go. Then you need to wrap your mind around doing what it takes to get there.

Where and how do you want to live? How much free time do you want, and how do you want to spend it? When do you want to retire? What do you want to do for your kids' education? What are your goals in paying taxes?

What do you need to do with your business so it supports your vision and goals?

How do you build the personal habits that will foster success? How do you translate your ambitions into a financial plan that will ensure you achieve them?

How do you take your first steps toward putting that plan into action? How do you adapt as your life and circumstances change?

Some of the most successful solopreneurs I've met haven't thought these questions through. Others don't have the time or the knowledge to manage their personal finances. In the pages to come, I'll outline a step-by-step guide that goes beyond managing your finances to mastering them and—here's the real bottom line—creating the life you want to live.

I can't guarantee that your business will succeed; no one can, and in any case, this isn't a book about how to build your business. It's a book about mastering your finances as a solopreneur. It follows a methodical, structured approach I've developed in serving my clients. And it works.

A LIFE OF MY OWN MAKING

Melissa and I were students at South Dakota State, a year apart, dating, and serious about each other. "You know," she said to me one day, "you're going to graduate next year. And as you start looking for jobs, you need to understand something. I don't want a husband who's gone all the time. I don't want to raise the kids all by myself."

I didn't want to be that husband either.

During college, I worked mornings for a guy named Dave, who ran a vending machine business. I'd get up early to drive around town with him, filling soda, candy, and cold food machines. After classes I'd head back out on my own, placing hot coffee machines in businesses. It was my own gig, and so much better than working for someone else. In school I was studying economics, but it's coffee machines that taught me the business skills I needed to succeed: how to sell and how to build relationships.

I paid most of my way through school, but I really didn't know my career path. I just knew that I wanted to have as much freedom as possible to make the money I needed to have a great life and spend the time with my family that I wanted.

One morning Dave looked at me as we sat in his battered van and said, "You should be in the insurance business."

"What?! The insurance business?"

"I'm serious, Gabe," he said. "The State Farm agents are some of the wealthiest guys in this little college town, and they are some of the happiest too. They're always at their kids' activities. They're always doing things in the community. You should look at the insurance business."

I took his advice. My first stop after graduating in 1995 was with American Family Insurance, where I began as an insurance agent. Planning was always part of my work, but it wasn't my focus. I was young, I was foolish, and ambition carried me to the home office in Wisconsin with dreams of a life in management. I lasted a year, having learned two things. First, I'm not cut out for the culture of corporate America. Second, Melissa, who was pregnant with our first child, wanted to be home near family in South Dakota, not chasing promotions around the country with me. Achieving that goal led me to a job with New York Life in 2000, where I spent two and a half years recruiting and training agents. I wasn't great at that either, and by then I knew where I wanted to focus.

I earned my credentials as a financial advisor, returned to the field, and was on my way. It's work I love; it's work I'm good at—and I lasted five more years with New York Life. But the corporate emails took their toll. I was still working for someone else. I wanted to serve clients and build relationships on my terms, not someone else's.

That brings us to 2008, when I struck out on my own into a worldwide financial meltdown—and nearly struck out myself.

I endured, and as time went by, my business began to do really well, growing right alongside our recovering economy. I could have coasted along comfortably for the rest of my career—but that's not how I'm wired. I grew bored, so I did what entrepreneurs do: I began to break stuff so I could fix it. (Sounds familiar?)

In 2019, I joined a coaching program for financial advisers called the Limitless Adviser Coaching program. It's tremendous. Their mantra: elevate your thinking and accelerate your growth. Their message: if you want to achieve a great lifestyle, find a niche and serve it better than anybody else.

I struggled for ten months in 2019, trying to pick my niche. Nothing I came up with felt exciting. Then the question came to me: where do I have the most fun? I took a look at my clients and realized that it was in helping people just like me: solopreneurs. I live in their world. I think like they do and I speak their language. I know how to fix their problems. I'm perfectly suited to help them identify their goals and manage their finances.

That fired me up. I had my answer. I had been serving solopreneurs for many years, and now it would be my focus.

CREATING YOUR PATH TO SUCCESS

What you'll find in the pages to come is a detailed guide for solopreneurs who want to define their vision of life success and manage their finances toward achieving it. That's what I call *mastering* your finances. Why should anything less than that be your goal? My goal is to teach you everything you need to know to achieve it without hiring a financial adviser like me.

I've broken my approach into three parts.

In part 1, we'll discuss setting yourself up for success: your vision, your mindset, and your goals and habits.

Part 2 is dedicated to your financial plan. Your realities, your aspirations, and the inescapables: death and taxes.

Part 3 takes us through living your dream: determining your baseline, projecting and planning, and, finally, taking action, reviewing, and adjusting.

Along the way, I'll illustrate the points I've made through a case study involving a client named Watt—a fictionalized version of the solopreneurs I typically serve.

It all begins with bringing your life vision into focus. When I sit down with a new client, we start by talking about what's called their Life Wheel. That's where we'll start too.

PART 1

SETTING YOURSELF UP FOR SUCCESS

CHAPTER 1

VISION

When your vision is clear, your decisions are easy.
—Roy Disney

Early in my life as a father, I came across a psychology article on the meaning behind the drawings preschool kids make of their families. Often, they draw the dad small, as if he were off in the distance. That's not a good thing. A small dad suggests the father isn't playing a significant role in the life of the child who drew the picture.

In that moment I made a promise to myself: I am *never* going to be the small dad. I don't have to be bigger than Melissa, but I want to be the same size. I want to be right there beside her in our children's lives. I want to be a great husband, and I want to be a great friend—and in my heart of hearts, what I want most of all is to be a great dad.

That's my vision, in its simplest form. It's my answer to the why question. Why do I work? What is the purpose of my money? My answer is family. It has driven my life—and my business—ever since.

Of course, my vision may not be yours. We're all different. But this much is universal: mastering your finances begins with developing a vision of where you want your life to go. Not your business first. Your life. That's because you want your business to support your life, not the other way around. This is not a matter of 'set it and forget it' either. As life changes, so should your vision.

I told you in the Introduction about the crossroads I reached several years ago, at a stage when I was successful but bored and decided—as entrepreneurs do—to blow things up. I knew I needed to make a change.

I was as determined as ever not to be the small dad in

my children's lives. But beyond that, what? I was forty-six years old, and I had lost my sense of purpose.

My first bright idea was to become a scratch golfer. I had no business trying to play scratch golf, but I began taking lessons twice a week and playing golf three. Before long, halfway through the second round of the week, I found myself getting bored again.

They say when the student is ready, the teacher appears. For me, that teacher happened to be the Limitless Adviser Coaching program. Its name, of course, is intentional; its implication is that your life is limitless. They gave those words meaning by starting me where I'm starting you: with your Life Wheel.

YOUR LIFE WHEEL

Imagine a circle, a wheel, with eight sections, each a core component of your life. In each of those areas, you're going to rate your current status on a scale of one (couldn't be worse) to ten (couldn't be better). That's your Life Wheel. I want you to get out a piece of paper and a pen or pencil. Draw your circle with its eight slices, or make a photocopy of the blank wheel in the book; we're going to fill it in. I've included mine too, so you have an example.

Why? Because your vision will rise from this exercise. If you want to master your money and create the life you're meant to live, you've got to have something to shoot for. If you don't know where you're going, how are you going to get there?

Ready? Here we go:

THE LIFE WHEEL

The Life Wheel is a powerful visual tool to help you assess your level of satisfaction and fulfillment in eight key areas. On the wheel, rate your level of satisfaction on a scale of 1–10 and color in/mark your level of satisfaction in each section. The goal is not to have perfect 10s in each section, but to have balance on your wheel. Once you have filled in the wheel, use the "Desired Outcome" boxes to define how you would feel at your optimal level. Ex. "I feel strong and healthy enough to enjoy my favorite activities and family."

DESIRED OUTCOMES
I feel confident and secure that I can provide the lifestyle my family enjoys.

DESIRED OUTCOMES
I feel in control of my health and mindful in eating, sleeping, exercise, and activities.

DESIRED OUTCOMES
I feel excited for the direction I am headed and relaxed that I will continuously figure it out.

DESIRED OUTCOMES
I feel connected to my family and am strengthening relationships.

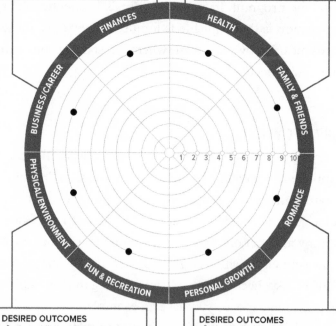

DESIRED OUTCOMES
I feel proud that we have purchased or made a plan to buy our beach magnet.

DESIRED OUTCOMES
I feel connected to melissa and continuously work to grow our relationship.

DESIRED OUTCOMES
I feel invigorated by my activities, which include golf, traveling, and snowboarding, and I am having a blast.

DESIRED OUTCOMES
I feel empowered to continuously become a better man, husband, dad, adviser, and friend.

THE LIFE WHEEL

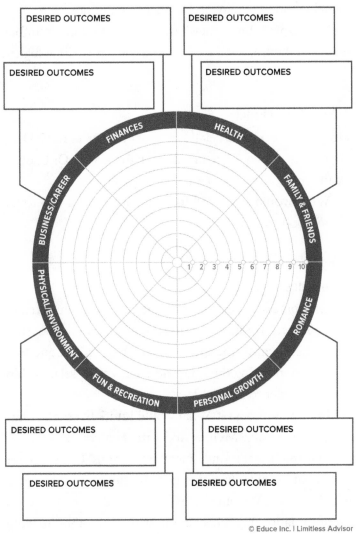

DESIRED OUTCOMES

DESIRED OUTCOMES

DESIRED OUTCOMES

DESIRED OUTCOMES

FINANCES
HEALTH
BUSINESS/CAREER
FAMILY & FRIENDS
PHYSICAL/ENVIRONMENT
ROMANCE
FUN & RECREATION
PERSONAL GROWTH

1 2 3 4 5 6 7 8 9 10

DESIRED OUTCOMES

DESIRED OUTCOMES

DESIRED OUTCOMES

DESIRED OUTCOMES

© Educe Inc. | Limitless Advisor

1) Health

Are you in tip-top shape? Eating well, sleeping well, doing all the right things? You're a ten.

Or are you a one? Passing out every night, eating and drinking too much, living like there's no tomorrow?

You're probably somewhere in between. Put a number on it, and think about the things you could do to lift it higher.

2) Friends and Family

Do you have a good relationship with your family? How about your friends? Feeling alone in the world? Or buoyed by the relationships you enjoy with others?

What would you need to do to rise from a two to an eight? A one to a six?

3) Romance

Is there someone special in your life? Are you connected to your partner? Traditional marriage, long-term relationship, gay, lesbian, trans—the specifics don't matter. The question is, are you investing the time and energy your relationship needs in order to flourish?

Put a number on it. What would lift it? Everybody has their own answer. Melissa and I made a commitment to one date night per month, just the two of us. Of course we talk about the kids, even though that's not everybody's idea of a date night. We can't help it—and we do keep the focus on our relationship, checking in with each other, making sure we're staying on the same page in life. It works for us. Our relationship has always been built on communication, and it feels as alive today as it did when we were in college.

4) Personal Growth

So many people start a career and stop growing. Are you reading books? Listening to podcasts that aren't just about fantasy football? Finding other ways to expand your mind?

Again, put a number to it. How could you get it higher?

For the longest time I read one or two books a year. I'm up to forty per year now and climbing—books on mindset, on marketing, creative confidence, making decisions. It's opening my mind and helping me grow.

5) Fun and Recreation

What are you doing to have fun? None of this is worth it if you're dead. Are you making the time to do the things you truly enjoy? Not just once a year—regularly, so you walk through life having fun as you go.

Life as a solopreneur can be stressful because it's all on your shoulders. Are you allowing yourself to have some fun?

Put a number on it. Think about how you could make it better.

6) Physical Environment

Are you physically where you want to be in the world? I want to have a beach condo or a mountain condo someday. But right now I live in South Dakota. It doesn't have everything I want. But Melissa wants to be here because it's where her family is, and I want to be with her. No regrets; Melissa makes my life so much better. But that condo, someday, would make it better still.

Put a number on it, from one to ten. What could you change to climb the scale?

7) Business and Career

Are you on track to do work that you truly love? Are you working with the kinds of clients you want to work with? Are your days filled with tasks that you *want* to do, or tasks that you *need* to do? Are you eager to get up every single morning and do whatever it is that you do?

The goal is to be happy, confident, and excited about your work. Put a number on it. How could you push it higher?

One to ten. Where are you? What would it take to get from, say, four to seven?

8) Finances

Are you spending too much? Saving enough? Are you on track to send your kids to college? Are you on pace to pay for that dream vacation, that away-from-it-all month somewhere you've always wanted to see? My guess is that you are neither entirely confident nor fully secure in your finances—because if you were, you wouldn't have picked up this book!

On a scale from one to ten, how do you feel about how well you're managing your finances? What would make you feel that much better?

ALIGNING YOUR LIFE AND BUSINESS

As you can see, the goal of the Life Wheel exercise is to force you to think clearly and methodically about each of these central aspects of life. Closing the gaps you've identified between where you are and where you want to be amounts to your vision for life. Not forever; for now. (We'll get to the need to revisit your vision regularly in part 3.)

With your Life Wheel complete, you are on your way to creating your personal vision. It should help you identify your "why" question too. Why are you working? What is the purpose of your money?

The next step is identifying how you need to change your business to get your Life Wheel rolling in the right direction. Let's call that your business vision.

What would it take for your business to support the life you want? Of course you can't change course overnight. But what steps could you take at one year, three years, and five years to align your business and life?

I'll share some of my answers to show you what I mean, starting with the biggest takeaways from my Life Wheel.

I wanted to make sure that we took one great family vacation a year, because our kids aren't getting any younger. I wanted to keep making breakfast *and* dinner for my family, every day.

I wanted to play golf once a week, not because I still wanted to be a scratch golfer, but because it allowed me to get outside in the company of other guys and refresh myself. It does good things for my psyche.

I wanted my business to be a joy, and to me that meant something simple: I wanted to spend my time talking with clients and leave everything else that needed to get done to someone else.

Finally, when the kids are grown, I want them to come back and visit—not out of obligation, but because they *want* to come back. To me, that starts with a destination: the house in the mountains or on the beach.

What are the implications of all this for my business? To buy that destination home, I knew I had to drive my business revenue north to $1 million a year. That meant finding and focusing on clients of the highest value. To make the time for golf without sacrificing making the family's meals, I needed to drive my hours down to thirty per week. In order to focus on the work I loved, I needed to outsource tasks like scheduling, paying the bills, and marketing. That meant finding experts in those fields all over the country and letting them do their thing. To get the most satisfaction from my days, I needed to focus my business on a niche of high-value clients whose challenges excited me.

The idea of building a million-dollar business while working fewer hours made my knees knock. It's hard to do. I wasn't going to get there overnight. That's where the one-, three-, and five-year goals come in. Here's where I came down:

ONE, THREE, AND FIVE-YEAR GOALS

One-Year Goals

- Outsource to begin streamlining my business
- Systemize my business to support the outsourcing, by making every process repeatable
- Begin to market my business to the type of high-value clients I would like to attract
- Begin to right-size my business so I have the time to deliver the value my clients need

Three-Year Goals

- Dial in my marketing to produce a stream of highly qualified prospects
- Write a book and create a podcast to support that marketing
- Streamline my business until all I do every day is talk to clients and help them solve their problems

Five-Year Goals

- Optimize my practice by providing high-value service to between 100 and 200 ideal clients
- Reach $1 million in annual revenue
- Write another book focused on retirement planning or a different aspect of mastering your finances

THE FIRST FIVE STEPS

It can seem overwhelming, and if you try to do it all at once you'll fail. My advice is to identify the first five steps you'll take and put them in writing. Ask yourself simple questions. How could I save five hours a week? Why am I keeping my own calendar? Do I know or can I find someone to help me set these changes in motion?

I wrote out my first five steps back in 2019, and the interesting thing is that I still read them every day. They remind me of where I started—and the importance of small, deliberate steps in carrying me toward my goals. I'm still working on some of them. Here they are:

Outsource routine client services, such as address changes, quarterly billing summaries, and communication with the custodian on creating new accounts or resolving account issues. (Thank you for this and everything else you do, Christina and Vicky!)

Systemize routine client communication through email templates and quarterly billing procedures. (That alone saved me as much as two days every quarter.)

Decide on my niche. (I struggled with this for ten months. Business owners? Retirees? In the end I chose to work with successful solopreneurs—people like me—because I knew and understood their challenges.)

Market to my niche. To that point I had relied entirely on relationships, building my business by word of mouth. (I hired a marketing consultant to develop and execute a strategy.)

Deliver massive value. (Honestly, this felt like pulling a marshmallow out of my ear. Who determines what's valuable? I decided to start by focusing on tax and retirement planning, because that's what my clients want to talk about most.)

UP FROM YOUR FOUNDATION

Your Life Wheel fits on one page. When you write down your business vision and your first five steps, keep that to one page too.

One page? Yes. Always. It forces you to focus your thoughts.

Taking the time to develop a well-defined vision for your life and your business is the foundation of success. But a vision alone does nothing to bring success about. You've got to get your mind right too, and that's where we're headed next.

CHAPTER 2

GETTING YOUR MIND RIGHT

Our thoughts are the most powerful tools we've got.
—Jen Sincero

My phone tried to warn me with an alert Sunday night: an oil price war in the Middle East, on top of growing anxiety about the emerging pandemic. The stock market would be off big time the next day.

It was March 9, 2020, and the COVID stock freakout was about to begin.

I was in Tahoe with a buddy, ready for an awesome day of snowboarding. It's a cherished winter ritual; we never miss it. The weather was perfect. I couldn't wait to get to the top of the mountain the next morning.

The market opened somewhere between 5 and 8 percent down. But I was going up—up the mountain on the chairlift at Squaw Valley, far from home in South Dakota, where most of my clients live. My phone began ringing. I checked my calls at the top: clients.

I got on my board and began flying down the slope. Mid-thirties, perfect snow. Just beautiful. I wear mini-speakers in my ears under my snowboarding helmet so I can enjoy music on the way down—but of course that means when the phone rings, I hear it. More calls. Maybe ten in all, but it felt like hundreds.

Back on the chairlift, I checked the market: down 10 percent.

I found a quiet spot in a building at the top and returned the most urgent of the messages.

"You need to talk to my wife," the client said. "She's crying, seriously freaking out. What do we do?"

It had to begin with putting her mind at rest. "This is what we sign up for when we get into the stock market,"

I said. "Volatility. The market will recover. It always has. Selling now is the worst thing we can do. Let's wait."

I knew they had the assets, income, and time to ride out any storm. "You're going to be fine," I told him. "Let's see what the day brings, and I'll get back to you."

Back at the condo that night, I returned the rest of my calls. "We need to wait," I told my clients. "Panic selling would be a disaster, because the fundamentals are good; the market will recover." Most clients were fine with my guidance—except for one, who was furious. "If you're so worried you can't sleep," I told her, "Then we'll sell. But I don't think you should. Just let this sit for a couple of days, please."

At the time I had more than one hundred clients. Only the most scared had called, and some had called more than once. But addressing their concerns didn't mean the storm was over. It was just getting started. This was a time when all of my clients needed me most; I had to be on my game. I needed to deliver the value they were paying for.

By the time I'd finished my calls that night, I had absorbed a lot of stress. My buddy and I basically drank ourselves to sleep, and that never ends well. I woke up at three in the morning, wide awake, fought my way back to sleep again, and was up for good at five.

I sat on the edge of my bed. I knew the first thing I needed to do.

I needed to get my mind right.

THE STORIES WE TELL OURSELVES

The reason some clients freaked out was rooted in their mindset: "Oh my gosh, my money's going to be gone! I'm never going to have enough to retire!" That's the story they were telling themselves. It was a story rooted in their upbringing, their culture, their times. Maybe they'd heard something like this from their parents or experienced it through their friends: "So-and-so retired in 2008, right before the market crashed—and he had to go back to work!"

We all tell ourselves stories, and we do it all the time: solopreneurs who tell themselves that they can't be successful and still be honest. Female solopreneurs who tell themselves they can't run a successful business and still be a good mom. You may tell yourself one of these stories too, or you may have your own. Stories are how we make sense of the world.

I grew up in Iowa in a melting pot family: a yours, mine, and ours, with five boys and one girl. My fantastic stepmother worked as a teacher. My father had a double major in chemistry and biology and worked as a chemist at a big power plant, climbing the ladder into an executive role while still managing to make his family a priority. Two of my stepbrothers were twins and just one month older than me. All five of us boys were in high school at the same time; in my freshman year, we made up half of the starting varsity soccer team.

We were blessed with a lot of kids—but not a lot of money. We were solidly middle class, with conservative, middle-class values. My parents believed in hard work, honesty, and decency. Those values stuck with me. As a kid, the greatest compliment I could get was, "I can't believe how nice you are!"

I still feel that way today.

The stories we tell ourselves matter. They can lift you, they can inhibit you—and you can change them. The critical thing is recognizing that the stories you tell yourself aren't always true.

That's getting your mind right.

CHANGING YOUR STORY

The services I provide clients aren't only about managing their money. It goes deeper than that. By helping them clarify their life vision and taking on their money management, I'm helping them get their minds right too. Together we change their stories. If a successful solopreneur mom comes to me, frustrated that she's not spending the time she wants with her children, we identify the steps she needs to take to change that—including delegating the work of managing her finances to me.

There's no reason you can't do this on your own—if you set out to do it deliberately. Let me set you on the path by recommending two books that influenced me.

The first is *The New Psychology of Success* by Carol Dweck. I like this book because it's grounded in how the brain works. In the simplest terms, your brain is on autopilot 95 percent of the time, running in the background and doing its most basic job: keeping you alive. You breathe. You look before crossing. You touch something hot and you pull your hand away.

The other 5 percent, you control through conscious thought. And, Dweck argues, you can change the way you think. In her book, she identifies two mindsets.

First is the fixed mindset. It's a mindset based on a self-limiting story: you tell yourself, 'I'm stuck here. This is all I can ever do. I'm not going to get any better or cleverer. And I won't try to learn new things because I can't, and I don't want to fail or appear weak or inept.'

The second, the growth mindset, is based on a different story: you tell yourself, 'I can improve! I can grow mentally and in all sorts of other ways. I can be better and cleverer! And if I fail or look inept when I try, I won't mind. Because I will learn from my mistakes, and I have time to try, fail, and improve over time.'

The beauty in this is if you change your story, you change your mindset. If you can get smarter, how are you going to do it? You pick up a book. You get on the phone. You go online. You go do *something* to educate yourself—and the story starts to shift.

A fixed mindset leads you to avoid challenges, to get defensive about feedback you don't want to hear, to give up easily, to see effort as fruitless, even counterproductive. A growth mindset leads you to embrace challenges, to see effort as the path to mastery, to learn from criticism, and find lessons and inspiration in the success of others.

The second book I recommend is written by Jen Sincero, and a quote from it opens this chapter. I love this book, starting with its title: *You Are a Badass: How to Stop Doubting Your Greatness and Start Living an Awesome Life*. It's a book-length call to action: you are a badass. Believe it. Don't settle. Act.

Sincero writes from experience, having started from what was a horrible mindset. She told herself that she wouldn't amount to much because she was unworthy in every way. But she made a decision to change that, simply by shifting her mindset from paralysis toward action. 'Stop grumbling,' she told herself, 'And get active! Be kind to yourself. You are in control of your brain and not the other way around.' I recommend reading her book, because her writing style is quite colorful, and you may enjoy what I only paraphrase here.

The bottom line, however, is that without the right mindset, you're not going anywhere. You will talk yourself out of everything you need to get you where you want to go.

THE POWER IN MEDITATION

I'm in agreement with Sincero on another thing too: the best way to rewire your brain is through meditation. That may seem odd; meditation is a form of inaction, not action. But its power lies in being still and allowing you to learn how to focus—on nothing, on a mantra, on your breathing, whatever.

Meditation is never perfect. It doesn't have to be. I've heard Tim Ferriss, an investor and author of *The 4-Hour Work Week*, say that you might sit to meditate for twenty minutes and daydream like crazy for the first nineteen. But in that last minute, if you pull your mind back out of that daydream to your central focusing practice, your session was a success. You're developing the ability to focus.

I meditate ten minutes every day as part of my morning routine. You can choose from a number of apps to guide your practice: Headspace and Calm, to name two. We have a Peloton bike, so I use the Peloton app. It's amazing how far and how often my thoughts will stray—and it's remarkable how often the instructor says, at just the right time, if your thoughts have tiptoed away, please bring them back.

MIND OVER PANDEMIC

Let's return to the morning after the great COVID stock freakout. There I sat in our Vrbo condo, feeling the effects of my drinking the night before, facing the need to get my mind right. To restore a sense of calm in the midst of chaos. To position myself to deliver the value my clients needed from me.

I wasn't in the right place. Where had my mind gone wrong, and how would I fix it?

The first thing I decided was to quit drinking until the market settled down and we passed through to the other side of the craziness. I don't drink a lot, but I do like bourbon—and I especially like drinking bourbon with my buddy after a day of snowboarding on our annual getaway. But I needed a clear mind. I didn't have another drink for eight weeks.

I needed a quiet mind too, one that set me up to deliver my best for my clients every day. I decided to double down on my morning routine. I'd get up at five every morning, I'd meditate, I'd read, I'd reflect, and I'd exercise. By eight thirty every morning, my mind would be ready for whatever the day might bring.

After I got home, I didn't wait for more clients to call. I got off my heels and onto my toes. I began crafting emails and sending them to clients every week. Every email contained this message: *Worried about your situation? Want to chat? Reach out.*

That led to lots of chats. Good conversations, every one of them different, because every client is different. The panic passed. Within two months, the market recovered. By getting my mind right, I helped my clients get their minds right too.

That's the power of mindset. With your life and business visions in place and your mind right, you're ready to identify the goals and build the habits that will lead to success.

CHAPTER 3

GOALS AND HABITS

If you aim at nothing you will hit it every time.
—Zig Ziglar

I was standing in our living room after the year Melissa and I spent in Madison, Wisconsin, in a rental home in Sioux Falls, waiting for our new home to be built, and holding our first daughter, Lauren, who was six months old. I happened to turn to the Ironman Triathlon in Hawaii on TV. One of the stories they featured was about Dick Hoyt and his son Rick, who was born with cerebral palsy. And over the course of Rick's life, his parents had figured out that he loved it when Dick took him and his special stroller out for a run. They began running half-marathons, then marathons, and Rick just loved it. And that's what first brought Dick and Rick to the Ironman Triathlon, which they took on together—first on a raft, then on an attachment on the front of Dick's bike, and finally in his special stroller.

And together, they did it.

What a story! I stood there in my living room, holding my daughter, crying my eyes out. And that summer I signed up for my first mini-triathlon. It was held in Watertown, South Dakota, and all I had for gear was a pair of swim goggles and a ten-year-old mountain bike.

It. Was. Amazing.

It was like a drug: after I finished I felt as if I could breathe easier, the colors were brighter, and the food better. I was hooked. I bought better gear—used!—and kept on competing. The next year some buddies led me to the most challenging race yet: a 1.2-mile swim in Lake Michigan, a 56-mile bike ride, and a half-marathon run. A half-Ironman, my first.

I had one of those great days when everything clicked. I kicked butt—and even qualified for nationals. In my mind my season was over, so I passed on the nationals. But the next year I came back for the same half-Ironman again, sure I'd top my first performance.

This time the race did the butt-kicking. I got a flat tire, ruined my replacement, and borrowed a tube from someone else who passed me on the course. It was July and felt like 100 degrees on the course, but I tried so hard to make up for lost time that I didn't eat or hydrate the way I should have. I made it, but the race just about killed me.

I could have folded—enough with the half-Ironmans—but I decided to double down. It was 2006, and I decided I was going for a full Ironman. I made a commitment to Melissa too: my training would not affect the family, because family came first.

I'd set my goal. Next, I needed to develop the habits that would get me there.

STEP BY STEP

In chapter 1 we talked about developing your life and business vision, and in chapter 2 we got your mind right. Now you're ready to define the goals and build the habits that will lead you to success.

It's time to get out another single sheet of paper. I've found there's no better way to focus your thoughts than to bring them down to a single page. It forces the choices and thinking you need to move beyond the confusion of trying to do everything at once. It's the best path to action.

You've already identified the steps you need to take to improve your Life Wheel and where you want your business to be in a year's time. What do you have to do to get your Health score from a four to a six? Could you carve out some time to work out before or after work? How about your Fun and Recreation score, to get it from six to eight? Well, how much can you set aside this year to get you on the path to that dream vacation? Let's say your Education score is a two right now, because you've done nothing to set aside money for your oldest child's education. Move it up a notch or two by creating a savings plan and taking your first step toward funding it.

Write out your goals, which flow from your Life Wheel. They're bite-sized and achievable in a year's time. These are the little successes that will power your next step. When I say little, I don't mean timid. We tend to overestimate what we can achieve in thirty days, but underestimate what we can achieve in a year.

Now, to get to those goals at the end of a year, where do you need to be at the end of the first quarter? What do you need to do now to get there? This leads us to your habits— the regular practices you need to establish to achieve your goals.

Do you want to lose ten pounds? What needs to change? Going to set aside $100 a month for college savings? Well, where is it going to go and how will you free up that money?

I began the chapter by describing my goal from 2006: ramp up my training to compete in a full Ironman in a year's time without impacting my family. A full Ironman involves a 2.4-mile swim, a 112-mile bike ride, and a full marathon run of 26.2 miles. Getting your body ready for that is no small task.

So I changed my daily habits. I got up at five every weekday morning and four on Saturdays so I could get in my training and be home in time to fix breakfast for the kids. I needed to fuel myself for success, so every twenty minutes as I trained, I'd eat and drink.

Goals and habits. Together, they'll get you there!

FINDING YOUR EDGE

I'm going to recommend a third book: *The Slight Edge*, by Jeff Olson. Carol Dweck describes the importance of a growth mindset; Jen Sincero makes it real with her badass, take-control-of-your-mind message. Olson's book is a call to action, describing, among other things, the three essentials of achieving a goal:

Write it down. (We've done that, on one page. I'd add, look at it every day.)

Add a timeline. (I'd add, pick one item from the timeline and put it on a sticky note on your computer.)

Take a step. It doesn't have to be perfect, just take a step. Follow with another step, and another step, and another step. Olson calls that the compounding interest of daily activity. That's what he means by a "slight edge." Every solopreneur is familiar with the hockey stick curve of exponential growth—the explosive surge in revenue or whatever you're measuring that we all dream of. Olson's methodology fuels it.

THE MORNING ROUTINE

I'm a believer in the importance of a morning routine. If you don't start the day right, you'll be playing from behind until you go to bed that night.

Mine still begins at five every morning, with some form of exercise for the first hour. I follow that with a ten-minute meditation, a reading in a daily devotional, and ten minutes of reading in each of two books to open my mind for the day. I go make breakfast for my family, give everyone a hug and a kiss, and send them out the door. I shower and am in my office around eight.

And I'm not done yet!

Most days I read a passage in another book, *The Daily Stoic* by Ryan Holiday, a collection of meditations. Next, I make a daily accounting of my habits, based on my activities the past day. One entry is as simple as this: did I check my email no more than twice yesterday? I'm trying to do it just once a day, because I've trained my assistant to handle all the emails I don't need to see—and as a result, I'm down to fifteen to thirty minutes a day on email. (Imagine how good that would feel!) But I need to hold myself accountable for maintaining that habit.

Finally, I journal for three to ten minutes, starting with three things I'm grateful for from the day before, a story about something I'm grateful for, and my feelings about the news of the day—the market, the election, COVID, whatever.

By eight thirty, I am ready for whatever comes my way. I'm ready, no matter what happens.

That's my routine. I'm not saying it has to be yours, but if you don't have a morning routine yourself, I'd encourage you to start one. Just try it. I've got another book to recommend if you'd like further guidance: *The Miracle Morning* by Hal Elrod. He outlines an approach that's simple and easy to follow. I know, because I followed it in developing my routine!

You don't have to do all I do, especially not on day one. I didn't. But don't talk yourself out of this with thoughts of how busy you are. After all, one of the beauties of life as a solopreneur is that you have control over your time. If you can control your thoughts, you can control your time—and a morning routine helps your mind grow all the stronger. Think of it as the root of all good badass habits.

ACROSS THE FINISH LINE

I've told you about my full Ironman goal and the habits I established to get me there. In September of 2007, I was ready for what's called Ironman Wisconsin.

And it, too, was amazing.

An Ironman is a twelve-hour immersion in excitement, fear, camaraderie, grit, and passion. We started out in Lake Monona for our 2.4-mile swim, and for the first thirty to forty-five minutes it was like swimming in a washing machine. You're getting punched, kicked, and hit as everyone tries to swim their way toward open water. Then it's out of the water, into your gear, and onto your bike for the 112-mile ride. Ironman Wisconsin features one of the toughest bike courses of all, highly technical and very hilly. I once topped sixty miles an hour going down a hill, and it had a curve at the bottom that could send you hurtling into a cornfield if you weren't ready for it. You've got to pace yourself, lock in, and stick to your game plan.

Finally it's on to the run, a full marathon. The route takes you through the University of Wisconsin campus, so not only do you have fans and family members watching, you've got college kids drinking and music blasting as they bang on pots and pans to cheer you on.

I crossed the finish line twelve hours and nineteen minutes after I started, found Melissa, and just started crying.

"Why are you crying?" she said.

"I'm just so stinking happy that I did it," I answered.

I still get goosebumps thinking about that day. It's the only Ironman location in which I've competed...but I've done so four different times so far! It all began with a goal, and I got there because of my habits.

So now we've got your mind in the right place. You've got your vision, you're in a badass mindset, and you're building out the goals and habits that lead to success. Next, it's on to the nitty gritty of creating your financial plan.

PART 2

PLANNING WITH PURPOSE

CHAPTER 4

YOUR REALITIES

The goal isn't more money. The goal is living life on your terms.
—Will Rogers

The financial plans I prepare for clients have ten elements. I have more to say about some of them than others, but they're all important. Together they encompass all aspects of the planning necessary to set you up for the life you want to live. Remember, that's our goal: the reason most of us solopreneurs went into business for ourselves is because we wanted the freedom to live the lives of our dreams. The financial plan is what gets you from here to there.

THE FINANCIAL PLAN

In this part of the book, I'll explain the elements of a financial plan, and I'll start with listing them all so you know where we're going. You'll need to think about all of these to map your path forward:

- Cash Flow
- Purchases
- Debts
- Emergency Savings
- Retirement
- Education
- Risk Management
- Portfolio
- Taxes
- Estate and Business

I'll devote more space to some than others, because of their complexity, but they're all important. Some will get their own chapters while others will be grouped. In this chapter we'll cover the first four, what I call your *realities*: Cash Flow, Purchases, Debts, and Emergency Savings.

CASH FLOW

Cash is king. I say that because your cash flow drives everything else in your financial plan. Simply stated, your cash flow is the amount of money that comes in every month versus the amount that goes out the door. If you've got $10,000 coming in every month and $15,000 going out, you've got a cash flow of negative $5,000 (and a problem you need to address right away!)

I've seen situations that were nearly that grim. I once hired a plumber to replace our water heater. He was as nice as could be, but he looked like a biker from the movies, with his bald head, a long beard parted in the middle like a pair of horns, and a build that said don't mess with me.

He was a great plumber—and he was a beaten man, because he didn't know how to run the financial side of his business. "I'm sorry to tell you this," he began, "but I need to have $1,000 to start this job. The wholesaler needs a down payment so I can get your water heater."

I wrote him the check, and he did a great job. We got to know each other as he worked, and at one point he asked what I did for a living. After the work was done he came in with his wife and his tax returns, bank statements, and other documents I needed to assess his situation, and we all sat down together. He was embarrassed to share them, sure that I'd tell him he needed to shut his business down.

The problem? His cash flow. He didn't bill on time, so he couldn't pay his bills on time either, and wholesalers stopped extending credit. He didn't need to shut down his business, but he did need to take control of his cash flow.

That meant raising his fees. It meant cutting expenses, managing his books, and getting his invoices out promptly. And it meant hiring somebody to answer the phone and manage his calendar. I'd heard him in my utility room taking calls from customers when he was supposed to be working on my water heater!

I've seen the flip side too, and it causes its own problems— although they're the kind of problems you're happy to have. A specialist in electronic medical records once came to me. He was offered the opportunity to take his knowledge from a health system to a position with a consulting firm that would jump his income immediately from $60,000 to $300,000 a year. "Holy crap, Gabe!" he said. "What do I do?"

He was an overnight cash flow success story, and as an employee he lacked the control over his income that he'd gain as a consultant working as an independent contractor. I urged him to make the switch. He did, and gained the freedom he needed to run his own business and manage his cash flow to do what he really wanted to do in life. We set to work on his retirement plan, disability coverage, life insurance—and he was off and running.

My point in telling you these stories is to drive home the fundamental importance of managing your cash flow. For a solopreneur, whose business income and personal income feel like the same thing, success can only start there. That's why it's first on my list.

PURCHASES

Lloyd and Elaine came to me with a successful business in a small town that generated between $500,000 and a million dollars a year—but they liked to spend their money. They had only $40,000 in retirement savings, a half a million in debt, and lots of expenses. They were in their late fifties and had reached the point in life where they wanted to begin thinking about winding things down, eventually turning the business over to their son. There was this too: Lloyd wanted nothing more than to take Elaine to Fiji for the vacation she'd always dreamed of.

But could they do it? They didn't know the answer.

My answer was yes, and so we set to work on the financial plan that would get them there. We had a lot to do—but this was about achieving the life they wanted to live. So we put that trip to Fiji under their purchases.

By purchases, I don't mean the groceries or the electric bill. I don't mean a new pair of corduroys or high-heel shoes either. These are ongoing or routine expenses, and they're covered in your monthly cash flow.

Instead I'm talking about significant, one-time expenses. Your dream vacation. The used cars you need to buy for each of your kids as they reach driving age. A hot tub for your deck, an addition for the in-laws, and other home improvements. Expenses big enough that we need to plan for them. You could think of them as capital investments, although items such as a vacation don't last. (Sadly.)

DEBTS

Liquidating your debts equals freedom. It's that simple. Everyone's financial plan is different because their goals are different. But this is universal: you want to be on a path to reducing your debt so that you have the freedom you want when you need it. If your goal is to be out of debt by retirement, how are you going to get there?

The debts my clients typically carry include a mortgage, a line of credit through their business, and car payments. Most pay off their credit cards every month. Some are still paying off their student loans, but not many.

Debt is not inherently bad. I'm a big fan of debt with a purpose. If you're a medical student going deeper into debt with each passing year, that's one of the greatest investments you'll ever make—because you'll earn a lot of money coming out the other side of your education.

We happen to be in a time when interest rates are historically low. That means it's wise to consider taking advantage of it. I have seen many clients take years off their mortgages by refinancing. Some of them have done it twice, because rates are so low.

All that said, the fundamental rule applies: paying down debt and ultimately avoiding it altogether equals freedom.

I worked with another couple in their fifties who owned their own small business. They had one part-time employee. I sat down with them in their shop and we talked about their goals and objectives. They were still paying off loans on their business.

"We've got to get rid of this debt," they told me. "We know we need to save for retirement. What do we do?"

We came up with a plan. "Follow this over the next three to four years," I said, "and you'll be close to getting out of debt. Just follow the plan."

Three and a half years later they called to say, "Okay, that's done! What do we do next?" We took the money they'd been paying toward debt and began saving for their retirement. That put them in position to retire on time—and only because they'd climbed out from under the debt on their shop.

I think of being debt-free as holding a "screw you" card. Pay off your debt and you can laminate that card and pull it from your wallet when the time is right and simply say, "Screw you. I don't want to do this anymore."

EMERGENCY SAVINGS

I'm fond of a quote by a man named Joe Moore that my marketing consultant shared with me:

A simple fact that is hard to learn is that the time to save money is when you have some.

Amen!

As I've said, as a solopreneur, your business income and your personal income feel like the same thing. If you don't have adequate savings in place, both your business and your household are at the mercy of events beyond your control—a pandemic, say. You'll be thrown into a debt spiral, charging your car repairs, the new furnace, and any other expenses you can't avoid to your credit cards. We need to avoid that.

When I was thinking through the information for this chapter, it was May 2020. COVID-19 had its hands locked tight on the economy's throat. I watched as my revenue dropped by 25 to 30 percent—and I thought, wow, am I glad I have savings! Of course, I couldn't see the future and I didn't know how long the pandemic would persist and what it would mean for me by the time all was said and done. So I took an additional step: I haven't used my line of credit in years, but I called my banker just the same and got it increased. But my savings were solid. I knew my business and my family were protected.

I urge my clients to set aside enough savings to cover twelve months of living expenses, six months at the very least. Twelve months is ideal; six months is adequate. (That's the goal. It may take time to get there.)

Imagine the fate of solopreneurs who couldn't fall back on an emergency savings cushion. I remember watching *CBS Sunday Morning* early in the pandemic, as Jane Pauley interviewed a caterer in New York City whose business had cratered. She was running out of money. With no money she had no options, no opportunity to ride things out or pivot to a new approach that would keep some cash flowing.

One of my clients was a consultant back at the time of the Great Recession in 2008, and he told me how he watched in horror as the housing market went down, the stock market went down, and his investments went down. He survived by the grace of God. And every year after as the economy recovered he added a little extra to his emergency savings in preparation for the next jolt. He knew one was coming; they always do. It was just a matter of what and when (the pandemic, as it turned out, in 2020.)

"I'm at peace," he told me when I checked in. "I know I'm going to be okay."

That's the beauty of emergency savings.

I keep my emergency funds in a cash account at the bank. I don't care if my clients keep theirs in a coffee can in the garage. I just want them to have the ability to get it tomorrow if they have to. Don't invest it. I know it's tempting—but don't.

I've got another client who is an anesthesiologist in a partnership, and they do really well in their life-saving work. When we first started working together, years ago, we set a goal of $100,000 in emergency savings.

"Where are we going to put it?" he asked.

"Nowhere," I said. "I just want it in your savings account. Just get to a hundred. When you get past it let me know, and we'll start investing."

Well, the pandemic hit. Elective surgeries stopped, so demand for their services fell, and their income fell with it. His partners were forced to cut back on funding their 401(k) to pay the bills. He didn't—because he didn't have to.

Again: that's the beauty of emergency savings.

ON TO YOUR ASPIRATIONS

With your cash flow, purchases, debts, and emergency savings accounted for, we've covered what I call your realities. Next, we're on to your aspirations, beginning with retirement. That's a big one.

CHAPTER 5

RETIREMENT

Americans are not saving enough for retirement.
—Tammy Baldwin

In the midst of the pandemic, Melissa and I decided to donate blood. It was one small thing we could do. When we arrived, the phlebotomist sat us down in her office and began walking us through a questionnaire.

"What do you do for a living?" she asked me.

"I'm a financial advisor."

She didn't skip a beat. "What should I do with my money?" she asked.

I was sure that question wasn't on her form. I chuckled. "I don't know," I said. "I don't know your story."

"Should I put my money in the 401(k) here at the hospital?"

"I don't know," I said. "I don't know your story!"

She told me that she'd been working at the hospital for more than thirty years, and she had a 401(k) there. Her husband owned a sporting goods store that had been on Main Street in their town for forty years. "He doesn't have any money saved," she said. "When he's ready to retire, we're hoping he can sell the building to someone who wants the location."

That was not a laughing matter. "Okay," I told her. "Hope is not a plan." Sure, her husband could probably sell the building at some point. But not during a pandemic—so when, and at what price? They had to do some financial planning, because he had not set himself up to leave his business for retirement on his own terms.

To me, that's the essence of the solopreneur's dream: retiring on your own terms. It's the ultimate freedom.

Of course, there's much more to life and more to fulfilling your dreams and aspirations than retirement. But for most of my clients, it's the most important piece of the puzzle they bring me. It's my favorite topic too, complex and meaty, so I'm devoting a full chapter to it.

FULFILLING YOUR DREAMS

Here's a figure that gets my attention, and I hope it gets yours too:

According to Investopedia, the average American between fifty and fifty-nine had a 401(k) balance of $160,000 in 2021. What does that mean for the average fifty-something's retirement? Nothing good. A portfolio of that size can produce no more than $8,000 annually without running out of money at some point in the rest of their life.

That's not much.

Ready for the good news? The good news is that even if you're not prepared for retirement now, you're reading this book. You're better prepared just by doing that, and if you apply the principles I'm sharing you can set yourself up for a truly amazing life, now and into the future. How great is that?

I once had a client named Andy, a fairly typical client, who was confused by his choices. He was a success, with a business income of $500,000 a year, but he wasn't sure how to make the most of that money to set himself up for later in life. He didn't know how much he should be putting away. He just knew that he needed to be doing something, and that's as good a starting point as any.

My answer began with questions.

"How old are you now?"

"I turned fifty last summer."

"When do you want to retire?"

"No firm plans, but let's say sixty-two at the latest."

"What's your tax bill? Do you want to pay less?"

"Around $60,000 a year. I'm happy to pay my fair share, but I don't want to leave a tip!"

"How is your business structured, and how do you pay yourself?"

"I'm an S Corp. I take $130,000 in salary, which maximizes my Social Security benefit, and a distribution of $70,000 from profits."

There were more questions, and more answers, but these are the ones most relevant to a retirement discussion. You'll have your own answers. But the options you have for funding your retirement are the same as Andy's, so let me lay them out.

As of the time I'm writing this, there are six types of retirement plans available to solopreneurs. All are intended to get you to the same place, encouraging you to build the assets you need to retire by reducing the taxes you pay:

- Traditional IRA
- Roth IRA
- SEP IRA
- Simple IRA
- Solo 401(k)
- Defined Benefit Pension Plan

All have different characteristics, requirements, and benefits. I'll go through the basics of how they work one by one, detailing Andy's circumstances and his choices as we go, by way of example. (We'll repeat the exercise at the end of part 2 with the Watt case study.)

Traditional IRA

Most people understand that when you put money into a retirement account you get a tax break for doing so. These are called tax-qualified accounts, and they're intended to encourage retirement savings. Put money into a tax-qualified account, such as a Traditional IRA, and you get a tax deduction for funding it. Your investment grows tax-free—but it's not a free lunch. You'll be taxed when you withdraw your money during retirement.

Let's do the math on a simple example. Let's say you are in a 24 percent tax bracket. That means you'd get a 24 percent tax deduction on the money you invest in a Traditional IRA. When it's time to retire, you're likely to be living on less money. For the purposes of our example, let's say that in retirement you enter a 12 percent tax bracket. The money you take from your Traditional IRA will be taxed as ordinary income—which means you just won the tax game by 12 percent, the difference between what you would have paid before (24 percent) and your retirement tax rate (12 percent).

Five of the retirement plan options work the same way: the Traditional IRA, the SEP IRA, the Simple IRA, the

Solo 401(k), and the Defined Benefit Pension. The outlier is the Roth IRA, for reasons I'll discuss in the next section.

What's the downside of a Traditional IRA for a solopreneur? There's a limit on how much you can put in and still get a tax deduction, and on the total income you can have as well. The annual contribution limit for 2021 is $6,000, or $7,000 if you're fifty or older. The income level is based on your modified adjusted gross income and how you are filing taxes: as a single head of household or married filing jointly.

Here is another wrinkle you will need to consider: if you're over fifty, you're allowed to make what are called catch-up contributions beyond the normal limit on your tax-deductible contributions.

Could Andy do a Traditional IRA? The answer was no. At $500,000, his business income was way over the limit. In addition, he was married and filing jointly with his wife, who had her own retirement plan at her job and was funding it at $7,000.

Roth IRA

The Roth IRA is the outlier, remember? That's because it's an after-tax retirement account. I call after-tax money "grocery money," because it's the same you use to buy your groceries—after you've paid your taxes on it.

Why do that, if there's no immediate tax break? Because the tax break comes later, after your investment has grown and when you take money out in retirement. At that point, everything in your Roth IRA is free from further taxes, both your original principle and all the growth your account has generated. That's the beauty of a Roth: pay now, save later.

It's conceivable that Congress could come back and change that. The Roth IRA was created by tax law, and Congress has the power to change it. I don't see that happening, because Congress's interest to date has been allowing Americans to save more money. But I can't guarantee that will never change.

Here are the catches: That $6,000/$7,000 annual contribution limit on a Traditional IRA doesn't budge if you contribute to a Roth IRA as well. It's a total cap, covering both types of accounts and varying based on your age. Income limits apply to both Roth IRAs and Traditional IRAs.

Was a Roth IRA an option for Andy? Nope. He was making too much money. But he still needed to save for retirement, and he needed a tax deduction. On to the next option.

SEP IRA

SEP IRAs were established with small businesses in mind; the name stands for Simplified Employee Pension. The amount you can contribute to a SEP IRA is capped every year, based on a percentage (I use 20 percent for solopreneurs) that's tied to either your business's bottom line or your W2 salary, depending on how you've set up your business. (We'll get to business structure in chapter 7.)

For the 2021 tax year, the income figure is $290,000, meaning the maximum contribution at that level is $58,000. If you make less, your cap will be lower.

Andy was paying himself $130,000 a year in W2 salary. He was taking a $70,000 distribution from his company's profits annually too. Of that $200,000 total, his best path using a SEP IRA was contributing 20 percent of his W2 salary, or $26,000, to a retirement plan every year. (Here's the math: $130,000 in W2 salary 20 percent = $26,000.)

That's pretty darn good. Andy's salary put him in the 24 percent tax bracket. Utilizing a SEP IRA would enable Andy to put away $26,000 a year toward retirement while saving about $6,000 in taxes. Better still, you don't have to decide how much to contribute until tax time in April the following year. In a good year, you can dial it up; in a bad one, you can dial it down.

But could Andy do better?

Simple IRA

A Simple IRA works like a 401(k) plan for small business owners. In a traditional 401(k), the employee makes a contribution, and the employer matches up to a certain limit. A Simple IRA works the same way.

In Andy's case, a Simple IRA would allow him to make a $13,500 tax-deferred contribution. Because he's over fifty, he can make an additional $3,000 catchup contribution, bringing his total to $16,500. In addition, he has to do the employer match of 3 percent of his W2, which amounts to $3,900. Add all that up, and it means he can contribute $20,400 to a Simple IRA—saving about $5,000 in taxes.

But here's a wrinkle: a Simple IRA has what's called an "exclusive plan year." If you put as little as a dollar into a Simple IRA during the year and you don't reverse it, by pulling your contribution out come tax time, you cannot take advantage of any other retirement plans designed to support a small business. As a solopreneur, you can have a Simple IRA and still contribute to a Traditional IRA or a Roth IRA, provided you meet their requirements, but not a SEP IRA or the two additional options still to come.

Another wrinkle: the contributions you make to a Simple IRA are part of your salary, meaning they have to be paid by December 31 every year. The same goes in Andy's case for his $3,000 catchup contributions. (Your match can come at tax time next April.)

Of the two choices, for Andy the SEP IRA is better than the Simple IRA. He can set aside more for retirement, save more on taxes, and hold off on a funding decision until April of the following year. But those aren't his only two choices.

SOLO 401(K)

This is where it starts to get exciting for me—and it got Andy's attention too. The Solo 401(k) is my favorite option. That's because it adds profit-sharing to the equation.

At fifty, Andy can defer taxes on $19,500 of income invested in a Solo 401(k), plus an additional $6,500 in catchup. Now he's at $26,000, the same as a SEP IRA.

But the beauty of a Solo 401(k) is that it enables Andy to make a profit-sharing contribution from his company to the account. That contribution will apply to every employee, but he's a solopreneur. He's the *only* employee.

The law allows Andy to distribute up to 25 percent of his W2 income through profit-sharing. With a W2 salary of $130,000, that's an additional $32,500 Andy can put into his Solo 401(k) as a profit-sharing contribution.

Now we're at nearly $59,000 going toward his retirement plan—and it's tax-deferred. Now we're dropping his tax bill by almost $14,000.

That gets me excited.

Andy had one reservation: "*What if I have a down year? Am I obligated to make the profit-sharing contribution?*"

The answer is no. As a solopreneur you have control over the size of profit-sharing contribution, or even whether to make one.

A Solo 401(k) does have a timing requirement, though: your tax-deferred contributions have to be in by December 31, but you can defer a decision on profit-sharing until tax time in April of the following year.

All told, is that a better alternative for Andy than the SEP IRA? He thought so, and I did too.

But is he done? Not yet!

Defined Benefit Pension Plan

For a solopreneur, this is really where we start to put some serious money away. The first layer is the Solo 401(k) salary deferral. The second layer is profit-sharing. And *then* you can add a pension plan on top of that.

In simple terms, a defined benefit pension plan amounts to setting aside income over time with a goal of building a pile by the time you retire. The payoff is a pension you can draw on for the rest of your life.

The amount you can contribute each year usually ranges from $50,000 to $300,000, depending on how old you are. By way of example, if you were fifty in 2021, like Andy, the limit was $162,000.

That's on *top* of a Solo 401(k) contribution. *And* it's tax-deferred. It's a tool, like the others, that's intended to build your retirement for the future by giving you a tax deduction for setting money aside now. If you were in the 24 percent tax bracket, like Andy, and made a $162,000 contribution, that could save you nearly forty grand in taxes.

As with every option I've outlined except the Roth IRA, you will pay taxes when you take your pension. You can take it as a lump sum cash settlement or as a monthly payment. You're in total control.

The wrinkle: it's generally recommended that you hire a third-party administrator to manage a pension plan and ensure you stay in compliance with federal law. It's not cheap: you're talking $3,000 to $5,000 a year. The payoff is the opportunity to make a massive tax-deferred contribution.

When my clients are ready to retire, we close the pension plan and roll the money into a Traditional IRA. That ends the administrative fees, and it gives clients total control of when and how much to withdraw until they reach the minimum distribution age, which is now seventy-two.

Options!

This is not a simple topic; my client Andy was not alone in his confusion, but his circumstances pointed us to his best solution. To get to the same place, you'll either need to devote time to careful study to determine the options that best fit your circumstances, or you'll need to reach out to someone like me who can guide you through your choices. Either way, it's work you need to do.

I know, you've got plenty of work on your plate already. But consider the payoff!

CHAPTER 6

TAKING CARE
OF YOUR FAMILY

If a man empties his purse into his head
no one can take it away from him. An investment in
knowledge always pays the best interest.
—Benjamin Franklin

In the past two chapters we've covered the first five elements of your financial plan: Cash Flow, Purchases, Debts, Emergency Savings, and Retirement. Five more to go: Education, Risk Management, Portfolio, Taxes, then Estate and Business. We'll cover Education and Risk Management in this chapter. Both relate to taking care of your family.

EDUCATION

I could share lots of stories from my work about people saving for college for their kids, but the one that speaks loudest to me involves a former client named Bob who called me out of the blue in the midst of the pandemic. He hadn't been a client of mine since 2008 or so, when he moved to Florida.

Bob had gone on to great success. He'd spent years making good money. Then he lost his job to COVID just as his college-bound daughter graduated from high school.

"I've got to tell you," he said, "that I am so thankful you told me to put a couple hundred bucks a month into that college savings plan when my daughter was born. I never would've saved without that nudge. Now I'm out of work—but she's going to college and I've got her first year covered. I cannot thank you enough!"

You may not have college-bound kids, or kids at all. Maybe you're not planning to pay for their schooling. My parents didn't pay much toward mine. But my commitment to Melissa and my family was to pay for four years of college for each of our three daughters.

If you've made a commitment like that to your family, or something like it, the moral of Bob's story is clear: it doesn't take a lot to build up enough to help pay for your kids to go to college. And the sooner you start, the better.

As with retirement, you've got choices in how to go about it. There are three basic types of college savings accounts:

- 529 Plans
- Coverdell Education Savings Accounts
- UGMA (for Uniform Gift to Minors) or UTMA (Uniform Transfer to Minors) accounts

Let's walk through them one by one.

529 Plans

Congress created 529 Plans in 1996; the name is taken from the section of the tax code that established them. They're the most popular college savings plan today.

A 529 is, in essence, a Roth IRA for education. Like the Roth IRA, you fund it with after-tax money. Your grocery money. The money inside the account grows as the years pass. When you take it out—so long as it's used for higher education expenses—it's tax free. You can use it to pay for an accredited four-year school, a two-year school, and since 2017, you can even use it to pay for a private elementary or high school too.

A 529 isn't entirely string-free. If the money you contribute isn't used for education, you'll pay a 10 percent penalty and ordinary income taxes on the gains.

A 529 is my preferred education savings choice. It's what I use for my kids, and it's what almost all my clients use. A 529 is child-specific, although you can change the beneficiary once a year. But in general, you'll want to establish one for each of your children.

In addition, there's no age limit on a 529. If you've got a kid who takes a gap year—and that gap year turns into ten gap years, or twenty—their 529 plan will still be there waiting for them.

You can put up to $15,000 per year into a 529. You can even pre-fund five years at a time with serious dollar amounts, if you choose. Most of my clients contribute between $100 and $300 every month.

Finally, anyone can contribute to a 529 on behalf of a child. Grandparents, aunts or uncles, friends, extremely kind strangers—you name it.

ONE IMPORTANT CAVEAT!
You can borrow money for a college education, but you can't borrow money for retirement. If it comes down to planning for your retirement or planning for your kids to go to college, I tell my clients—always—you've got to plan for your retirement first. The kids can borrow money if they have to.

Coverdell Education Savings Accounts
Coverdell accounts, which used to be called Education

IRAs, have been around for a long time. But you can only put $2,000 a year into a Coverdell account—far short of what's allowed with a 529. There are income limitations too. Joint filers with adjusted gross incomes of less than $190,000 can contribute the full amount of $2,000. If you make more than that, you might not be able to fund it at all because you make too much money. (As with a 529, anyone can contribute to a Coverdell—provided they meet the income limits.)

Another disadvantage: unlike a 529, the money in a Coverdell account has to be used by the time the beneficiary turns thirty. And as with a 529, if the money's not used for education, it'll be subject to taxes and penalties.

The reason some people use Coverdells is that for many years, they were the only college savings plan you could also use to pay for private K–12 education. But as I said, since 2017, 529 accounts can be used in the same way. As a result, the Coverdell is becoming a dinosaur.

UGMA and UTMA Accounts

UGMA (again, it's Uniform Gift to Minors) and UTMA (Uniform Transfer to Minors) accounts are both vehicles you can use to transfer assets—money, even real estate—to a child for any purpose. In some states it's UGMA and in others UTMA, but they function the same way. When your child hits their age of majority—that varies based on the state too, at eighteen, nineteen, or twenty years—the money inside the account is theirs.

What if they're not mature enough to handle the money at that age? Good question! I sure wasn't. But when they hit the age of majority, it's theirs. (Not to get ahead of things, but when it comes to life insurance payouts, you have more control. I'll get to that in the next section.)

There's no tax benefit to funding an UGMA or an UTMA account; the money you put in is after-tax. There is a tax advantage at the other end. Your gains and losses are taxed at the child's tax rate, which is likely to be lower than yours. But the advantage is modest.

Pros? You can contribute as much as you want to an UGMA or UTMA—though if you contribute more than $30,000 in a given year as a married couple filing jointly, you may have to file a federal gift tax return. (You should seek the advice of your tax professional if you're considering this.) In addition, anyone can contribute to the account on behalf of your child.

It's Your Call

I've made clear my preference for a 529 among the options for saving for the education of your child. I think it's the smart move.

But that's my preference, not your choice. The path you choose depends on your goals, as does the amount you contribute. Do you want to pay for a two-year school? Four year? State school? An Ivy?

Once you've decided what you're aiming for, you've got another decision to make: how much of the bill do you want to pay? A lot of parents I know believe it's important for their child to have some skin in the game.

Solopreneurs are resourceful people, so I'll note that there are options beyond the three I've outlined. You can overfund a life insurance policy, although I haven't seen that for years. You can buy a rental property, pay off the debt by the time your kids are graduating from high school, and use the rental income to pay their college bills. You can even prepay college tuition ahead of time if you know where they're going.

When I discuss this topic with clients, I walk them through the basics of their choices, just as we've done here. I'll outline other options. Then I tell them my story.

I paid for college myself with a little help from my parents—and I mean a *little* help. As a freshman in college, standing in the tuition payment line, I had a little money in my checking account, and I knew I'd borrowed money to pay for college. But as I made my way through that line, it dawned on me that I was going to have to write a big check. So I wrote one, knowing it was going to bounce. But the clerk didn't know that, so they took the check and I went on to get my picture taken for my student ID. I called my mom as soon as I could, got a little help to cover the check, and started college, picking up work around classes and over the summers to carry me from there. (Aside from the summer after my first year, when I squandered my earnings having an excellent time. My dad gave me a little help then—and told me it was time to get my act together. Which I did.)

In any event, I promised myself that if I ever had kids, I wouldn't put them in the same spot. As each of my daughters were born, Melissa and I set up their 529 plans. For all of them, we'll have at least their first two years covered, and we'll pay for the rest through cash flow.

That's my plan. If you've got kids, or plan to, I hope I've encouraged you to formulate your own.

Risk Management

I was making supper for my family about five o'clock one Friday evening when my phone rang. It was Rob, the husband of a client named Christine—and that got my attention, because he'd never called at five on a Friday evening. When we'd talked before, Rob was always happy, always good. But this time the first words out of his mouth were, "Christine's got cancer."

It sounded ominous. The cancer was located in Christine's right shoulder, and the doctors had told them that their best chance to save her life required removing her arm. Christine worked as a CRNA: a certified registered nurse anesthetist. They intubate patients, put them to sleep; they work with their hands. It's not a job you can do one-handed.

I was worried about Christine—but I wasn't worried about their finances, and I told Rob so. We had met just a couple weeks before to review where things stood. I knew Christine had disability insurance and, if worse came to worst, life insurance too. We agreed to review the details the next day, after she'd seen the specialists at the Mayo Clinic.

Rob called on their way back from the clinic. "The good news is Christine's going to live," he said. "The bad news is she's going to lose her right arm. We're scheduled for surgery in six to eight weeks. Do we call our insurance company? Do we need a lawyer? What do we do?"

When I talk about delivering value to my clients, it matters most in times like this. "I'll pull up your contract," I said, "and I'll work with the insurance company. I'll walk you through every step. We've got this. We're good."

The relief in their voices was amazing.

My point in telling this story is to stress the importance of risk management in forming your financial plan. Catastrophes happen. Reducing the threat they pose to achieving your goals is a matter of preparation and investment.

THE THREATS TO A SOLOPRENEUR'S LIVELIHOOD COME DOWN TO FOUR THINGS:

Death: your income is gone. Where does that leave your family?

Disability: you're alive—but if your income is gone, where does that leave your family?

A major health event: without health insurance in place, you might go in for heart surgery that costs $500,000— and find yourself filing for bankruptcy within a year.

Some form of incapacitation: if you have a stroke and lose the ability to communicate or think clearly, who speaks for you, or makes decisions on your behalf?

Let's take the components involved in managing these risks one by one.

Life Insurance

As a general rule, I tell my clients that they need between five and ten times their annual income in life insurance. If they don't have sufficient coverage in place, I encourage them to contact a professional and address that. The type of coverage they buy doesn't matter to me; I simply want them covered. No one cares what type of coverage you've got when you die. The only thing that matters then is that the insurance company pays.

That said, I do have twenty-five years of experience helping people make choices about their insurance, so I'll lay out the basic options for you.

TERM LIFE INSURANCE:

Term insurance is like renting an apartment. It's temporary. You sign the lease, get a roof over your head, and when the lease runs out, you've got nothing. Most people buy term insurance in blocks of years: a five-year term, a ten-year term, fifteen, twenty, twenty-five, or a thirty-year term. Your premiums are locked in for the duration of that term.

At the end of the term, the insurance company either says, "We're out," or, "You're going to have to pay more money." Just like renting an apartment.

UNIVERSAL LIFE INSURANCE:

There are twists and turns here, variations, but the basic idea of universal life is flexibility. It's like driving a car with a stick shift. First gear is great for starting out, but if you stay in first forever, you're going to blow the engine up. If you want to break one hundred on the highway, you're going to go up to sixth gear and floor it.

Universal Life allows you to play with the gears—by which I mean the premiums. You could start with the death coverage you need, but as you gear up in life you can choose to pay higher premiums and build up the cash value of your coverage.

I'm not a huge fan of Universal Life Insurance, because I think there are better ways to invest your money. But it's an option.

WHOLE LIFE INSURANCE:

If Term Life is like renting an apartment, Whole Life is like taking out a mortgage and buying a home. You might sign, say, a thirty-year mortgage. So long as you make your monthly mortgage payments, no one is going to take away your home—and at some point, it's going to be all yours.

That's Whole Life. It costs a little more, but the premiums are guaranteed. Eventually you might be able to stop making payments or continue to make them and build up your equity, as you would with a home.

Again, I tell my clients that their choice doesn't matter to me. What does is ensuring that you've got enough life insurance to take care of your family if something happens to you. If you've got coverage and decide you need more, reach out to the professional you're already working with. If you don't have life insurance but you have homeowner's insurance or auto insurance, you might get a deduction on your policy by adding life insurance, because every company wants to sell you life insurance. If you're not working with a professional, just Google "how to buy life insurance online." There are dozens of companies out there that are happy to sell it.

Disability Income Insurance

The purpose of disability insurance is to replace your income if you're no longer able to work—or, to get technical about it, unable to perform the "substantial material duties" of your occupation. If something happens that renders you unable to work, Disability Income Insurance typically replaces about two-thirds of your income. So it's not a complete solution, but it's far better than none.

You need to be self-employed for two years or longer before most insurance companies will sell you disability coverage. And I urge my clients to get what's called an "own occupation" definition of disability. Remember Christine: without an arm, she'd no longer be able to work as a registered nurse anesthetist. But there'd be nothing to stop her, say, from teaching. With "own occupation" disability coverage, the company would pay her claim—and she could go teach. That's because "own occupation" coverage applies to the job you're no longer able to do.

If you don't have disability income insurance, I'd recommend that you find a professional who specializes in it to work with. This is a more nuanced realm, and you'll benefit from working with a trusted guide.

Health Insurance

I'll keep this simple: you need healthcare coverage to protect you and your family. Without it, you're one significant medical event from bankruptcy.

Here, the type of coverage you get matters. I urge my clients to buy a high-deductible health insurance plan—typically a deductible of $10,000 for a family, $5,000 for an individual. That keeps your premiums down while ensuring that you and your family are protected from a major health event.

I also encourage my clients to fund their deductible through a Health Savings Account, or HSA. The beauty of an HSA is its triple tax benefit. The money you invest in an HSA is tax-deductible. In 2021, the funding limit is $7,200. In addition, the money invested in your HSA grows tax-deferred. Finally, if you use the money to pay for medical expenses—from your deductible to your prescriptions, your eyeglasses and so on—the withdrawals are tax-free too.

One last benefit: the money in an HSA is yours. Anything that's left rolls over from year to year.

Every state has a health insurance marketplace where an individual can buy coverage. You'll need to research the options in your state to identify the choice that works best for you.

Incapacitation

Typically this is a form of risk that's addressed in your estate plan, which I'll cover fully in the next chapter. But it is possible that you'll lose the capacity to control your thoughts, your speech, your movements in a way that compromises your ability to make or express decisions. You've got to have a way for someone you trust to step in and act on your behalf.

The mechanism for this is a document called a durable power of attorney. There are two options that most people use: a "springing durable power of attorney" and "durable power of attorney in fact."

I use a "springing durable power of attorney." It states that if a doctor certifies in writing that I've lost the ability to act on my own behalf, Melissa becomes, in a legal sense, me. She can make every decision that I can make. That's pretty important in my business.

On the other hand, a "durable power of attorney in fact" takes effect the minute it's signed. If that's the option I'd chosen, Melissa could act as me at any point, even if I am not incapacitated. That may sound risky! But some people, especially couples who've been together for many years, choose this option because it captures the reality of their lives. They've come to act as each other anyway.

As a solopreneur, you're probably working with a business attorney already, and you can consult with them on drafting either of the durable power of attorney documents. If you don't have a lawyer, I'd recommend you find one who specializes in working with solopreneurs.

DON'T PUT IT OFF!

When I work with a solopreneur, we step through each of these risk issues as we formulate their financial plan. We'll establish where they are and where they need to be. Some of the choices are personal and involve how much risk you're willing to take. I have more disability insurance than I probably need—after all, I could be disabled from the waist down and still do my job—but I want to be absolutely sure that I've protected my family.

I want to stress this: to me, healthcare insurance is a flat-out no-brainer, and the power of attorney is just something you have to get done.

There's a cost involved in all aspects of risk management, to be sure. But there's a payoff too—peace of mind!—and it's invaluable.

I opened this section by introducing the story of Rob and Christine, but I didn't tell you how it ended. I'm pleased to tell you it ended well. When a wealthy friend learned of Christine's diagnosis, she said, "I don't want you to lose your arm. We're going to find a second opinion." The friend found another specialist in St. Louis, put Christine on an airplane, and they flew there together. "I've dealt with this before," the doctor said. "She doesn't have to lose her arm."

And she didn't. Christine is cancer-free. She's cured and back to work. She didn't have to call on her disability insurance—but it was there for her if she'd needed it. That's risk management.

Now that we've covered taking care of your family, it's

time to talk about taking care of your money, namely your options, and my recommendations, for structuring your investment portfolio.

CHAPTER 7

TAKING CARE
OF YOUR MONEY

The investor's chief problem—and even
his worst enemy—is likely to be himself.
—Benjamin Graham

We solopreneurs have a tendency to think we can do all things. We've figured out a way to build a great business. We've figured out a way to outsource everything, if that's our choice, and work on our own terms. And we've figured out a way to build this great life, or at least get on the path to that destination.

But when it comes to investing, experience has taught me this: solopreneurs need to accept that the biggest thing they can control—and the hardest—is their own behavior. And it's my belief that controlling our behavior is the biggest determinant of our investment return.

YOUR PORTFOLIO

To me, maximizing your return is about *time in the market* and not *timing the market*. This investment philosophy was born out of the chaos of the market crash in 2008 and 2009, and reborn with the market craziness in the first month or two of the COVID pandemic in 2020.

The methodology I share with clients in managing their behavior and their portfolio comes down to what I call the Four P's of Investing:

- Purpose
- Process
- Proceed
- Perspective

Let's take them up in turn.

Purpose

A solopreneur who is ready to start investing needs to begin by asking themselves, "What's my purpose?" Once you've got an answer to that question, everything else starts falling in place.

This goes right back to where we began, with your life vision and goals; the purpose of your investments is to support them. For example's sake, let's say your primary purpose is retirement. If you're thirty or thirty-five and you want the ability to retire at sixty, your investment options flow from there. Maybe you've got two preschool kids; paying for their college is a second purpose. And on it goes. With the work we've done already on your vision and your goals, we've essentially identified the purpose of your investments.

Process

Now we're getting into the basics of investing and managing your portfolio. First, you've got three things to think about—and they all tie back to your purpose:

- **Risk:** What is your willingness or ability to take on risk in pursuit of your objectives?
- **Time horizon:** How much time do you have before you need to fulfill your purpose?
- **Investments:** What types of investments are best-suited to achieving your goals?

To answer that last question, you need to understand your investment options.

STOCKS

Stocks (or equities) are slices of ownership in a company. You purchase them with the idea that the company is going to grow in value, getting bigger and bigger with time. I like to compare the categories of stocks in terms of high school classes: freshmen, sophomores, juniors, and seniors, with a sprinkling of foreign exchange students.

Your freshmen are small-cap stocks—smaller companies that typically haven't been around as long and aren't as mature as the upper classes. They're volatile and can go either way: they can turn out to be good kids, or they can turn out to be bad kids. But the best of them have upside.

Your sophomores are mid-cap stocks. They've made it through their first year of high school and are starting to get the lay of the land. They're less volatile, a little more mature, and they're beginning to get an understanding of where they're going.

Your juniors? Large-cap stocks. They've got things figured out. They've learned from their mistakes. They're not dropping out; they're going to graduate. They've also got a sense of where they're going next. They're not kings and queens of the school yet, but they're on their way.

Seniors are your mega-cap stocks. They've been around a long time. They're not going to surprise us. But they know who they are, and you know what they're going to give you.

Finally, the foreign exchange students: your international stocks. They might come from Sweden, Russia, Belgium, Brazil. They could fall into any class. But they don't live in America, and they bring something different to the mix.

BONDS

When you invest in bonds you're acting not as the owner of a company but as its banker. You're lending money to the company, and they're agreeing to pay it back with interest.

The parallel I'll use here is buying a car. Most people today borrow money to do that. Think of the company as the car-buyer, and think of yourself as the banker. They either have good credit, middling credit, or crappy credit. They may seek a short-term loan at three years, a medium-term loan at four or five years, or a long-term loan at six, seven or even eight years. The risk in lending them money will dictate the interest you require them to pay.

Just as you finance a car when you need one, companies in need of money to run and grow their businesses will sometimes borrow the money they need through issuing bonds. They'll promise to pay you, as an investor, your money back plus interest through the revenue they make. If they've got a good history of paying their bills, they'll pay a low interest rate; if they've got a bad history, they'll pay a premium interest rate. Those are called high-yield or junk bonds. The return on your investment is higher—and so is the risk.

You're acting like a banker lending money to these companies, and your tolerance for risk determines the bonds you choose and the yields you realize. Most people buy bonds for safety, to balance the risk inherent in stocks by investing some of their portfolio in bonds and the return of principal with interest that they offer.

BUILDING YOUR PORTFOLIO

Armed with an understanding of their basic choices, the solopreneur needs to decide how they're going to make their investments.

You can build your portfolio by buying individual stocks and bonds on your own. This comes down to researching the company. What are its earnings? Its history? Are there any accounting scandals in its past? Do they have a good history of paying their bills?

With the technology today, it's easy to find the answers to these questions. But it's a lot of work. Think back to your Life Wheel. Is this how you want to spend your time?

You've got an alternative: outsource the work and buy mutual funds. Companies such as Vanguard, Fidelity, and Schwab have their own teams of researchers. They buy and sell stocks and bonds and put them inside of mutual funds. As an investor, you're buying a share of the fund.

I like to think of a mutual fund as a cookie jar. I grew up in a family with six kids. The first thing we'd do when we got home from school is go straight to the refrigerator for something good left over from the previous night. We went through three or four gallons of milk a week. There was never anything good left over in the fridge. So where next? To the cookie jar.

My stepmom did her best to keep that jar filled with all kinds of cookies. But the mix changed every week, based on what was on sale. Some days we'd reach into that jar and pull out an Oreo, on others a Nutter Butter, on others a Chips Ahoy. On the best days, our lucky days, we'd pull out a homemade chocolate chip cookie.

That cookie jar is your mutual fund. When you buy a mutual stock fund, you're getting a little bit of each stock inside. It might be a small-cap stock fund, filled with high school freshmen stocks, a mid-cap fund, a large-cap fund, even a mega-cap stock fund. Or the cookie jar could be filled with bonds issued by companies that promise to pay them back.

In simple terms, those are your choices as you build your portfolio: you're either buying individual shares or you're buying some form of a cookie jar.

You'll have a variety of cookie jars to choose from. Some are index funds, filled with stocks that represent one of the stock indexes, such as the Dow Jones Index or the S&P 500. You can buy ETFs, or Exchange Traded Funds, which give you the ability to buy and sell at the price you want and don't cost a lot of money to put in place. There are even insurance products—Variable Life Insurance, Variable Annuities—that have cookie jars inside them.

That's the basic outline of the investment landscape today.

PICKING YOUR MODEL

I like to operate in a world of models—basic investment choices intended to meet the risk tolerance and time horizons of my clients.

It's pretty simple. If we were sitting down together, I'd ask you to put a figure on your risk tolerance from one to ten, with one being, "I don't want to lose my money, I'm close to my finish line," to ten being, "I've got time, let 'er rip!" If you're working toward more than one purpose, on different timelines, you may have a different answer for each of the investments you make.

I've developed models—blends of mutual funds—that are tied to the risk tolerance of my clients. The basic formula goes like this: if you're high on the risk scale—let's call it an eight—your mix is 80 percent stock funds, 20 percent bonds and cash. If you're a two, the proportions reverse: 20 percent stocks, 80 percent bonds and cash. The classic blend for a balanced, modest-risk portfolio is 60 percent stocks, 40 percent bonds and cash.

You can find a financial advisor who takes a similar approach to mine. (Or you can find an advisor who takes a different approach that appeals more to you!) Advisors typically charge either a percentage of the assets they're managing for you or through a financial planning fee.

Your alternative is saving much of that money and managing your portfolio on your own. That entails investing through a company such as Vanguard, Fidelity, or Schwab that has developed its own offerings based on the model

I've described. These are typically called balanced portfolios or asset allocation portfolios.

These investment companies also offer mutual funds with risk levels based on your retirement time horizon. These are typically called target date funds. These are structured to be more aggressive when you're younger and get more conservative as you get closer to your goal of retirement.

In assessing your choices among these firms, it's easy to compare returns over time and the fees they charge.

PROCEED

Once I've explained to my clients what I've just explained to you, they typically trust me to put their money to work. If you chose to work with a financial advisor, that's part of what you're paying them for.

I've done the research and chosen risk profile-based models that are appropriate for their particular situation. We invest their money and go from there.

Once a month I review every client's account. If there's a little extra cash available because they fund it monthly or there's money left over from a sale, I either invest it or produce cash for the client. Once every quarter I rebalance the account, adjusting the mix of stocks and bonds to get it back to the appropriate percentage based on how the market has performed. Stocks and bonds tend to work in tandem: when stocks drop, as they did in the early months of the pandemic, the value of bonds rises. As a result, what was a 60-40 stock versus bonds and cash balance might shift to 55-45. Rebalancing involves selling some of the bond fund and buying more of the stock fund to restore the desired ratio.

As the years pass and the client's risk tolerance and time horizon changes, we move to a different risk model. That's typically how my clients and I proceed.

If you choose to proceed independently and manage your own portfolio, you either need to put a similar rebalancing process in place or find a fund that will automatically do the rebalancing for you.

Here's the second key to success: an approach for funding your portfolio called dollar-cost averaging. It involves buying an investment on a monthly basis with the same dollar amount each time. This approach takes advantage of the ups and downs in the market from one month to the next. It's a much simpler and more effective approach over the long run than trying to time the market and buy low. For example, if you decided to invest $19,500 per year into your Solo 401(k), you would divide that by twelve and make a monthly contribution of $1,625 throughout the year.

PERSPECTIVE

Now we're down to the hard part: keeping your emotions in check.

I'll keep it simple: ignore the financial news media. Please.

The news media are not here to manage your portfolio. They're here to sell you advertisements, and to do that, they need to command your attention. As a result, they're always sensationalizing what's going on. When CNBC and Bloomberg sniff fear in the market, they capitalize with hour after hour of talking-head experts who can all see the sky falling. They feed the fear, and as a result, investors react emotionally instead of rationally. When investors are frightened, they sell—and that leads to bad decisions.

Fear passes. It always does.
And in time, the market recovers.
It always has.

You have a plan based on your tolerance for risk and your time horizon. You have a structured process in place for making adjustments in your portfolio based on the market's behavior. My advice is to turn off the market alerts on your phone and trust the process.

The biggest factor in maintaining perspective is making sure that your portfolio is tied to your risk tolerance, that one to ten scale that we started with. The question I stress with my clients is, when things start to go crazy, are you going to lose sleep? If their answer is yes, we either need to figure out how to manage their behavior or adjust their risk profile. Sometimes the answer is both!

The final element in keeping perspective is one more step in the process: once a year, go back and revisit your purpose. What's the purpose of your investment choices? Has your risk tolerance shifted? It might. Circumstances change.

Find a financial advisor with a solid approach to manage your portfolio for you, or do it yourself. Either way, turn those market notifications off. Ignore the media, double-please. Stick to your plan of continuous investment and periodic rebalancing—and focus on your business and your family, not your portfolio.

That's taking care of your money. We're now through eight of the ten elements in your financial plan. Next up is taxes, and the way the structure of your business influences what you pay. After that, we're on to your business and estate planning, the final element of your plan.

Yes, we're talking death and taxes—just not in that order. The prospect of death is hard for all of us to face, but we need to; as for taxes, that's another topic that gets me excited. So, let's go!

CHAPTER 8

THE LEGAL SIDE OF LIFE

Tax avoidance can make you wealthy.
Tax evasion can make you a prisoner.
—James Buss, CPA

I'm starting this chapter with a quote from my CPA, James Buss, because he puts his finger on the core reason for the importance of working with a CPA. I spend a lot of time helping my clients reduce their taxes. But I'm a CERTIFIED FINANCIAL PLANNER™, or CFP®, not a Certified Public Accountant, or CPA. I know enough about taxes to be dangerous—so my first piece of advice for clients, always, is to get a good CPA or tax professional on what I like to call your A-Team.

Who else should join your A-Team? A financial advisor, if you choose to work with one. And a lawyer, perhaps two. You need a business lawyer to help you structure your business, as we'll see in discussing taxes. You may also need a personal attorney to help with estate planning, as we'll see when we come to the estate section of this chapter.

I'll cover both topics in this chapter, and I'm going to start with taxes. I recommend working with a CPA because they've met an industry standard for education and experience in order to win that certification. A good CPA can handle filing your taxes, but that's just the starting point of the value they add. They'll help you with the planning required to minimize the taxes you're required to pay—and they'll keep you out of prison too.

TAX BASICS FOR SOLOPRENEURS

I'll often see solopreneurs—especially new ones—stumble over a simple and easily overlooked necessity: they don't realize that they need to set aside money during the year to pay their taxes.

As a solopreneur, no matter how your business is structured, you are subject to what are called self-employment taxes, above and beyond any income tax that's due. When you work for somebody, a tax of 7.65 percent that funds Social Security and Medicare is automatically deducted from your pay, and your employer pays an additional 7.65 percent on your behalf. That adds up to 15.3 percent—and when you're a solopreneur, you pay it alone. That's your self-employment tax.

As a solopreneur, you will be paying a 15.3 percent self-employment tax in some shape or form. In addition, you'll be paying your ordinary income taxes in whatever marginal tax bracket you fall—10 percent, 12 percent, 24 percent—when taxes come due every April.

Here's my biggest piece of tax advice for solopreneurs: you need to set up a separate tax account at your bank or your credit union on day one. I call it a tax account, but it's simply a bank account: a separate account where you'll put the money you need to pay your taxes. Segregating keeps the math simple and the money safe.

Another important point: as a solopreneur, it's recommended that you make quarterly estimated tax payments to the IRS. They're based on last year's tax bill: whatever you paid then, you need to put away this year in advance on a quarterly basis, or you may find yourself subject to underpayment penalties. One more reason to feed your tax account monthly.

BUSINESS STRUCTURE AND TAXES

Once you've established your footing as a solopreneur and at least set yourself up for success, you should start thinking about structuring your business to help reduce your taxes. You can certainly reduce your taxes through the expenses you attribute to it, but the way you've organized your business itself will affect your taxes.

YOU'VE GOT FOUR OPTIONS FOR STRUCTURING YOUR BUSINESS

- Sole proprietorship
- LLC, for a Limited Liability Company
- S-Corporation
- C-Corporation

I'll give you an illustration of what each of them looks like when it comes to taxes.

Sole Proprietorship

When you as an individual just put yourself out there, doing business, you're a sole proprietorship under the law. That's true whether you set yourself up as a DBA, or Doing Business As, or not.

Any revenue you make through your business goes directly to you, and that sum is reduced by any business expenses you incur. That bottom line of income will be subject to the 15.3 percent self-employment tax and your personal income tax, which is determined by the bracket in which you fall.

You're doing business as yourself, not as a corporate entity, and that means you have none of the liability protection a corporate structure offers. If someone sues you over your business activity, your personal assets could be at risk.

Limited Liability Company (LLC)

Doing business as an LLC protects your personal assets from your business assets. But you'll still pay taxes as if you were a sole proprietor. It's called pass-through taxation. You take your business revenue, subtract your business expenses, and that bottom line is taxed as if you were simply self-employed. Your bottom line is still subject to the self-employment tax and your personal income tax.

So, the first two options have no impact on your taxes. The difference lies in your liability risk—and that's significant.

But if you're like me, the taxes you pay are significant too.

S Corporation

It's not a sexy title—an S Corporation takes its name from Section S of Chapter 1 of the Internal Revenue Code—but the tax consequences of adopting this structure should get your attention.

An S Corp structure offers the same liability protection as an LLC: it separates and protects your personal assets from business liability. But it also allows you to pay yourself a salary, and you'll actually issue yourself a W2 for tax purposes, accounting for the salary you paid yourself during the tax year. And of course you have control of how much you pay yourself. That's where tax planning starts to come in.

Let's say you're a solopreneur with a bottom line of $200,000, once your business expenses are subtracted from your revenue. And let's say you paid yourself $100,000 in salary and took the additional $100,000 in what's called a distribution.

You'll still face self-employment taxes, but they'll be accounted for as if you were working as an employee. You'll pay 7.65 percent on your salary, and your business will pay the additional 7.65 percent. It still adds up to 15.3 percent—but half is being paid out of your personal checkbook and the other half out of your corporate checkbook.

If you were to take the full $200,000 as a W2 salary, you'd pay 15.3 percent up to the Social Security wage limit—which was $140,700 in 2021—and you'd continue to pay Medicare taxes on the balance.

By taking $100,000 as salary and the other $100,000 as a distribution, you're reducing your self-employment tax. You'll still pay your ordinary tax rate on the distribution, but not the self-employment tax.

That's what I call tax avoidance: minimizing your tax bill as allowed by law. In other words, paying the bill without leaving a tip.

Here's an additional wrinkle: some solopreneurs will form their business as an LLC and file their taxes as an S Corporation to take advantage of these strategies.

C Corporation

A C Corporation is its own true entity, entirely distinct from you as an individual. As a business entity, the C Corp would pay you, the solopreneur, a salary. The remaining revenue would stay with the corporation, and it would pay taxes based on the prevailing corporate tax rate.

The C Corp was fading in popularity for solopreneurs, but it made something of a comeback when President Donald Trump's tax bill went through, cutting corporate taxes to make American companies more competitive around the world. But then Congress followed by enacting what's called the Qualified Business Income Deduction, which helped lower the effective tax rate for non-C Corp businesses too.

MANAGING YOUR TAXES

A few final points before we move on from your business structure and taxes.

First, we discussed the impact your choice of retirement plan can have on your taxes in chapter 5. I'm not going to reiterate that material here, but I wanted to remind you of it. The way you structure *both* your business and your retirement plan will affect your taxes.

Second, as I've mentioned, your business expenses also influence your taxes. They're deducted from your business income before your taxes are calculated. At the end of a good year, what will you see solopreneur farmers do? They buy tractors and combines. They'll borrow money and buy a $500,000 combine because it allows them to decrease their tax bill. This isn't necessarily in their long-term interest, but it does lower their tax bill. Again, work with a CPA—ideally one who specializes in serving solopreneurs who can help you understand both the short- and long-term consequences of a decision. Meet with them two or three times a year, project where you see the year going, and make your decisions accordingly. That way you'll know how much money you need to set aside in your tax account to pay the bill.

Okay. We've put it off as long as we can. It's time to talk about death.

ESTATE AND BUSINESS

I talk to all of my clients every year, and I'm constantly reminding them to go get their wills done. It's just not something people like to discuss. No one likes to think about dying. Perhaps they don't know where they want their kids to go if both they and their spouse die early, so they get confused and they stop.

I see it all the time. It's why I bring it up in every meeting: "Do you have a will? I should have a copy of it." I raise what's an uncomfortable topic because, in the end, there's nothing more important than taking care of your family and ensuring that your wishes are honored.

I strongly recommend using an attorney to prepare your will. It's true; you can do it for free online. Solopreneurs of a certain can-do nature will simply take care of it themselves on LegalZoom. You *can* do that too. I don't advise it. A good attorney will charge you somewhere between $500 and $1,000 to draw up your will. To me, that's a small price to pay for the peace of mind that comes with knowing it's been done right and in compliance with the laws of your state. Your particular circumstances may create nuances that an online service doesn't anticipate, and the result can be more of a mess for your heirs than is necessary.

I'm here to make this as easy as I can for you, so let me break it down. There are five things you need to think about before you draw up your will. Once you've settled on the answers to the questions I'll pose, you'll find that finalizing your will isn't so hard.

1) The Kids

You need to discuss and decide who's going to raise your kids if you and your spouse are gone. This starts with an honest discussion: who is up for the call of duty? Where do they live? Will the kids have to change towns or schools? Will you need to set aside additional money to help with that?

2) The Money

Where do you want your money to go? Should it go directly to the kids upon your death, or do you want to establish a trust?

There are two types of trusts to consider.

The first is called an Intervivos trust. That's a Latin word meaning "living" or "while alive." It is its own legal entity, and you can transfer personal assets such as your home, your cars, your household possessions and (if you're married) jointly held accounts to your trust. While you're alive, you control it. When you die, control passes to a trustee you've named.

The second type of trust is called a Testamentary trust. It takes effect at death. It's created through your will, instructing your attorney to set it up upon your death. I call that a "poof" trust. You die, and "poof!" The trust is created through your will, following instructions you've outlined.

For most of my clients, and most likely for most people reading this book, a "poof" trust will do the job. In the end, the legal costs are about the same; you'll either pay an attorney something on the order of $3,000 to $5,000 to create the trust now, while you're living, or you'll pay them out of your estate after death.

Establishing a living trust can avoid the nine months to a year required to process a will in probate court, a proceeding intended to ensure that the assets you're passing along in your will are actually yours. That's a plus. But establishing a living trust also requires you to retitle all the assets it contains, and you'll need to make sure any new assets you acquire are owned by the trust as well. That's a hassle.

The biggest objection I hear to taking a will through probate is privacy. It's true that probate proceedings are public. But I always ask people this: when was the last time you went down to the courthouse and pulled the probate records to see exactly what your neighbor had? I have never done it. Have you ever done it?

The bottom line here is that every situation is different—which points back to my recommendation: work with an attorney who can guide you to the solution that works best for you.

3) Powers of Attorney

I discussed powers of attorney in chapter 6 under the topic of "Incapacitation," so I'll simply reference it here. This addresses who you want to make decisions on your behalf if you become incapacitated. You can invest someone you trust with that authority right away or in the event a medical professional certifies that you have become incapacitated. The key decision here is choosing who you'll invest with the authority, and for that matter, whether they need a backup. Let's say you choose your spouse; what happens after they're gone? Again, every situation is different.

4) Healthcare Powers of Attorney

This is similar in concept but relates exclusively to your healthcare. I like to call it the "pull the plug" scenario. By designating a healthcare power of attorney, you are both expressing your wishes for end-of-life scenarios and naming the person you want to make decisions about prolonging care if you're no longer of sound mind or body. These are not burdens you want to place on your loved ones without providing clear, written instructions. What are your wishes, and who is responsible for seeing that they're followed?

5) Your Beneficiaries

Here is the easiest and quickest estate planning step you can take: check the beneficiaries you've designated on your life insurance policy, your annuity, your retirement plans—whatever the case may be—and ensure that they are up to date. You can do this before you go to an attorney. We live in a world where the divorce rate is about 50 percent. That alone means there's a good chance that the beneficiary you've designated on one account or another may be out of date.

If your accounts are jointly held, they'll automatically pass to your joint tenant. But if they're individual, you can create what's called a "transfer on death authorization" to direct it where you want it to go. If not, it will go by your will, and if you don't have a will, it will go to your estate and be handled by a probate judge. That can cause family issues you might want to avoid.

I check beneficiaries with my clients every time we meet. You'd be surprised how often we find something that needs to be changed.

A CASE IN POINT: MINE

Melissa and I have chosen to create what I call simple "I love you" wills. If something happens to me, everything goes to Melissa. If something happens to her, everything goes to me.

If something happens to both of us, our kids will go to Melissa's parents. As I write this, the first of our daughters is twenty-one, so this isn't as crucial as it once was. But when we drew up our will they were much younger, and it mattered.

Our wills also establish a testamentary trust called the Nelson Family Trust. It's a "poof" trust. If the second of us dies, or we both die at the same time, all our assets go into the trust for the benefit of our kids.

We have three daughters, and for the sake of simple math, let's just say we are worth $3 million at the time of our deaths. Each girl will inherit a third share, amounting to $1 million apiece. First, the trust specifies that its function is to support each of them until they turn twenty-five: to pay for their college, their clothes, their car, their health insurance, and so on.

As each of them hits twenty-five, they're also entitled to the first third of their share, with no strings attached. At age thirty, they'll get the second third, and at thirty-five, they'll get the rest. Why did we do that? To keep them from screwing it all up and shortchanging their future. If I had inherited $1 million at the age of eighteen, I would have figured out how long I could stretch it while living on a beach in Mexico. I'd have had a great time, but today who knows where I'd be.

We've also established a springable durable power of attorney. As I write this, Melissa and I have been married for twenty-five years, and we pretty much act as one financial entity anyway. But this ensures that if a physician determines that one of us has become incapacitated, the other is authorized to act on our behalf.

We've signed a healthcare power of attorney too. We've both been very healthy, and we're grateful. But mine makes clear that if something happens to me and the doctors determine I won't recover, I want them to harvest every organ they can to help someone else live and breathe—and then pull the plug on me.

The fact is that I breathe easier every day knowing I've got all this in place. You'll thank yourself for doing the same, and your loved ones will thank you too.

WE HAVE A PLAN!

We did it! We've now covered all ten elements of your financial plan.

In chapter 4, we discussed the Realities:

- Cash Flow

- Purchases
- Debts
- Emergency Savings

In chapter 5, we covered a Big One:

- Retirement

In chapter 6, we discussed Taking Care of Your Family:

- Education
- Risk Management

In chapter 7, we took up another Big One:

- Portfolio

And finally, in chapter 8, we addressed the Legal Side of Life:

- Taxes
- Estate & Business

It's essential work. But all it's done is to give us a plan. In Part 3, we'll cover putting your plan into action.

First, though, I want to pause for review.

PART 3

LIVING YOUR DREAM

CHAPTER 9

CASE STUDY: WATT

We've covered a lot of ground. Much of the thinking is now behind us; the task ahead is putting the plan into action.

In working with clients, I break that action phase into three stages:

- **Baseline:** establishing where you stand now
- **Projecting and Planning:** determining the steps you'll take to achieve your goals
- **Taking Action:** moving forward, then reviewing and adjusting as you go

We'll take those up in turn later in Part 3. But at this point I think it's helpful to step back and review, and I'm going to do it through a case study involving a fictional character I've named Watt. He's not real, but he is realistic—a composite representing one of my typical clients.

I hope that putting flesh on the bones of what we've been discussing through Watt's case study will bring the approach I've outlined to life for you. So let me introduce him.

Watt is forty-eight and a solopreneur executive coach who is based in Austin, Texas. He's got a gift for it; he's been making $1 million a year. But the truth is that he's been coasting along; when you're making a million bucks a year, it's easy to let some things slip. For all his success, Watt doesn't have a very clear picture of his personal goals, never mind whether he's on the path to achieving them.

On top of all that: 2020. It was a tough year. COVID knocked out Watt's speaking engagements and thus his primary means of generating leads. His income dropped by half. He figures he'll make it until the pandemic passes—but now he's wondering, "*What can I do to prepare my personal and business finances for the next punch to the chin?*"

You know what's next: Watt came to me for help, and I broke out the Life Wheel. Let's see where he's at.

WATT'S LIFE WHEEL

1) Health: 5

On a scale of one to ten, Watt's a five. He works out twice a week, but he knows that in order to keep his energy up and his mind sharp he should be exercising more regularly. He's eating better because of COVID, because he's not on the road and going out to eat all the time. He needs more and better sleep too. He's reading too much social media at night, and he's watching way too much news.

2) Friends and Family: 7

Seven! COVID has left him traveling less, and that means spending more time hanging out with his family. But the first Monday of the month business breakfast club hasn't met in months, and he'd made some great friends and contacts there.

3) Romance: 6

Call it a six. Watt suffers from tunnel vision. He just works, works, works—and as the pandemic took hold, he worked all the harder. Maybe he should schedule in a date night with his wife, Gabriella, once a month. And when six o'clock comes every evening, he needs to close his laptop and stop working. Simple as that.

4) Personal Growth: 8

Watt's curious, a born learner, and COVID has prompted him to dig deeper into the whys of life and what's going on around the world. He's started reading Tolstoy's *Calendar of Wisdom* and its lessons, which draw on the wisdom of the world's great faiths and minds. He signed up for "The Download" too—that's MIT's daily email newsletter about the latest developments in tech. He wanted to follow progress on a COVID vaccine from a source he can trust, and now he's hooked.

5) Fun and Recreation: 8

COVID has its upsides. The one thing in Austin that didn't shut down was golf, and Watt played more golf in 2020 than he's ever been able to play. Ever. His handicap dropped to nine and he had a blast on the course with his socially distanced buddies. It kept him sane, and now he's worried that when work ramps up again, he'll lose something he's come to love. One more reason to work fewer hours somehow.

6) Physical Location: 10

Austin, Texas, right? Are you kidding? Great weather, great food, great music, and great people all around. What's not to like? (Well, aside from the heat in the summer!)

7) Business and Career: 6

He took it on the chin with COVID, and he's learned that he's resilient. He's thought a lot about his core values and what he's really trying to achieve with his business. But he's not sure when things will come back or how different they'll be, so he figures he's going to have to pivot. But when, and how?

8) Finances: 6

His cash flow is half what it used to be, and he's worried about the future. Fortunately, he has built up assets, and he's got retirement savings. But the truth is that he's allowed a lot of details to slip, because at a million bucks a year, he wasn't feeling any pain. Now he is. What does he have to do to get from a six to a nine? A ten?

WATT'S BUSINESS VISION

Watt's Life Wheel left him with some of the same business challenges I faced. He needs to make that business pivot, and he decides to begin by identifying a lucrative niche that maximizes both his passion for the work he's doing and the income he makes. But now he also recognizes that he doesn't want to sacrifice time on the golf course in the bargain, so he needs to run his business more efficiently and charge a premium price for the value he brings to the table.

That's all well and good—but what's his niche? Here's a bit of reality for you: it took me ten months to identify my niche. But this is an illustration, so we'll identify Watt's niche in the time it takes to read this paragraph: he decides to focus on becoming the country's premier executive coach for Fortune 500 CEOs who are tasked with making fundamental change. The stakes they face are high. The challenge they face is daunting. It'd be a great challenge, and a trusted coach who can guide them to success would be invaluable.

Watt's business vision has fallen into place. Time to get realistic: what are his business goals for one year, three years, and five? (Remember, Watt is in 2020.)

- **Year One:** Regain momentum lost to the pandemic by doing virtual speaking engagements until COVID has passed and he is able to travel again.
- **Year Three:** Launch a podcast aimed at his core audience and continue to grow through digital and in-person marketing avenues. He's aiming to be back on track with revenues at the two-year mark, but will be conservative and plan on getting there in his third year.
- **Year Five:** Author a book on leading for change that commands attention. Grow his podcast to 1,000 downloads a month in his very specific niche. Push beyond $1 million in revenue.

It's starting to take shape. But what are his first five steps?

- He needs to find a Zoom coach who can help him get his virtual presentations down.
- He needs to hire a virtual executive assistant who can manage his calendar, his email, and his business operations. That should save five hours a week. That's a round of golf.
- He's got to systematize his approach, from seeking clients to understanding the particulars of their challenge to guiding them toward action.
- If he needs to close his laptop at six every day, he needs to be on his game from the moment he opens it every morning—and that means establishing a morning routine.
- He needs to make the most of his networking time, focusing on CEOs and chairpersons of the boards of companies needing rescue or transition.

WATT'S MINDSET

The truth is that Watt has always suffered from imposter syndrome. Success came easily—too easily. He can't help but wonder, am I actually worth this kind of money? He thinks often of his father, an oil man without a college education who wanted the best for his kids but always told them, "You've got to work your butt off if you want to get someplace in this world." When his father talked about a celebrity or a sports star, he always had an edge in his voice. "They didn't earn it," he'd say. "They just fell into a pot of gold."

So, Watt has always wondered, "did I just fall into a pot of gold too?"

As Watt's business vision came into focus, so did the problem his mindset posed. If he wants to be the best executive coach he can be, thriving by serving the CEOs who face the biggest challenges, he's got to get beyond the self-doubt that was planted by his dad. He's got to believe in the value he brings to the table. Otherwise, he'll never get where he wants to be.

Despite his doubts, he has read the right books and recognized the problem he's creating for himself. Watt reaches out to a friend in his late fifties, a mentor who's at the top of his game, and asks if he's ever doubted the value he brings to the table. His friend surprises him with a chuckle.

"Man," he says, "I used to, all the time. Now, let me ask you a question: how often does a referral from one of your clients lead to another?"

Watt ponders that for a moment. "Pretty often, actually," he says. "In fact, I got my best three clients from referrals."

His friend chuckles again. "What's better evidence of value than that?" he asks.

Now it's Watt who's chuckling. He can feel the story he's been telling himself beginning to change.

WATT'S GOALS AND HABITS

As Watt reflects on his Life Wheel, the four goals that matter most emerge. He gets out a piece of paper and writes each of them down:

- I want to be able to retire at sixty—not sure I will, but I want the option.
- I want to pay for all four years of my kids' college.
- I want to spend a summer in Spain with Gabbie and the kids before they're both out of college and off into lives of their own.
- I want to get my handicap under nine.

Great goals! Now what are the habits that will set him up for success? He decides to start by getting his mind right, each and every morning.

He's going to get up at six every weekday morning, meditate, do a thirty-minute online core strength and flexibility class, and read ten pages in a business book that's high on the charts. He'll watch a ten-minute MasterClass taught by an expert in a field he knows nothing about, and he'll close with five minutes spent reading his daily devotional: *Golf Is Not a Game of Perfect*, by Dr. Bob Rotella.

Now he's ready to take the next step and build his financial plan.

WATT'S FINANCIAL PLAN

Here, as I would with my clients, I'll walk through the ten elements of Watt's financial plan. We need to begin by determining his financial goals. What are his objectives?

Cash Flow:

It's the pandemic. Watt's income just got its ass kicked. He's gone from making a million dollars a year to half that. "I think I can turn the spigot back on," he says, "but right now I'm here. And my cash flow's still good." I ask him if he had to write a check to cover his family's monthly expenses, how big would it be? "Between $10,000 and $20,000 a month," he says.

Purchases:

Watt's son is a junior in high school and his daughter a freshman. In the next two years, he needs to write checks for two cars: a safe used car for his daughter in a year so she can drive herself to school and her team practices, and a better used car for his son in two years, as he heads off to college. He'd rather write the checks than finance the cars, because he doesn't want to add more drag to his cash flow.

Watt's got a dream too: that bucket list summer in Spain with Gabbie, who was born in Barcelona, and their kids.

Debts:

Watt's done well here. Because he went through the Great Recession in 2008 and 2009, he didn't let the good years that followed tempt him into borrowing. All he's carrying is a half-million-dollar mortgage on his house. We know he wants the option to retire in twelve years, at age sixty, so we set the goal of paying the mortgage off by then.

Emergency Savings:

Watt's goal is to get twelve months of living expenses set aside in emergency savings. That's $240,000.

Retirement:

We know Watt's goal. He'd like the opportunity to retire at sixty. The steps he'll take to make that possible will come into focus in the next stage, once we've identified where he stands today—his baseline.

Education:

Watt graduated from a state university and had a great experience there. He wants to provide his children with the same opportunity. After that, he believes they need to be on their own. His goal is paying for four years at a state school, twice over.

Risk Management:

In the simplest terms, Watt wants to make sure that if he's dead, his family is taken care of. But he hasn't thought about what would happen if he became disabled or incapacitated, and he needs to. I'll be sure to bring that up in the next phase, when we discuss his baseline.

Portfolio:

Watt wants to be sure his investment portfolio is aligned with his goal of having the option to retire at sixty. He can't stomach another roller-coaster ride like the one he endured in the Recession, so he wants to temper his risk.

Taxes:

Watt is just like 90 percent of my clients: he wants to pay less taxes. He doesn't mind paying his fair share, but no more, and he's not sure what else he needs to be doing.

Estate and Business:

Watt does not have a will. It's crazy, at this stage of life, but he doesn't have a will. Neither does Gabbie. And he's made no provision for someone to step in and make decisions about his business if he's incapacitated.

MAKING IT HAPPEN

So here we are: Watt has clarified his vision and identified the goals and habits that will lead to the life he wants to lead. He's broken down the steps he needs to take to bring his business to the level that will support his vision. And he's developed the elements of a financial plan—the specific objectives he needs to reach for.

It's time to take action—and that begins with assessing exactly where he stands today. That's the task you'll face at this point too, so let's explore just what that means.

CHAPTER 10

BASELINE

You can't really know where you are going
until you know where you have been.
—Maya Angelou

One issue that came into focus as I worked with Watt was that, for all his success, he didn't have a firm grasp of where his finances stood relative to his goals. How well-positioned was he to make his dreams a reality? It's essential to know the answer.

In simple terms, Watt didn't know his baseline. On its own, your plan is nothing more than your feelings. You need to know your feelings about where you want to go in life, but you can't stop there. You need to know your numbers and your facts.

It's a straightforward process. You've itemized the elements of your financial plan. It describes where you want to go.

The next step is walking through each of the ten elements and identifying where you are. I'm not introducing any new concepts here. This is a fact-finding mission. So, let's walk through the baseline with Watt.

Cash Flow: Even at his pandemic income level of half a million dollars, Watt's in good shape. He's bringing in about $40,000 a month and he's spending $10,000 to $20,000. That means he's still got $20,000 to $30,000 left over to run his business.

Purchases: He needs to buy a couple cars over the next couple years at a cost of about $15,000. Other than that, no purchases beyond household expenses, which are covered in the cash flow.

Debts: Just the half-million-dollar mortgage. He refinanced it over the summer to a fifteen-year mortgage and a 2.25 percent interest rate. He'll have it paid off when he's sixty-three. It's a $3,000-a-month payment, covered in his cash flow.

Emergency Savings: Watt's initial goal is twelve months of living expenses in savings, or $240,000. He's only got $60,000 set aside now.

Retirement: Watt's got a half-million in his retirement account. It's from his prior life in the corporate world, before he became an executive coach; he's got $450,000 in his old 401(k) and $50,000 in his Roth IRA. Gabbie works too. She's a school nurse making $40,000 a year, with summers off. She left work for a decade to raise the kids, but they're older now and she's back on the job. She's got about $100,000 in her retirement account, and it's building again.

Education: Watt and Gabbie both value education, and they've done a good job of saving for it. There's $60,000 sitting in their son's 529 account, and $45,000 in their daughter's. Even through the pandemic they've continued to put a couple hundred bucks a month in each account, and they're on pace.

Risk Management: Watt has $2 million of life insurance in place, and a million-dollar policy on Gabbie. He has no disability income insurance. That's the bad news. The good news is their health insurance is covered through Gabbie's work as a school nurse. During her years out of work, Watt covered the family through a high-deductible plan and funded the gap through an HSA. Over a decade their premiums rose from $440 a month to $1,500 a month—and that's aside from their HSA contribution of $600 a month—but that's all in the past now.

Portfolio: It's a hodgepodge. He picked funds as his friends recommended them, and he's never looked at them again. He's in ten different funds, all with Fidelity. They're all stock funds, which means he's in a riskier position than he's told me he wants. Watt has been too absorbed in building his business to devote the time it would take to do much better.

Taxes: Watt and Gabbie meet with their CPA once a year, finalize their numbers together, and pay whatever taxes are due. Their CPA calculates their quarterly estimates, and Watt pays them. Even with his reduced income in the pandemic, it's going to amount to at least $60,000.

Estate and Business: Watt has his business structured in a smart way: an LLC, operating as an S Corporation. But he doesn't have a will. That means if he dies, the state is going to determine where his money goes—and it won't necessarily go to the children.

That's the lay of the land, Watt's baseline. Once you've determined yours, you are ready for the next step: planning and projecting.

CHAPTER 11

PROJECTING AND PLANNING

B ack in chapter 4, I introduced you to Lloyd and Elaine, the couple who came to me in their late fifties, with a successful business in a small town that generated between $500,000 and a million dollars a year. But they liked to spend money. They had only $40,000 in retirement savings, a half million in debt, and lots of expenses. Lloyd wanted desperately to take Elaine to Fiji for her dream vacation, but that seemed far beyond reach. But it actually wasn't—not with proper planning.

Beginning with the first financial plan we developed together, we set $800 a month aside into a vacation account. That's $10,000 a year, going toward their dream vacation. Four years down the road, I called Lloyd to say, "Time to take Elaine to Fiji."

"Not ready yet," he said.

Five years down the road…still not ready yet.

Finally, ten years down the road, they took the trip—and enjoyed the greatest experience of their lives.

That's the power of planning.

GETTING FROM HERE TO THERE

You've established your goals in your financial plan, and your baseline tells you where you stand today. Now it's a question of filling—I like to call it minding—the gap. You need to determine if you're on track toward achieving your goals. That's a step-by-step process too.

Minding the Gap

Cash Flow: Is your cash flow where you need it to be? If not, remember: back in the visioning stage you already identified a first set of steps for building your business. But you need to start on the expense side, beginning with what I call an audit of your cash flow. Open your business checkbook and look at your credit card statement. What are you paying for that you're no longer using? Business software? For a solopreneur, your business income and your personal income feel like the same thing. So, what about Netflix—are you still watching?

Purchases: What's coming in the next two years? Do you need to plan for those purchases, or are you building your emergency savings with those purchases in mind? It could be new computers, new desks, new furniture for your living room, a new car, a new roof.

Don't forget the lesson of Lloyd and Elaine: how about your vacations? I'm big on vacation accounts that are funded every month, because there's nothing better than a trip that's paid for before you go. For Lloyd and Elaine, it was Fiji. For my family, it was the Women's World Cup in France in 2019. It was our trip of a lifetime—so far.

Some of the clients who come to me have their nose to the grindstone, and I encourage them to step back and dream a bit before life passes them by. And I have others who leap off into adventures, then figure out how to pay the bills later. I try to keep them from doing that!

Debt: Are you paying higher interest rates on your mortgage than you need to be, given where rates stand today? Paying off your credit cards every month, or carrying a debt on those? What changes can you make to lower those costs? When will your debts be paid off? Do you want to accelerate the pace if you can? What will you do with the money that's freed up when they are? The biggest issue—and opportunity—I find with my clients is typically paying off the mortgage and their credit card debt.

Emergency Savings: You're a solopreneur; if your business goes down, you don't want your family to go down with it. My advice is to try to get to between six and twelve months of living expenses in emergency savings. You know where you're at today. How much money per month can you save to get to your six- to twelve-month goal?

Retirement: Are you setting enough money aside every month to get to your retirement goal? Have you built a strategy for retirement, or are your accounts all over the place? This one is going to take some calculations. We've talked about assessing your risk tolerance, and how to create an investment mix that matches it. You can find financial calculators online that can help you understand how much you need to be putting away. I use the Simple Savings Calculator on bankrate.com.

Let's say you want to live on $100,000 a year in retirement, aside from Social Security and pensions or anything else. It needs to come from your portfolio. I use a factor of 5 percent in determining how much you should plan to draw from your portfolio each year. In simple terms, that means if you want to draw $100,000 in retirement, you need a portfolio of $2 million—because $100,000 divided by 0.05 is $2,000,000.

Now you turn to the Simple Savings Calculator. Say you're sitting on $600,000 in retirement assets and you're currently putting $1,000 a month into your retirement account. You're twelve years out from retirement, and you anticipate getting a 6 percent return on your portfolio. (That's a bit below the market's historic average return of 8 percent.) Those factors get you to between $1.4 million and $1.5 million—so now you know you're not where you need to be.

Play around with the numbers, and you'll see that it's going to take about $4,000 a month to achieve your goal.

The financial planning I do is more sophisticated than that. But I'm sharing this to give you a sense of how to approach the math on your own, if that's your choice.

Now, the reality is that all of us are going to get Social Security at some point, depending on when we choose to begin taking it. In my opinion, it's going to be less generous in the future than it is today. Why? The math that underlies the program is broken. We have too few people paying in, and too many people taking out. I foresee a 25 percent cut in benefits coming. In my view, prudence dictates taking that possibility into account too.

Education: If you've got kids and paying for their education is your goal, you need to run the same calculations as you've done with retirement. The timing depends on their age, and your goal depends on what exactly you're choosing to fund: private high school? Two years or four in college? State school or private?

If the cost of a state school in your state is $20,000 a year for room, board, and tuition, and you're paying for four years of school, you need to have $80,000 set aside. (Remember to add in a little bit for inflation.) It's pretty easy to use the Simple Savings Calculator to figure out how much you need to set aside to get there.

Risk Management: The first thing to take care of is health insurance, because if you don't have that in place you could be bankrupted in the blink of an eye. In my opinion, a high-deductible plan coupled with an HSA to fund the deductible is a wise choice; it helps minimize your premiums and it increases your tax deductions. If you have a plan in place, does it deliver the most coverage you can get for the least money?

Next up is life insurance. My advice in simple terms is to buy between five and ten times your annual income in coverage. You can find analytical tools that will generate numbers based on your particular circumstances, and I do a deeper analysis for my clients. But that's my rule of thumb. Five times if you're willing to cut it close, ten times if you want to be generous.

Do not overlook disability insurance. You need to assess the risk you face, given what you do. I'm a big supporter of disability insurance, but the fact is that I'm in a business where my risks are limited. As long as I can talk, I can run my business. That said, if I had a stroke and recovered my mental capacities but not my ability to talk, I would no longer be able to pay the bills. I've seen disability insurance make a huge difference for clients. But it is harder to get and it's more expensive too, so you do need to assess your own risk carefully and plan accordingly.

An important note: if you're leaving a job to strike out as a solopreneur, and you have disability coverage, try to bring it with you. Otherwise, insurance companies will want to see that you have at least two years of self-employment behind you to make sure that you're worthy of disability coverage.

Portfolio: I laid out my methodology in chapter 7, but here's a recap: the first thing to consider is your risk tolerance. Put it on a scale of one to ten. A one means you don't want to lose your money and so want to minimize risk. That suggests you should put 100 percent of your portfolio in bonds and cash. A ten means you're all-in aggressive, willing to maximize risk in order to maximize your odds of making a lot of money. That suggests 100 percent of your portfolio in stocks. Most people land somewhere in between. Let's say you're a six. That suggests 60 percent stocks and 40 percent bonds and cash. You can purchase individual stocks and bonds or take the cookie jar approach I outlined in chapter 7 and opt for mutual funds.

Next, you should gather all your statements and go to a financial website like morningstar.com—it's free for a trial period—where you'd plug in your data and see where your portfolio actually stands. If it matches your risk tolerance, great; if not, you now know you need to adjust it.

Taxes: Most of my clients come to me paying a lot in taxes and hoping to pay less. Where do you stand? Have you consulted with your CPA or tax professional lately on ways to reduce your taxes? Are you taking full advantage of the tax benefits available in how you've structured your business and are funding your retirement? In my opinion, this is not do-it-yourself work. I meet with my CPA three times a year and I talk with him regularly. My business has taken off. I need to know how much to put aside in quarterly payments as my income rises. We also adjust my salary to meet the Social Security wage base. I believe you will get far more value in tax savings out of working with a good CPA than you will pay in fees. They're worth their weight in gold.

Estate and Business: How is your business set up? Is it a sole proprietorship? A partnership? An LLC? An S Corp? Based on what you've read in chapter 8, do you need to make a change?

Secondly, how about that will? You need to do it. Do you want to put a trust in place? Who's going to act on your behalf or make end-of-life decisions for you if you're incapacitated?

Here's one more thing to think about: do you have a business succession plan in place? If you become disabled or die prematurely, is there another person in your industry who could step in on behalf of your clients? If you don't have a succession plan in place, you should reach out to someone you trust and draw up an agreement that gives them the first option to buy your business at the time of your death or incapacitation. This has to be a good friend. You're not going to turn to your biggest competitor unless your biggest competitor is also a good person and friend. In my realm, security regulators at the federal and state level require me to have a succession agreement in place.

There are a number of financial advisors in Sioux Falls alone, and I considered two. One had a bigger business than mine, the other a smaller one; I knew and trusted both. I decided to approach the bigger of them because I knew he had the means to write a check to Melissa and take over my business if I died. "Go take care of your clients," he told me after signing the agreement, "and hope to God that we never need this thing. Realistically, it's not going to happen. But it's there if you do need it." I've always appreciated his comment, and left his office feeling peace of mind.

TIME FOR ACTION

We know your goals, because they're embodied in your financial plan. We know your numbers, because that's your baseline. Now we've identified the gaps through the planning process.

But of course, nothing's happened yet! Next, we'll turn to taking action.

CHAPTER 12

ACTIVE STEPS

A journey of a thousand miles begins with a single step.
—Lao-Tzu

Not long ago I began working with a young couple named Paul and Kelly who had developed a fantastic marketing business. We followed the process I've outlined and made plans for creating an emergency savings account, buying a new house, paying off their car and student loans, and putting money away for retirement.

But they couldn't do it all at once. If they had tried, they'd have been frozen in terror. Here's one example of why: to achieve their goals, I needed to get them to the point where they were putting $20,000 a year toward retirement. They were doing $1,200 a year—$100 a month—when they came to me.

"Here's the deal," I told them. "We're going to work up to $20,000. Let's go from $100 a month to $200, maybe $300. Every time we sit down to review, we're going to talk about bumping it again."

I'm big on taking small steps. It's just like dieting. You're not going to lose fifty pounds in a week—but you could lose fifty pounds in a year. Focus on losing one pound this week, and the same in the week after that. Keep at it, and you'll get there.

I'm also big on reviewing and adjusting. Your circumstances change and your goals do too. As the saying goes, your financial plan is wrong the next day. Don't despair; that's not literally true. But long-term success requires establishing the habit of reviewing and adjusting periodically.

These are the final two steps in the process I've laid out for you, but your first *active* steps:

- Take Action
- Review and Adjust

I'll outline my approach to both in this chapter, and I'll illustrate what I'm describing through Watt. We left him in chapter 10, when we established his baseline. Let's imagine that he's gone through the projecting and planning process, identifying the gaps between where he wants to be and where he is today. Now it's time for him to take his first active steps.

It comes down to this: don't succumb to paralysis. Imperfect action is better than no action at all. Take that first step, however small—and then keep moving.

TAKE ACTION

Perhaps by this point you can guess where I'm heading next: you need to walk through your financial plan one more time, identify the first steps you're going to take toward closing the gaps between where you are and where you want to be—and then you're going to take them.

Once again, we're setting a goal—an interim goal this time—and defining the habits we need to achieve it. What might this look like? It differs for everyone, though the steps are the same.

Cash Flow: Your goal here is to continuously improve on your cash flow until it's where you need it to be. What can you do to improve it now? You've identified next steps for your business, which should pay off in time with increased income. But start with expenses. What's the first step you can take to reduce them? And the habit: how will you keep the process moving?

Watt: *He's in a good position, despite the pandemic, but he's recognized that he hasn't paid attention to his expenses as he should have. His first step: he reviewed his business checkbook and credit card statements and realized he was paying a monthly subscription for business software he no longer uses. He canceled it. The habit: booking an afternoon to repeat the process every six months, three years out in his calendar.*

Purchases: I'm a big fan of creating a separate account with a regular contribution to fund your upcoming purchases. It's the best way to stop Peter from robbing Paul. If you don't have one already, your first step is setting up that account and the mechanism for funding it. How you go about it depends on your cash flow. I collect my fees once a quarter and take my salary monthly. Typically I make distributions to my college savings accounts, say, on a quarterly basis too.

Watt: *He needs to buy a used car for each of his kids over the next two years and he's debt-averse, so he plans to scratch a check to do it. His plan had been to take the money from Emergency Savings when the time came. Instead, he takes a new first step: he sets up a "kid's car" account at his bank and a monthly automatic transfer of $500 from his primary checking account. That won't be enough to cover both cars, but it's a first step.*

Debts: Are you on pace to achieve your goals? If not, what's the first step you can take in that direction? If your goal is to have your student loans paid off in two years instead of four, and it will cost an extra $500 a month to get there, you need to start adding that $500 to your monthly payments now—or as close to it as you can come.

Watt: He's already refinanced to a fifteen-year, half-million-dollar mortgage at a rate of 2.25 percent, and that should save him more than $50,000 over the thirty-year mortgage he'd been carrying. No action is needed here now. But his goal is to have his mortgage paid off at sixty, not sixty-three. As his business recovers from the pandemic and his cash flow improves, he'll revisit.

Emergency Savings: You know where you stand and where you need to go. How much more can you contribute on a weekly, monthly, or quarterly basis to build toward your goal? I can tell you that once you hit it, it'll be the greatest feeling in the world—because you'll know your family's taken care of.

Watt: He's at $60,000. His initial goal was $240,000, or twelve months at his maximum monthly spending. That's a lot of money. But remember: I'm working with him. Through the projecting and planning process, we decided that he doesn't need to set the bar that high. The pandemic has demonstrated that there'll always be a demand for his services, that $10,000 a month in family expenses is workable. We reset his goal at $100,000, so he has a gap of $40,000 to close, and his math tells him he can get there in a year. We'll reassess when he reaches that goal. His first step: he sets up a shareholder distribution of $10,000 per quarter to fund it.

Retirement: Don't have a retirement plan? Determine which option I've described is best for you, set it up, and begin funding it. Not setting enough aside to achieve your goal? Set aside as much as you can now toward closing the gap. I'm a big fan of getting that money in your retirement account every single month, rather than making a one-time contribution in April to cut your taxes. If you don't make the commitment to regular funding, you're gambling with your own future happiness.

Watt: He has been funding a SEP IRA at the rate of $20,000 a year. If he continues at that rate over the next twelve years, when he hits his "maybe I will" retirement age of sixty, he'll have $1.5 million in retirement assets. He wants a retirement income of $100,000 a year, and that will yield only $75,000 in pre-tax income. He's not quite there. Watt's first step is working with me on the planning—this is in my wheelhouse—and a CPA to make sure everything's set up right.

In the projecting and planning phase, we decide to shift to a Solo 401(k) funded at $19,500 a year, bump his W2 salary to $137,500 and establish a profit-sharing plan at 25 percent of that. That will generate an additional $34,425 he can contribute to retirement at tax time every year—for a total of $53,925 toward retirement annually. Over twelve years, that should bring his portfolio to $2.14 million, enough to fund his retirement at

$107,000 per year, pre-tax. If he decides to defer his retirement until sixty-five, he should be sitting at $3.1 million, yielding $155,000 in annual income just off his retirement accounts.

Education: If you've got kids and are funding their education, it's the same process. If you're not on pace to achieve your goals, what's the first step you can take to close the gap? Take it!

Watt: He's on pace. If inflation pushes tuition higher than he's planned for, he'll fund the difference from his cash flow.

Risk Management: If you don't have life insurance, you could reach out to the agent or company that handles your car or homeowner's coverage; they'll be happy to sell you life insurance too, and you might save through bundling. Rule of thumb: secure five to ten times your annual income in coverage. With disability insurance, I recommend contacting a professional who specializes in working with solopreneurs. Coverage is complicated and it's critical that you buy insurance with a definition of disability that meets your needs.

Watt: Through the planning process, we identify that Watt's $2 million in life insurance coverage leaves him short of his goals: paying for the funeral, paying off the mortgage, funding college for the kids, and enabling Gabrielle to sustain her current lifestyle. Taking care of those initial obligations will leave about $1.4 million to fund Gabbie's lifestyle; at 5 percent a year that's *enough to generate about $70,000 to supplement her $40,000 income. To make sure there's enough coming in until the youngest is out of the household, we decide to add $250,000 in coverage in a four-year term policy.*

He has no disability insurance, and that's a big risk. Watt's first step: make an appointment with a specialized agent to discuss options for coverage. Although disability coverage is expensive, a solopreneur such as Watt with an income between $500,000 and $1 million can afford it. Gabbie should be part of the discussion too.

Portfolio: Is your investment portfolio aligned with your objectives and risk tolerance? If not, reallocate. Diversification matters. You can do the math on your own, work with an advisor, or use a robo-advisor that will generate an asset allocation mix that meets your needs. As you know, I recommend funding your portfolio on a monthly basis to take advantage of dollar-cost averaging. And here's a good first step: manage your behavior! Turn off Bloomberg, CNBC, Fox Business—or at very least, put them on mute.

Watt: His hodgepodge of mutual funds has performed well, thanks to a good market, but it's all in stocks, so it's not well diversified. His risk tolerance is an eight; he's sitting at ten. He needs to consolidate and reallocate to meet his risk profile. Because he has come to me, I'll do the work, based on the model portfolios I use and his time horizon, while setting up a quarterly rebalancing check. And he took the stock-ticker app off his smartphone. I know, because I watched him do it on our Zoom call!

Taxes: If you do not have a relationship with a CPA or a tax professional, I recommend you establish one with a specialist in working with solopreneurs so they can help optimize your business structure and decisions for tax purposes. Consider hiring them on a retainer basis that will enable you to schedule at least two to four meetings a year. Your first step: schedule interviews with CPAs or tax professionals to find the best fit for you. You have online options, but this is also a good time to lean into friends and family for recommendations.

Watt: Given where Watt was when he came to me, with the salary he was taking and his SEP IRA, he was paying between $60,000 and $70,000 in taxes on his half-million-dollar income. By implementing the changes we identified together— increasing his salary, shifting to a Solo 401(k), and establishing a profit-sharing distribution and putting that toward retirement—as well as maximizing his annual contributions to his HSA, Watt should save between $5,000 and $10,000 a year in taxes. Once his income returns to $1 million, he should save between $30,000 and $40,000 a year.

Estate and Business: If you need to create a will, change your business structure, or create an agreement for succession, my advice for a first step is to seek the advice of an attorney—again, ideally one who specializes in working with solopreneurs. They will interview you to understand your needs and put together a solution that complies with the laws in the state where you live and perhaps even the countries where you're operating. It's always good to have an attorney you can call on as needed too. You can do this online, although I don't recommend it, because most solopreneurs are not attorneys and may not foresee the twists and turns they need to navigate.

Watt: He has no will, but in the planning process he and Gabrielle did decide who should take on responsibility for the kids if they both die at the same time. His business is structured as an LLC filing as an S Corporation; that's good. He has no succession agreement. His first steps: find an attorney to draft his will. He'll also identify and reach out to another executive coach of similar caliber who is either willing to purchase his business at the time of his death or at least serve as a recommended option, giving Watt's clients an opportunity to step into a relationship with someone else rather than being left without guidance.

REVIEW AND ADJUST

As you can see, in some cases a first step is only that; in others, a single step may be all that's required—for now. But circumstances change, and it's easy to overlook that once you put your head down and lose yourself again in the busy-ness of growing your business. So the work of defining your life vision and developing the financial plan to support it is never really done.

There is always going to be a need to step back, review where things stand, and adjust.

I've talked about the importance of getting to that first small step, and taking it. You'd be amazed how often people get paralyzed along the way. It doesn't matter if they're a solopreneur just starting out or a C-suite executive making a million a year. The idea of figuring all these things out and putting them on paper can paralyze. I hope I've gotten you past that!

The need to review and adjust is another spot where people get stuck. They just don't do it. They're busy. They're preoccupied. It's work.

But it's important. So much so that I'll recommend one more active step: book a day in your calendar to step back all the way to the beginning—review your life wheel, goals and habits, financial plan, and baseline. Are you still the partner you aspire to be? Did you fall off the wagon of better eating? When's the last time you made time for the gym? (Be honest!)

It comes down to this: is your vision the same? Are your goals? Are you still on track?

In my experience, going through this exercise once every year is enough. If you're in a time of rapid change, once every six months is better. I wouldn't recommend doing it more often than that, barring a major life event, because you run the risk of overreacting to a short-term turn of events.

What might change for Watt, say, in six months' time? Perhaps, coming out of the pandemic, he gets back in front of CEOs and sees his income rise, with no signs of slackening. But what if CEOs who had held out as long as they could reach the cash flow point of no return, pull back, and his business drops by an additional 20 percent? What if his son, the high school junior, gets a perfect score on the SAT and starts to talk not about State but about Stanford?

THINK JOURNEY, NOT DESTINATION

It's been our family tradition to take a one-week vacation to go someplace special between Christmas and New Year's and just be together. Someplace warm. The year before the pandemic, it was Marco Island in Florida. We spent an amazing week walking around, riding our bikes, and soaking in the sun.

I'm someone who needs a purpose in my life—why am I working, what am I reaching for?—and mine is buying a family magnet: a beach condo in Florida that would draw my kids (and my grandkids!) back long after they'd left home and, perhaps, spread across the country. That is my why.

Then came COVID. Melissa and I found ourselves reflecting on our priorities on the daily walks we took to get out of the house. As summer turned toward fall, we canceled our holiday vacation in the sun. It was the smart call; we had to. And we began thinking, why put the magnet in Florida? Why not someplace closer, someplace central? Why not buy a place in the mountains of Colorado instead? It's a day's drive away from Sioux Falls, not two. It had been a century since the last pandemic swept the world, but could we count on it being another century before the next one?

Believe me, I recognize our good fortune; so many people lost jobs or loved ones in the pandemic. My point is that life changes, and your vision changes with it. That means your goals and your financial plan need to change too. The beauty of mastering your finances lies in the choices you create for yourself when the ground shifts under your feet.

Set a date, no sooner than six months out, no more than a year, and make an appointment with yourself to get back to your starting point. Review and adjust. Take the next small steps. Allow yourself the grace and understanding that comes with recognizing that life is a process, a journey—not simply a destination. And the journey takes time.

Back when I was doing Ironman Triathlons, I learned to appreciate the journey most of all. Gearing up for each race meant committing to a thirteen-week training program that kicked my butt, physically and mentally. I loved it, because I knew I was preparing to do something special. The race? That's just the party at the journey's end.

So schedule that appointment with yourself—and keep it!

CONCLUSION

Dreams don't work unless you do.
The surest way to your dreams coming true is to live them.
—Roy T. Bennett

My business as a solopreneur was born in the greatest financial crisis in our lifetime. This book for solopreneurs like you was born in a pandemic. What's my point in noting this, aside from questioning my own sense of timing?

My point is that you can do anything you set your mind to doing if you define and move toward your goals in a methodical fashion. I hope this book has equipped you to do just that.

We started by getting your mind right: defining a vision for your life, changing the stories you tell yourself, aligning your personal and business goals, then developing the habits required to achieve them. We moved from there to developing the ten elements of a financial plan that supports your life vision. Then we discussed the steps you need to take to translate your plan into action, and to keep it on track as your circumstances and goals in life change. Along the way we put flesh on the concepts through a case study involving a fictionalized client named Watt. We covered a lot of ground!

I wrote this book so you could benefit from the things I've learned and the mistakes I've made in my twenty-five years as a financial adviser and twelve years as a solopreneur. I haven't completed my own journey, but I'm on track to fulfill my life vision because I've applied the lessons I'm sharing with you.

My goal in working with every one of my clients is to help them define their life vision and get them on track too. That's also my goal for you. This book is your rocket booster.

I hope you will strap it on your back, follow the approach I've laid out for you, and fly a lot faster than I did.

You're armed with all the tools and knowledge you need to master your finances and achieve your life's goals. You can do it.

If you decide you'd like me to help you, or you simply want to be in touch, you can reach me through my website, gabenelsonfinancial.com, by email at gabe@gabenelsonfinancial.com, or by phone at 605-553-9180. You can also check out my podcast, "Solopreneur Money," on your favorite podcasting service. It'd be great to hear from you, one way or another.

Now it's up to you. *You can do it.* Go kick ass!

ACKNOWLEDGMENTS

FAMILY

"The Nelson Nucleus"—Melissa, Lauren, Avery, and Lydia. You are the reason I do everything that I do. Thank you for making every day special.

Sam and Linda Nelson—You taught me how to be a man and always kept the cookie jar full.

Jill and Steve Reff—Thank you for bringing me into this world and helping me to understand how I want to live this life.

Gary and Theresa Emigh—You taught me about family and opened my eyes to the world of self-employment.

Lloyd and Elaine Nelson—I know you are smiling down on me from heaven. You are missed.

Brothers, Sister, and In-laws—You remind me that this is a great big world and we all play our part. Thank you.

Chad Bricker

Eric Bricker

Brian Bricker

Jeff Bricker

Carly Mjelde

Brad and Sheri Jans

COLLEGE AND LIFELONG FRIENDS

I have to thank my college roommates for all the learned lessons in those formative years. Without you, I (and the world) would never have heard of the "Underwear Dance."

Paul

Joey

Travis

Jon

Soup (Ryan)

Matt

Craig

Dan

Chuck

Mark

Jon Giles—My best friend, outside of Melissa. Thank you for your friendship, the snowboarding trips, the hours in the hot tub with bourbon, the weekly check-in.

PROFESSIONAL

Vicky Sawyer—You are a rock star. I could not have done this book without you.

Christina Miser—Another rock star. This book would not have happened without you either.

Gene McNaughton—Mentor, friend, and guide. You are quite possibly the single reason that this book is even a thing. Thank you for your wisdom and friendship along the way.

The Scribe Family

Mark Travis—The friendship built in this process will last a lifetime. I am truly grateful for your wisdom and expertise.

Natalie Aboudaoud—Your guidance along the way has been wonderful. I always knew what was coming next.

From cover design to marketing, everyone has been first class. I truly appreciate each of you.

COACHES

Stephanie Bogan—When the student was ready, the teacher appeared. You opened my eyes to a much greater life and business.

Alyse McConnell—Thank you for the insight you bring to all you touch. Fight on!

Limitless Mastermind Pods—I learn something new every time we meet. Thank you to:

Bryan

Tom

John

Calvin

Payton

Michael

Brian

Kevin

You are all lifelong friends.

CURRENT AND FUTURE CLIENTS

I will be safe and not list names for compliance purposes. You know who you are and I am forever grateful for the honor of being your guide through this crazy world of money, life, and business. Without you, this book would never have come to be. You created these stories and this great life we all share. Thank you!

ABOUT THE AUTHOR

Gabe Nelson earned a BS in Economics from South Dakota State University in 1995, began working in financial services immediately following graduation, obtained his CERTIFIED FINANCIAL PLANNER™ Designation in 2006, and founded Gabe Nelson Financial in 2008. His mission is providing independent, objective, trusted advice that helps solopreneurs enjoy the life of their dreams. He and his wife Melissa live in Sioux Falls, South Dakota, and have three daughters: Lauren, Avery, and Lydia. You may see him in a coffee shop meeting with a client, snowboarding in Colorado, or perfecting his stroke on the golf course.

CPSIA information can be obtained
at www.ICGtesting.com
Printed in the USA
BVHW071114030122
625353BV00006B/366